Feeding Lee's Army
of Northern Virginia

Michael C. Hardy

SB

Savas Beatie
California

First edition, first printing

ISBN-13: 978-1-61121-731-5 (hardcover)
ISBN-13: 978-1-61121-732-2 (ebook)

Library of Congress Cataloging-in-Publication Data

Names: Hardy, Michael C, author.
Title: Feeding Lee's Army of Northern Virginia / by Michael C. Hardy.
Description: El Dorado Hills, CA : Savas Beatie LLC, 2025. | Includes
  bibliographical references and index. | Summary: "Although seldom
  studied, food (or the lack thereof) and the logistics behind it played a
  critical role during the war, contributed mightily to the success and
  failure of campaigns, and impacted the overall outcome of the conflict.
  Understanding how soldiers fried their bacon and baked their biscuits,
  how they ate and, very often, went hungry, is a vital tool to
  understanding their individual experiences and the larger history of
  supply and logistics within the Confederate Army. Battles and campaigns
  would not have been possible without a proper diet and a functioning
  logistical system to support the men at the front. This book offers
  invaluable insight into this overlooked and understudied topic that made
  it all possible"-- Provided by publisher.
Identifiers: LCCN 2024047812 | ISBN 9781611217315 (hardcover) | ISBN
  9781611217322 (ebook)
Subjects: LCSH: Confederate States of America. Army of Northern
  Virginia--Military life. | Cooking for military personnel--United
  States--History--19th century. | Confederate States of America--Armed
  Forces--Messes--History. | United States--History--Civil War,
  1861-1865--Social aspects. | United States--History--Civil War,
  1861-1865--Food supply. | United States--History--Civil War,
  1861-1865--Regimental histories.
Classification: LCC E468.9 .H373 2025 | DDC 973.7455/2--dc23/eng/20241216
LC record available at https://lccn.loc.gov/2024047812

SB

Savas Beatie
989 Governor Drive, Suite 102
El Dorado Hills, CA 95762
916-941-6896 / sales@savasbeatie.com / www.savasbeatie.com

All of our titles are available at special discount rates for bulk purchases in the United States. Contact us for information.

Printed and bound in the United Kingdom

Dedicated to all the readers who encouraged this project as it simmered and asked after its progress. How grand it would be to have everyone gathered around the table to share a meal and to return thanks for our blessings. I am grateful for the opportunity to preserve the history of brave men who were often hungry, the cooks who struggled to feed them, and families who longed to have them well-fed and home.

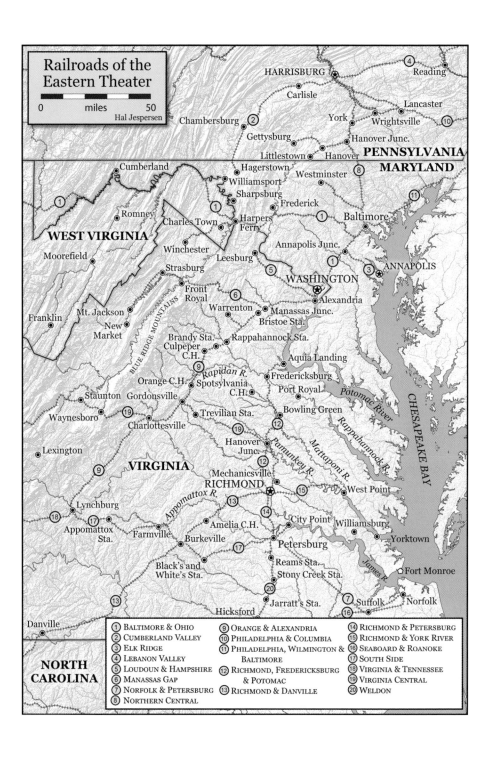

Railroads of the
Eastern Theater

0   miles   50
Hal Jespersen

HARRISBURG
Reading
Carlisle
Lancaster
Chambersburg ②   York   Wrightsville   ⑩
Gettysburg   Hanover Junc.
Littlestown   Hanover   PENNSYLVANIA
Cumberland   Hagerstown   Westminster   ⑧   MARYLAND
Williamsport
Sharpsburg   ⑪
Romney   Frederick
Charles Town   Harpers   ①   Baltimore
WEST VIRGINIA   Ferry
Moorefield   Winchester   Annapolis Junc.
Leesburg   ①
Strasburg   ⑤   ③   ANNAPOLIS
WASHINGTON
Franklin   Mt. Jackson   Front   ⑥   Alexandria
New   Royal   Warrenton   Manassas Junc.
Market   Bristoe Sta.
Lexington   Brandy Sta.   Rappahannock Sta.
Culpeper
C.H.   Aquia Landing
⑨   Rapidan R.   Fredericksburg
Orange C.H.   Spotsylvania   Port Royal
Staunton   Gordonsville   C.H.   Potomac River   CHESAPEAKE BAY
Waynesboro   ⑲   Bowling Green
Charlottesville   Trevilian Sta.   Rappahannock R.
⑲
Lexington   Hanover   Pamunkey R.   Mattaponi R.
Junc.
⑨   VIRGINIA   Mechanicsville
RICHMOND   West Point
⑬   ⑮
Lynchburg   ⑬   ⑭   City Point   Williamsburg
⑱   ⑰   Amelia C.H.   Yorktown
Appomattox   Farmville   Burkeville   Petersburg
Sta.   ⑰
Black's and   Reams Sta.   Fort Monroe
White's Sta.   Stony Creek Sta.   James R.
⑬   ⑳
Hicksford   Jarratt's Sta.   ⑦   Suffolk   Norfolk
Danville   ⑯

NORTH
CAROLINA

① BALTIMORE & OHIO   ⑨ ORANGE & ALEXANDRIA   ⑭ RICHMOND & PETERSBURG
② CUMBERLAND VALLEY   ⑩ PHILADELPHIA & COLUMBIA   ⑮ RICHMOND & YORK RIVER
③ ELK RIDGE   ⑪ PHILADELPHIA, WILMINGTON &   ⑯ SEABOARD & ROANOKE
④ LEBANON VALLEY   BALTIMORE   ⑰ SOUTH SIDE
⑤ LOUDOUN & HAMPSHIRE   ⑫ RICHMOND, FREDERICKSBURG   ⑱ VIRGINIA & TENNESSEE
⑥ MANASSAS GAP   & POTOMAC   ⑲ VIRGINIA CENTRAL
⑦ NORFOLK & PETERSBURG   ⑬ RICHMOND & DANVILLE   ⑳ WELDON
⑧ NORTHERN CENTRAL

TABLE OF CONTENTS

MAP

ABBREVIATIONS

CV	*Confederate Veteran*
DU	Duke University
NCDAH	North Carolina Department of Archives and History
SHC	Southern Historical Collection, University of North Carolina, Chapel Hill
SHSP	*Southern Historical Society Papers*
UGA	University of Georgia
VMI	Virginia Military Institute

Photos have been placed throughout the text for the convenience of the reader.

Introduction

"I am as harty as a pig, able to eat all I can get and more too," David Parker wrote home as his regiment was mustered into Confederate service at Camp Magnum, near Raleigh. "We have corn bread and bacon and pease and wheat bread and rise a plenty, but I can not eat it without something to wash it down." Parker recalled all the buttermilk he had wasted over the years and wished for it now. David Parker was not a wealthy man. He owned a farm valued at just $250, with $279 in personal wealth, according to the 1860 census. However, on March 21, 1862, Parker, with his brother Elijah, enlisted in a local company being formed in the North Carolina mountains for the 54th North Carolina Troops. At 34 years old, he left behind his wife, Nancy, and four children under the age of eight.[1]

Unlike many in his company, Parker had some cooking experience. Not long after arriving in camp, he began cooking for his mess of fifteen, earning a dollar per man per month, doubling his salary as a private. In August, the regiment was assigned to garrison duty in Richmond. Parker wrote home in November that he was still cooking for a mess of fifteen, a chore that excluded him from guard duty. But he was starting to complain, as all they had was beef and crackers. "I don't think I can stand the scarcities much longer," he confessed to Nancy, adding that he had lost seven pounds. When sick, he wrote home in December that he had to spend "a site of money" to purchase items to help him recover. Even though he remained a private, Parker had a promotion of sorts in January 1863, now cooking for the officers of his company. "It is given up that I am the best cook in the company," he wrote. Gathering firewood, bringing water, tending the fire, and cooking were his sole responsibilities. A month later, the men were complaining of

1 Riley Henry, ed., *Pen in Hand: David Parker Civil War Letters* (Morgan Hills, CA, 2014), 8.

short rations. However, due to his unofficial position, Parker ate well, better than any of the other privates.[2]

Parker survived the battles of Fredericksburg, Chancellorsville, and Gettysburg unscathed. While stationed near Orange Court House in September, he became an entrepreneur. Parker purchased three bushels of peaches for $23, borrowed a horse to transport them back to camp, and then sold the peaches for $47. It is unclear how often he repeated the strategy, for, on November 11, Parker was captured at Rappahannock Station and sent to Point Lookout. Paroled around March 9, 1864, Parker returned to his regiment and was wounded in the forearm on September 24 at New Market. Before being wounded, he found the food in the Shenandoah Valley much to his liking. Apples and corn were plentiful; "they cost us nothing but to go into the orchards and get them." Nevertheless, army-issued rations were sparse.[3]

Parker's letters showed a marked difference when he returned to the army from his hospital stay. "It is the hardest time in this army that I have saw since I have been out in the service and if it does not get better the soldiers will not stand it long. They are all threatening to run away if they don't give them more to eat," he wrote on December 20, 1864. Rations had increased slightly by his December 28 letter, yet he was concerned that the surplus might not last. Many of his messmates in the Confederate army were leaving, heading home, or toward the Federal lines. Parker did not want to desert, "but hunger will make men do that they do not want to do. So long as Jefferson Davis does feed me . . . I will stay with him." Parker wrote that the good rations he had enjoyed at the end of December were just a "Christmas spree," and prospects were as bleak as ever. "We do not get enough to eat," he confided. Parker, however, stayed until the end. He was wounded, probably on April 2, 1865, as the Federals swarmed over the works around Petersburg. He lingered in a Richmond hospital until April 14, when he died, another casualty of a cause lost.[4]

David Parker's letters provide a rich narrative regarding the story of food in the Army of Northern Virginia. Rations were plentiful early on, and his cooking abilities worked to his advantage. There was always more to eat at the officers' table. Frequently, there was a farmer's field or orchard to raid while on active campaign. As the Federal armies closed in, cutting off outside foodstuffs to the army in Virginia, many began to slip off, unable to endure long, cold nights with practically nothing

2 Ibid., 5–6, 44, 45, 59, 62.

3 Ibid., 102, 123.

4 Ibid., 133, 142. Parker's date of wounding is unknown, only that he was admitted to a Richmond hospital on April 3.

to eat. Parker's experiences resembled those of numerous other Confederate soldiers. There were many reasons Confederate armies were unsuccessful in their endeavors to fend off Federal advances. In *Feeding Lee's Army of Northern Virginia*, I contend that foodstuffs played a significant role in the demise of the Confederate army in Virginia.

Bell Irvin Wiley explored foodstuffs in a broad sense in a chapter entitled "Bad Beef and Corn Bread," in his classic, *The Life of Johnny Reb* (1943). Wiley places the blame for hungry Confederates not on production, but on distribution, faulting Commissary General Lucius Northrop, who tied everything in red-tape bureaucracy. There was also a lack of salt to preserve meat, inadequate transportation, a deficiency in the Confederate finance department to pay farmers, and even a lack of packing materials to ship foodstuffs. The loss of the Mississippi River impeded transporting supplies from further west. Other historians have also surveyed foodstuffs. William C. Davis examined both sides in *A Taste for War: The Culinary History of the Blue and Gray* (2003), as did Joan Cashin in *War Stuff: The Struggle for Human and Environmental Resources in the American Civil War* (2018) and Judkin Browning and Timothy Silver in *An Environmental History of the Civil War* (2020). Four other books bear special mention. Andrew Smith's *Starving the South: How the North Won the Civil War* (2011) and R. Douglas Hunt's *Agriculture and the Confederacy: Policy, Productivity, and Power in the Civil War South* (2015) are essential contributions to the overall understanding of food in the South during the war. Jerrold Moore's *Confederate Commissary General: Lucius Bellinger Northrop and the Subsistence Bureau of the Southern Army* (1996) comes to the defense of a person considered by some the most hated man in the Confederacy. Arguably, the most important book is Richard Goff's *Confederate Supply* (1969). While there are more recent volumes on logistics, Goff's tome is still the best on the subject. However, that landmark text looks at the subject of food across the South, while this present study is concerned with only the principal army in Virginia, providing a much more focused analysis.[5]

My interest developed in the last two decades of the 20th century. I was heavily involved in Civil War interpretation, and the food-related questions of visitors drove me to letters and diaries in search of answers. Then in the late 1990s, while working on a book on the 37th North Carolina Troops, I came across a soldier's letter thanking the people back home for a box. The box contained eggs, only one of which broke in transit. How was this logistical miracle accomplished? The eggs were packed in sawdust, I discovered. Later, while writing a history of the Branch-Lane brigade, I devoted almost five pages to food in the army. These

---

5 Bell Wiley, *The Life of Johnny Reb* (Baton Rouge, 1943), 96–97.

pages moved me to believe that the subject warranted additional research. A rich array of sources, along with the strategic and historical importance of the Army of Northern Virginia, led to a focus on these men and their experiences with food.

When it comes to sources, a great emphasis has been placed on war-time letters and diaries, instead of relying upon elderly soldiers writing decades later. War-time letters and diaries narrate an almost daily history of food being issued (or not) by the army, foods from home, rations eaten on campaign, or meals provided in hospitals. There are a few instances when post-war accounts do figure into the narrative. For instance, Carlton McCarthy, a former private in the Richmond Howitzers, wrote in 1882: "The historian who essays to write the 'grand movements' will hardly stop to tell how the hungry private fried his bacon, baked his biscuit, and smoked his pipe." This volume seeks to remedy this oversight. Private McCarthy, I hope your skillet is good and greasy.[6]

Acknowledgments

Projects like this take a long time to develop, incurring many debts of gratitude over that period. I posted several times each week on social media as I wrote this book, and many people responded with helpful comments and suggestions. This is a new way to crowd-source history.

Several people helped in many ways. Mark Wade has a profound knowledge of Maryland soldiers. John Winebarger fielded numerous questions concerning the medical profession, and Charlie Knight patiently answered all my questions concerning Robert E. Lee.

The production team at Savas Beatie are great folks to work with. I am particularly grateful to Theodore P. Savas for taking a chance on this unconventional topic, and to Sarah Closson, Sarah Keeney, Veronica Kane, Rebecca Hill, and David Snyder for their hard work on this project.

Finally, many thanks to my readers: Lee White, Charlie Knight, John Guss, and John Winebarger. Your comments helped make this book all the better. And as always, to Elizabeth Baird Hardy. Thanks for your reads, comments, and feedback. Thank you for being as interested in this story as I am.

---

6 Carlton McCarthy, *Detailed Minutiae of Soldier Life* (Lincoln, 1993), 16.

Prologue

Pre-War Foodstuffs

"We live on fat bacon and bread—hard fare in comparison with home, but we must get used to it, for we are going to get no better during the campaign." James Edmondson, 4th Virginia Infantry, penned these words to his wife Emma from Harper's Ferry in April 1861. Edmondson's sentiment was expressed frequently over the next four years. From the lowest private to the highest general, the volunteer soldiers missed foods that once graced their tables.[1]

In 1860, the Southern states boasted vast and diverse resources in agriculture. Some areas, like those along the Mississippi River, grew cash crops such as cotton, procuring some of their foodstuffs from mid-western farmers. Other regions, like Louisiana, specialized in one or two crops, such as sugar and molasses. Steamers supplied port cities with food from far and wide along the coast. Coffee came from South America, tea from East India, and fine wines from Europe. The growth of railroads in the 1850s allowed luxury items to be transported inland while moving staple goods from the interior areas to larger markets. However, most farmers were subsistence farmers, growing what they needed, with a little extra to sell or barter to procure items they could not grow, such as coffee and salt.

Pork was the staple of just about every diet. Hogs were killed in the fall, salted, and smoked, providing meat for months. Cattle could not be preserved as efficiently, so Southerners ate beef less frequently. Poultry was often a treat, as eggs were more important than meat. Coastal area residents consumed fish and oysters. Wild game, such as deer, squirrel, and rabbits, bedecked the tables of many abodes. Corn was ground into meal, and thus cornbread was more prevalent than

---

1 Charles Turner, ed., *My Dear Emma: War Letters of Col. James K. Edmondson, 1861-1865* (Verona, VA, 1978), 5.

wheat bread. Also, corn became hominy or grits, or it was boiled or roasted. Rice, in certain areas, was also very common. Turnips, sweet potatoes, and peas were staples. Irish potatoes were more common further north. Fruits, including apples and peaches, were plentiful. They were eaten fresh, made into pies, and dried for wintertime use. Milk was drunk separated as "sweet milk" or as buttermilk. Lamb and mutton were more common among the affluent, and the luxury foods a person could buy in a large city included refined sugar, cheeses, raisins, almonds, and ice.[2]

Among those filling the rank and file of the Confederate forces, pre-war diets were simple and provided adequate nutritional value for their daily lives. While their army rations could mimic tables at home occasionally, there was never enough fare to help them endure the exertions of camp and campaigns.

2 Sam Hilliard, *Hog Meat and Hoecake* (Athens, GA, 1972), 37–69.

Chapter 1

"We are having a right hard time
of it in the eating line"

Army-Issued Food and Food in Camp

"We get plenty to eat such as it is, hard crackers and crackers hard," William Stilwell, 53rd Georgia Infantry, wrote home on July 1, 1862. Stilwell and his fellow Georgia soldiers had not seen much of the war. The regiment was recruited in the spring of 1862, arriving in Virginia during the Seven Days campaign. For Stilwell, foodstuffs never really improved. He wrote of living on half a cracker and parched corn and spending almost all his money on apples and bacon when he was sick. He also mentioned the area around Winchester being "eat out of everything," of rations lasting two days instead of six, and trying and failing to catch fish. "Southern people were never made to starve," he complained in a letter home in April 1863.[1]

From the infant days of the Confederacy in Virginia through the surrender at Appomattox, officials struggled to keep the armies fed. The Subsistence Department, with commissaries in the field, never had enough vegetables, vinegar, or salt. As the war progressed, soldiers often found their issued meat rancid, while the meal or flour was poorly ground and full of husks and insects. Meager nourishment frequently led to disease and, in some cases, death. For the remaining men, bad food or lack thereof led to hunger, low morale, theft, and eventually, desertion. By war's end, the steady decline of already limited foodstuffs through the war years left Robert E. Lee a fraction of the army he could have commanded.

Thousands of recruits, eager to defend their new country, poured into Virginia in the spring of 1861. They were full of enthusiasm, and they were woefully

1 Ronald Moseley, ed., *The Stilwell Letters* (Macon, GA, 2002), 2–3, 10, 28, 60, 145.

unprepared for camp life. Some were clerks, merchants, students straight from the classroom and their teachers, local politicians, mechanics, railroad engineers, and even ministers. Most were farmers. While many had plucked chickens or butchered hogs, few had the culinary skills to prepare food properly. "The cooking department was the greatest obstacle . . . none knew the first principles of cooking," grumbled a soldier from the 31st Virginia Infantry. While some newly minted soldiers attempted to downplay their lack of skill with a frying pan, others were brutally honest. "Our eating here is the worst feature," a South Carolina soldier griped in late June 1861. "[W]e have plenty and that would be good if prepared right. Our biscuits are very different from those we were raised on. I do not know what I would give for a dinner at home. It makes me hungry to think of *clean* milk and butter and well baked bread even if there was not even salt in it. Do not believe that I am suffering for quantity *but for quality*. Oh the cooking. Everything else is better than I hoped for."[2]

The soldiers were often separated into messes to help with cooking responsibilities. Some men gathered wood, tended fires, or hauled water from nearby sources. A trooper in the 3rd Virginia Cavalry told how his company was divided into messes of fourteen men each, with a corporal in charge of drawing rations. Those who were detailed as cooks were usually relieved from daily military duties, such as drill. Alexander McNeill, 2nd South Carolina Infantry, wrote that his mess contained fifteen members but had "two Negro cooks." Most discovered that the enslaved brought from home, or free men of color hired along the way, knew as little about camp cooking as their employers. As the war progressed, men reorganized their messes to suit their tastes. Writing after the war, the famed South Carolina sharpshooter Berry Benson noted that the men drifted "together as their own social desires prompted," and formed their messes.[3]

Ivy Duggan, 15th Georgia Infantry, recorded in August 1861 that his mess consisted of twelve men, with three men detailed to cook at a time. His shift came every fourth day. They did not have, nor did they want, a servant, he chronicled in his diary. "I think we cook very well under the circumstances." Their mess equipment for twelve men consisted of "a camp kettle, a frying pan and a coffee pot." Men arriving earlier in the war often had nothing to cook with or eat on. One member of the 5th Alabama Infantry recalled in July 1861 that their cooking utensils had

---

2 Ruth Dayton, ed., *The Diary of a Confederate Soldier* (Lewisburg, WV, 1961), 14; John Brinsfield Jr., ed., *The Spirit Divided: Memoirs of Civil War Chaplains* (Macon, GA, 2005), 19–20.

3 Blake Corson Jr., ed., *My Dear Jennie* (Richmond, VA, 1982), 7; Mac Wyckoff, ed., *The Civil War Letters of Alexander McNeill* (Columbia, SC, 2016), 77–78; Susan Benson, ed., *Berry Benson's Civil War Book* (Athens, GA, 1992), 7.

Private David C. Colbert, 46th Virginia Infantry Regiment, displays his tin canteen, pistol, and Bowie knife.

Library of Congress

been left during a recent move, and two or three different messes shared cooking chores using a spade.

As the quartermaster's bureau became organized, companies could requisition mess equipment. Major John B. McClelland was initially responsible for contracts with suppliers for mess equipment for Confederate forces in Virginia. One company that worked with the quartermaster department in Richmond was the Richmond Stove Works, Asa Snyder, proprietor. From 1861 through 1865, Snyder provided hundreds of cast iron kettles and skillets with lids, sometimes called spiders or biscuit bakers. Between October 1861 and March 1862 the Confederate army in Virginia received 3,520 pans, 1,318 kettles, and 500 skillets.[4]

The actual mess equipment of individual soldiers and officers—knives, forks, spoons, and plates—was purchased privately or brought from home, at least early in the war. A soldier in the 15th Alabama Infantry wrote home in January 1862 asking for a knife, fork, tin plate, and cup. Likewise, a Tar Heel soldier, in September 1863, wanted a "knife fork spoon & small tin plate so I can enjoy my beef & bread better." A few months earlier, a member of the 27th Virginia Infantry sent a shopping list home. He wanted a baker or skillet with a lid, one tin kettle, six tin plates, cups, knives, forks, and a camp kettle. Some soldiers supplied themselves with captured tableware. A fragment of a letter from William Jackson,

---

4 Ivy W. Duggan Diary, University of Georgia, 15–16; G. Ward Hubbs, ed., *Voices from Company D* (Athens, GA, 2003), 25–26; Asa Snyder, Confederate Papers Related to Citizens of Business Firms, 1861–1865, Roll 0962, M346, RG 109, NA; Harold Wilson, "Virginia's Industry and the Conduct of War," in Davis & Robertson, ed., *Virginia at War 1862* (Lexington, 2007), 26. McClelland died in August 1862, and in September 1862 was replaced by Maj. William G. Bentley. Major Bentley defined his duty as contracting "for the manufacture of Axes, Tents, Cooking utensils, Drums [and] Fifes" and for issuing of "Clothing, Tents, Camp [and] Garrison Equipage for the same." William Bentley to Sir, June 14, 1864, William Bentley, Roll 022, M331, RG109, CMSR, NA.

8th Alabama Infantry, recalled collecting not only food, paper, and envelopes but a knife, fork, and spoon. One Georgia soldier picked up a knife, fork, and two spoons after one of the Overland campaign battles in 1864. By November 1863, the government shops in Richmond were building mess chests. Georgia Assistant Surgeon Abner McGarity wrote of placing a requisition for such a chest. He was surprised when it arrived promptly and "well furnished with everything necessary." Lieutenant Colonel John Lilley likewise placed an order for a mess chest on March 17, 1864, and received his chest five days later, noting that it only cost $5. Most of the mess equipment a soldier carried was made of tin, cheap and lightweight. Sometimes, finer ware might come from home, especially for officers. Charles Blackford, serving in the 2nd Virginia Cavalry, noted that his supper was being cooked and, "in another fence corner my table is spread with china your mother sent me, ready for supper." When Gen. James Conner requested some china from home in September 1864, he asked his family to pack it in rice to withstand the journey.[5]

Early in the war, every infantry and cavalry regiment had an assistant commissary of subsistence officer, usually at the rank of captain. According to regulations, these men were bonded because they handled money. A regimental commissary officer was responsible for procuring food for his regiment. There were requisition forms to submit, and once rations were obtained, he had to keep them safe until issuing them to the men. In the early days, the commissaries were issued scales for weighing foodstuffs. These portions were then allocated to the individual companies through a non-commissioned officer. The company's non-commissioned officers were responsible for dividing portions equally among the men. Most regiments also had a commissary sergeant. The assistant commissary of subsistence was responsible for driving the wagons and livestock on campaigns and penning the livestock every evening while securing a guard. The wagons themselves belonged to the quartermaster's department. Officers purchased rations from the commissary for the war's first two and a half years.

5   Edmund Burnett, ed., "Letters of Barnett Hardeman Cody," *The Georgia Historical Quarterly* (Dec. 1939), 2:363; Laura Peace, ed., *To Tranquillity* (Charleston, SC, 2018), 159; Turner, *My Dear Emma*, 118; Wayne Wood & Mary Jackson, eds., *"Kiss Sweet Little Lillah for me"* (Birmingham, AL, 2000), 50; Moseley, *The Stilwell Letters*, 261; Abner Embry McGarity, "Letters of a Confederate Surgeon: Dr. Abner Embry McGarity," in Edmund Burnett, ed., *The Georgia Historical Quarterly* (Sept. 1945), 2:181; John Doak Lilley, "Diary of Lieutenant Colonel," in Robert Driver, ed., *Augusta Historical Bulletin* (Fall 1991), 27:18; Susan & Charles Blackford, eds., *Letters from Lee's Army* (Lincoln, NE, 1998), 112; Mary Moffett, ed., *Letters of General James Conner* (Columbia, SC, 1950), 152. Both Robert E. Lee's and Stonewall Jackson's mess equipment, which survive, were made of tin. J. E. B. Stuart's pewter cup is in the collection of the American Civil War Museum in Richmond, VA.

Commissaries of a regiment or brigade might look similar to their counterparts in the Federal army. *Harper's Weekly, April 18, 1863*

With the influx of new troops in the Manassas area, the Commissary Department struggled to keep up with supplies. While still in Alabama, the Provisional Confederate Congress created the Commissary Department of Subsistence, placing Lucius Northrop at the head of the bureau. Born in Charleston in 1811, Northrop was a West Point graduate and veteran of service out West and in Florida. Wounded in 1839, he was dropped from the rolls and reinstated by his friend Jefferson Davis. He was still listed on the sick rolls when the war began. One of Davis's first appointments made Northrop a lieutenant colonel, placing him in charge of the Commissary Department. For this role, Northrop's qualifications were meager. He had his West Point education and years of service as a dragoon officer. He studied medicine, although he had not practiced, and he spent the winter of 1842-43 surveying the food-producing areas of the Southwest. While Northrop was honest and practiced excellent economy while in office (sometimes to his detriment), he was ill-prepared for the size and scope of the Confederate armies he was charged with provisioning.[6]

Northrop faced numerous challenges. He wanted to buy non-perishable foodstuffs in quantity, stockpiling needed items as a contingency plan. Yet he had little cash at his disposal. Instead, he had Confederate bonds issued by the Treasury Department, redeemable in months. Most farmers needed specie to buy supplies to re-plant and refused to take the bonds. There was scarcity, even in the agrarian South. Much of the South, especially areas connected to a railroad or a navigable body of water, cultivated cash crops such as cotton and tobacco. These areas imported various foodstuffs, such as hogs, from the Midwest. Areas with

6 Northrop was Davis's third choice for the job. First to decline was Richard Griffin, then William Maynadier. Northrop himself wrote that he declined the position twice. Jerrold Moore, *Confederate Commissary General* (Shippensburg, PA, 1996), 48–49.

self-sustaining production, like the mountain South, lacked the means to grow surplus or transport crops. Northrop also faced excessive food bills coming from volunteer regiments. Often, when regiments were transferring from other states to Virginia, officers paid for the food their men consumed. These bills were submitted to Northrop's office for compensation. Northrop refused to pay, leaving officers to foot the bills. Commissary officers in regiments were also a challenge. They were appointed by regimental and brigade commanders and did not report to Northrop. Many were new to their jobs, and omissions in requisitions were frequent.[7]

Northrop himself created some early supply problems. Instead of paying the requested prices of Manassas-area farmers, Northrop stockpiled flour in Richmond, shipping it via the railroad to the soldiers encamped in the region. Accounting for the cost of transportation, the price was the same. Much of the salt pork for the army came from Tennessee, where prices were lower and hogs more plentiful. The distance and non-standard railroad gauges requiring the meat to be unloaded and reloaded in Richmond caused delays. There was one railroad into Manassas to transport troops, armaments, and foodstuffs. Eatables were often left rotting at depots.

Nevertheless, soldiers put a good spin on their plight in their letters back home. "We have always had plenty to eat. The fare, it is true is rough such as we are unaccustomed to at home. We did not expect to live in the way we have been raised. Here soldiers must and should willingly put up with soldier fare and without a murmur submit to the regulations of the Army," a member of the 2nd South Carolina told his family in June 1861. Others were more honest. A soldier in the 9th Alabama Infantry confessed at the end of July that they were living "very hard here nothing but Wheat Bread and meat and not enough of that."[8]

Manassas was a resounding Confederate victory. However, the Confederates' failure to follow up that victory with a march into the Federal capital left many public questions. Letters flowed back and forth between military leaders and politicians. Lieutenant Colonel Richard B. Lee, Jr., the new chief commissary for the Army of the Potomac, precursor of the Army of Northern Virginia (ANV), wrote Davis on July 23, 1861, informing him that army supplies were "alarmingly reduced, in consequence of the non-fulfillment of requisitions of the Commissary General." Confederate general P. G. T. Beauregard telegraphed Davis, asking that

---

7 For a more in-depth look at the early problems faced by Northrop across the Confederacy, see Richard Goff, *Confederate Supply* (Durham, NC, 1969), 10–40; Moore, *Confederate Commissary General*, 51–60.

8 Goff, *Confederate Supply*, 20–21; Wyckoff, *The Civil War Letters of Alexander McNeill*, 44; John Carter, ed., *Welcome the Hour of Conflict: William Cowan McClellan and the 9th Alabama* (Tuscaloosa, AL, 2007), 42–43.

Confederate General P. G. T. Beauregard warned Confederate officials about the lack of food following the battle of First Manassas. *Library of Congress*

no additional troops be sent to him due to lack of rations. At the same time, Beauregard wrote to other Congressmen on July 29 that the "want of food and transportation had made us lose all the fruits of our victory. We ought at this moment to be in or about Washington. . . . God only knows when we will be able to advance. . . . Cannot something be done towards furnishing us more expeditiously and regularly with food and transportation?" The letter was read before Congress, and a resolution was sent to Davis, asking about the condition of the Subsistence Department. Davis fired off his own letters. Beauregard contacted Davis again, saying "that some of his regiments were without food." Davis wrote Joseph Johnston, stating that local citizens had flour and beef, obviously unaware of Northrop's actions. If "the troops have suffered for food, the neglect of the subsistence department demands investigation," Davis told Johnston. In the end, Davis defended Northrop, and Northrop removed Richard Lee, along with another commissary officer, William Fowle, who had worked with the army in collecting local foodstuffs.[9]

Overall, the men in the camps around Manassas wrote disparagingly of their rations as the calendar slipped into August. A Maryland soldier stationed near Fairfax Court House stated that it was a "difficult thing to make bread and coffee good enough to support life." They lacked yeast and any way to roll out biscuits. They frequently received corn meal and made "first-rate corn bread." Local

---

9 Alfred Roman, *The Military Operations of General Beauregard*, 2 vols. (New York, 1884), 1:121–122; *War of the Rebellion: A Compilation of the Official Records of the Union and Confederate Armies* (Washington, D.C., 1880–1901), Series 1, vol. 5, 767; Series 1, vol. 51, pt. 2, 204, hereafter cited as *OR*. All references are to Series 1 unless otherwise noted.

people sometimes baked bread for the troops or sold them eggs and chickens. In September, an Alabamian recorded that at dress parade, the soldiers were told that they would be living for the foreseeable future on five days' rations of beef, and two of salt pork. "If they continue I think we will be learned to live on nothing, or only what we buy. We are now out of coffee and sugar and have had nothing but tough beef for three or four days, and from all appearances there is no prospect of a change soon." A few days later, a mess mate remarked that they were fed only beef. "[F]requently there can be seen men walking about, half bent with their hands upon their abdomens looking awful angry." By mid-October, the commissary was out of coffee. Instead, it began issuing whiskey, causing additional problems. One soldier wrote of getting "*bust head* whiskey." Those who did not drink sold their rations to others. By October 14, a member of the 33rd Virginia Infantry recalled that they could not "draw any more on account of some of the men getting drunk."[10]

Many soldiers wrote about supplementing their rations by purchasing foodstuffs from local community members. "We would have nothing to eat if it were not for what we buy," recalled a South Carolina soldier writing from Fairfax County on August 1. Soldiers visited neighboring farms to beg or buy food. Some citizens experienced a cash boom, while others saw their winter supplies seriously depleted. Soldiers bought anything they could. A man in the 45th North Carolina Troops bought turnips; an Alabamian, chestnuts and apples; a member of the 6th North Carolina State Troops purchased oysters, shucked, at $2 a gallon; besides vegetables, a South Carolinian procured butter, mutton, milk, and chickens. Another South Carolinian wrote of purchasing chickens, eggs, butter, honey, potatoes, "and almost any thing else we want." Other soldiers walked or rode to some adjacent farm and dined with a family. Sergeant Alexander McNeill, 2nd South Carolina, wrote of walking half a mile for a meal near Vienna while on picket. Tar Heel Calvin Leach went "up the railroad" in mid-September and purchased peaches and some grapes a week later. Soldiers often complained about the high prices they were forced to pay. Writing on December 1, a Virginia soldier lamented that it took "a month's wages to buy anything now."[11]

---

10 Randolph McKim, *A Soldier's Recollections: Leaves from the Diary of a Young Confederate* (New York, 1910), 46; Hubbs, *Voices from Company D*, 42–43, 61; Harland Jessup, ed., *The Painful News I Have to Write: Letters and Diaries of Four Hite Brothers of Page County in the Service of the Confederacy* (Baltimore, MD, 1998), 33.

11 Guy Everson & Edward Simpson, eds., *Far, Far from Home: The Wartime Letters of Dick and Sally Simpson, 3rd South Carolina Volunteers* (New York, 1994), 38; Thomas Cutrer, ed., *Longstreet's Aide* (Charlottesville, VA, 1995), 37; Ellen Stone, ed., *Letters Home to Baughn Mountain, 1862–1865* (n.p., 1979), 27; Carter, *Welcome the Hour of Conflict*, 97; Richard Iobst & Louis Manarin, *The Bloody Sixth* (Raleigh, 1965), 49; Wyckoff, *The Civil War Letters of Alexander McNeill*, 77–78, 84; Everson

This proximity to farmsteads produced some problems. Captain Thomas Goree, on Gen. James Longstreet's staff and stationed near Fairfax Court House, felt sorry for local citizens. They had a fine crop of grains, but the harvest suffered due to the impressment of horses and wagons. Their corn crops were also good, but soldiers were "making sad havoc of it." Ivy Duggan, 15th Georgia, recalled their camp near a cornfield where roasting ears were beginning to ripen. Officers were forced to place guards "day and night to keep out soldiers. This is rather hard upon those who have never visited it; but it is very common for the innocent to suffer for the crimes of the guilty." In October, while encamped near Bunker Hill, Duggan was instructed to lie down in the provision shed while guarding the meat. Sometimes, soldiers ran afoul of the guards. Members of two different companies in the 5th Alabama raided a farmer's hog lot in October, killing eleven. When the guards arrived, the cohorts split, leaving one of the pigs. The regiment's colonel allowed the guards to have the one left behind while arresting the perpetrator's company commanders. Virginia artillerist William Jones and two pards were out foraging within fifty yards of a house when they were apprehended. "I was never so vexed in my life," Jones confessed. The guard trotted the men along for the remainder of the day, visiting various headquarters and depositing detainees. When Jones reached his camp, he was greeted "with jests and laughter by our comrades."[12]

Confederate officials in Richmond were doing their best to supply the troops in Virginia. Northrop had contracted with mills in Fredericksburg, Petersburg, and Richmond to produce flour. The Haxall and Crenshaw Company in Richmond agreed to supply 25,000 bushels of flour. While the government had purchased a bakery in Richmond, loaves of bread spoiled before they could be sent to the army. The bakery turned to hard bread, or hardtack, but discovered that it often became musty when packed. Instead, raw flour was shipped to the army, and soldiers became responsible for baking bread. Special agents visited Virginia farmers willing to sell to the government. Depots were established in Staunton, Lynchburg, and Fredericksburg, and a pork-processing facility at Charlottesville. However, problems persisted. Confederate commanders held boxcars full of supplies at railyards near their commands as temporary warehouses. If troops needed foodstuffs, these cars required unloading. Northrop also employed agents to purchase meat as well. A meat-packing plant was established at Thoroughfare Gap, not far from Johnston's army. By the end of 1861, small stockpiles of salt pork

---

& Simpson, *Far, Far from Home*, 40; Calvin Leach Diary, September 9, September 25, 1861, SHC; Dayton, *The Diary of a Confederate Soldier*, 40.

12 Cutrer, *Longstreet's Aide*, 37; Ivy W. Duggan Diary, UGA, 15–16, 43; Hubbs, *Voices from Company D*, 55–56; Constance Jones, ed., *The Spirits of Bad Men Made Perfect* (Carbondale, IL, 2020), 132.

The Haxall Flour Mill in Richmond held contracts with the Confederate government. *Library of Congress*

rations, flour, and hardtack were stored in both Richmond and Northern Virginia. Supplies such as coffee and vinegar soon became scarce. When the price of coffee exceeded the price the Subsistence Department could afford, Northrop reserved his supply for hospitals. As winter set in, the only army meat rations were salt pork. Brigadier General W. H. C. Whiting confessed in March 1862 that his men, stationed around Occoquan, had been on half rations for parts of the winter.[13]

Johnston's army in Manassas was not the only Confederate force in Virginia needing food in 1861. There were detachments of soldiers spread out from Norfolk into the mountains of western Virginia. It was a struggle to provision them. Soldiers on the coast had more opportunities than those in the mountains. From Portsmouth, in May, a South Carolina soldier wrote of purchasing and abundance of fish. "Oysters, crabs, and fish of all kinds, abound in profusion, oysters 10

---

13 Goff, *Confederate Supply*, 36; Moore, *Confederate Commissary General*, 60, 113–115, 118; Wilson, "Virginia's Industry and the Conduct of War," 25; *OR* 5, 532. Northrop and many others argued, unsuccessfully, for the government to take control of the railroads. Robert Black III, *The Railroads of the Confederacy* (Chapel Hill, NC 1998), 96–100.

Joseph E. Johnston was initially responsible for getting food to his army.

Library of Congress

cts a quart and fish 12 ½ cts a string, furnishes to the not overburdened purse an opportunity to gratify the appetite," he claimed a month later. A Virginia cavalryman stationed at Williamsburg divulged that some of his fellow troopers rode their horses "out in the water and sat on them fishing for crabs. . . . After the tide commenced falling we caught oysters and gathered shells." Victuals were harder to come by in the western part of the state. Writing from Valley Mountain in Pocahontas County in August, Virginia artillerist Ham Chamberlayne stated there was a "great difficulty about the Commissariat, from length of road to be waggoned over." That same month, an officer on Robert E. Lee's staff in western Virginia complained that the country knew little of their struggles. Conditions scarcely improved as Confederate forces attempted to outmaneuver the enemy during the disastrous Rich Mountain campaign.[14]

Confederate forces at Manassas Gap occupied a defensive line 60-plus miles long, stretching from the Potomac River into the lower Shenandoah Valley, manned by 47,617 effective troops. A wagon shortage and poorly fed horses slowed the delivery of rations from the railhead to troops in various encampments. To help haul supplies, Johnston ordered the railroad extended from Manassas to Centerville. A member of the 11th Georgia Infantry wrote in February 1862 that the spur was almost finished to Centerville. He thought it would save horse flesh and recounted how he had seen eight dead horses on his way to the picket line and eight more while on picket duty. Johnston labored to provision his army. Sawmills that cut lumber for winter quarters now produced planks for corduroy

---

14 Clyde Wiggins III, ed., *My Dearest Friend* (Macon, GA, 2007), 3–4; S. William Fisher Plane, "Letters of William Fisher Plane, C.S.A. to His Wife," in Joseph Lewis, Jr., ed., *The Georgia Historical Quarterly* (June 1964), 218; Corson, *My Dear Jennie*, 22; C. G. Chamberlayne, ed., *Ham Chamberlayne—Virginia* (Richmond, VA, 1932), 28; John Washington to aunt, Aug. 31, 1861, John Washington Papers, Virginia Historical Society.

Confederate soldiers built substantial winter quarters in 1861–1862. *Library of Congress*

roads. Brigade and division officers were pressed to submit accurate requisitions to deliver only necessary supplies. Johnston managed to stockpile millions of pounds of sustenance at Manassas, a storehouse that could have provisioned his army when he chose to go on the offensive. Yet all that effort and organization came to naught. Johnston feared a Federal advance against his overextended lines. In February, he met with Davis in Richmond, receiving permission to retreat behind the Rappahannock River. By the first week of March, Johnston's men were on the road south. While some supplies were hauled away, the rest were destroyed. Some troops were marched to the depot and allowed to help themselves. Government stores were incinerated, along with countless boxes shipped to soldiers from home. A soldier in the 23rd North Carolina Troops wrote that at the express office at Manassas, he witnessed "hundreds of boxes burst open by the soldiers as they had the privilege of doing so." "We were not permitted to carry more than we could carry on our backs," another Georgia soldier wrote. "We left a great many things, some of the messes lost as much as twenty or thirty pounds of lard & a great many plates, ovens & such things."[15]

15 James Thompson, "A Georgia Boy with 'Stonewall' Jackson: The Letters of James Thomas Thompson," in Aurelia Austin, ed., *The Virginia Magazine of History & Biography* (July 1962), 321; Peace, *To Tranquillity*, 88; Stephen Sears, *To the Gates of Richmond* (New York, 1983), 12–14; Gregory Parks & Steve Baker, eds., "I am Writing on My Canteen: A Georgia Soldier's Letters Home," *Company Front* (June 2001), 13. While scorn was heaped on Johnston for the loss of supplies, he had

In some respects, the new Confederate positions were easier to provision. The Richmond, Fredericksburg & Potomac Railroad connected the capital to defenses behind the Rappahannock River. The Virginia Central Railroad connected the rich Shenandoah Valley to the east, while the Richmond & York River Railroad ran to the White House landing on the York River. Yet the Confederacy relinquished an area that produced sheep, swine, wheat, rye, oats, beans, potatoes, and other desperately needed foodstuffs. As Johnston was preparing to reposition his army, Federal forces captured much of central Tennessee, denying the army in Virginia a major source of pork.[16]

By April, soldiers across Virginia were reporting short rations. Near the Culpeper Court House, a staff officer under J. E. B. Stuart reported "our bread awful." From Fredericksburg, a member of the 55th Virginia Infantry told his loved ones, "We are having a right hard time of it in the eating line." His dinner consisted of "a few tough biscuits and a piece of Souse." Writing from Yorktown, a South Carolinian communicated that their "fare generally has been scanty and poor." Usually drawing bacon, beef, and flour, they had drawn rice "once or twice," but never coffee. They drank sassafras tea when they could get sugar for it. They were also fishing, catching both fish and eels in "Stiff Creek," using baskets for the eels. On April 28, the War Department reduced meat rations for the entire Confederate army. Bacon and pork rations went from three-fourths of a pound to one-half pound and beef from one and one-quarter pounds to one-half pound daily. Flour and meal rations, to compensate for the reduction, were increased.[17]

In April 1862, the bulk of the Confederate army in Virginia shifted to Yorktown. A large Federal army had landed at Fortress Monroe, stalling in front of Confederate defenses. Much of the Confederates' line of supplies shifted to the Richmond & York River Railroad; the small line was barely completed when the war began. Until mid-May, when the Confederate army retreated closer to Richmond,

---

been telegraphing the subsistence bureau since early January, requesting no supplies sent further than Culpeper Court House. Moore, *Confederate Commissary General*, 127.

16 Those counties north and east of the Confederate defensive lines that were located in a no-man's land include Stafford, Prince William, Fauquier, Fairfax, and Loudoun. Fauquier was second in the production of sheep, Loudoun was second in bushels of wheat, and Fairfax was second in potatoes. Joseph Kennedy, *Agriculture of the United States* (Washington, 1864), 3:154–165.

17 Robert Trout, *With Pen & Saber: The Letters and Diaries of J. E. B. Stuart's Staff Officers* (Mechanicsburg, PA, 1995), 56; Robert Tombes, ed., *Tell the Children I'll be Home When the Peaches Get Ripe: Letters Home from Lt. Robert Gaines Haile, Jr., Essex Sharpshooters, 55th Va., 1862* (Richmond, VA, 1999), 8; Everson & Simpson, *Far, Far from Home*, 117–118; OR Series 4, 2, 414. Goff argues that the reduction was to ensure a supply of meat for the balance of the year. *Confederate Supply*, 76–77. There was discussion about moving supplies from Gordonsville to Richmond, but Lee and Northrop were against the move. OR 11, pt. 3, 407–408.

the Richmond & York River moved barrels of hardtack, flour, thousands of pieces of bacon, sacks of salt, and other munitions toward the front. Some supplies were offloaded at places like Dispatch Station and transferred to wagons, while others were transferred via ships from West Point to one of the wharves near Williamsburg. Once active campaigning commenced in May, much of the Richmond & York River Railroad was destroyed by retreating Confederates.[18]

Northrop claimed that he had ten days' rations for 70,000 men in Richmond, with 10,000 cattle en route from the Shenandoah Valley and another one million rations in Lynchburg. However, those rations did not seem to reach the men in the ranks. "[W]e are barely subsisting upon meat and bread. Our men have to go upon short rations nearly every day," Col. William D. Pender, 6th North Carolina, wrote from near Baltimore Store, east of Richmond, on May 14. On the Chickahominy River, a soldier in the 5th Alabama shared how he and a couple of men were sent into the countryside to purchase meat for their company. He was happy to report that when he returned from his expedition, he found a trunk full of eatables from home. A South Carolinian in Magruder's command mentioned that scurvy was appearing in some regiments. Details were sent out to gather wild vegetables. "The names of the plants are these: wild onions, lamb's quarters, potato tops, and others. . . . I have tried the onions, but I do not relish them. The others, I am afraid, will be worse," he concluded. As the armies became stationary for a few weeks following the retreat from Yorktown, locals from Richmond with food for sale began arriving in camp. "[T]here are a great many market carts running from Richmond to the different encampments, bringing bakers bread and pies such as they are," recalled a member of the 55th Virginia. The prices were "very high, small chickens are selling from a dollar to a dollar & quarter, lambs eight dollars apiece, sugar, brown sixty cents per pound, pies fifty cents apiece, butter I don't know it is selling at." While a couple of engagements were fought at the end of May, active campaigning got underway at the end of June. There were lulls in the fighting, but campaigning lasted for months.[19]

Much had changed by the time the troops returned and went into camp in October 1862. Robert E. Lee now commanded what he styled, "the Army of Northern Virginia" as he replaced Johnston, wounded at the battle of Seven Pines.

18 Richmond & York River Railroad, Confederate Papers Relating to Citizens or Business Firms, 1861–1865, Roll 0862, M346, RG109, NA. While Confederate forces burned bridges as they retreated, the Federals re-built parts of the railroad, using it for their own transportation to the front.

19 Moore, *Confederate Commissary General*, 147–48; William Hassler, ed., *One of Lee's Best Men: The Civil War Letters of General William Dorsey Pender* (Chapel Hill, NC, 1990), 142; Hubbs, *Voices from Company D*, 86; Everson & Simpson, *Far, Far from Home*, 12; Tombes, *When the Peaches Get Ripe*, 50. At some point, some of the cattle were sent elsewhere in anticipation of an evacuation of Richmond.

Robert E. Lee took over the main Confederate Army in Virginia after Joseph Johnston's wounding.
Library of Congress

The soldiers returning to camp in the fall were now hardened veterans, having weathered the battles of Seven Days, Cedar Mountain, Second Manassas, Chantilly, Harper's Ferry, and Sharpsburg. They had experienced both plenty and scarcity on campaigns. In Virginia, supplies were running low overall. A severe drought in the upper South had reduced wheat crops, leading to flour shortages. Fresh beef was almost exhausted, and salt shortages diminished pork shipments to Virginia. The War Department closed Virginia's borders to exports of foodstuffs, allowing officials to impress flour held by speculators.[20]

Confederate soldiers settling into camp near Winchester following the Maryland campaign wrote despairingly of their rations. "We get plenty of beef and bread to eat but that is all we do get, not even peas or rice," penned a Georgia soldier on October 10. "I am getting tired of beef though we fix it up in many ways, boiling, frying, making soup, and such like. I can make splendid bread though it is not so good without anything to go in it but salt and cold water." Another Georgia soldier believed that he and his messmates could fix beef so well that a Georgia cook would be "ashamed of herself cooking beef." A soldier in the 7th South Carolina Infantry complained about the quality and quantity of the beef. He found it impossible to buy anything due to a lack of funds. Many soldiers complained of the government's neglect to pay for their services in the summer and fall of 1862. Few knew that those funds had been redirected to pay for army subsistence.[21]

20 Goff, *Confederate Supply*, 78–79.

21 Moseley, *The Stilwell Letters*, 64; Randall Allen & Keith Bohannon, eds., *Campaigning with "Old Stonewall"* (Baton Rouge, LA, 1998), 173; Keith Jones, ed., *The Boys of Diamond Hill* (Jefferson, NC,

On returning from Maryland, Lee abandoned the prescribed reduction of meat rations, trying to compensate for the lack of vegetables. A trooper from the 1st North Carolina Cavalry stationed near Martinsburg in early November reported one meal per day. The soldiers visited neighboring farms looking for food or begged loved ones to send boxes of provisions. One Georgia soldier recalled the day a raccoon stumbled into camp and ran up a tree. "The boys armed themselves with sticks cut down the tree and had quite an exciting time which ended in the outflanking and capture of 'old zip.'" Another possible reason for Lee's disregarding the directive to cut rations was an opportunity to open a campaign against the Federals. Lee wrote the war department, requesting increased rations to reduce straggling as his army prepared for campaigning. On November 17, the Federal army was discovered at Fredericksburg, threatening a move across the Rappahannock River. If successful, the Federals could be in Richmond before Lee could move Longstreet's and Jackson's soldiers from Winchester. Longstreet took up the line of march on November 18, with Jackson following a few days later.[22]

The march was hard on the Confederate soldiers. Many lacked shoes as they tramped along in the snow and ice. Opinions about provisions were mixed. One South Carolina soldier thought they were better provisioned on this march. A Georgia soldier wrote of marching all day and cooking at night. Foodstuffs were scarce in the area. A member of the 2nd Virginia Cavalry recalled dark flour and tough meat issued by the army. The countryside was "so poor that even hen's grass will not grow. . . . One of my men said, 'Crows fly over this district with haversacks and three days' rations.'" These shortages affected everyone. Chief of Artillery William Pendleton recalled getting a little butter once in camp near Fredericksburg but never any bacon. It was "beef, beef, beef, all the time," he wrote. An Alabamian at Port Royal recalled on December 4 a lack of wood and poor breakfast. They had steer beef and mashed up hard crackers into the beef tallow, producing gravy. Three days later, the same soldier recalled a "poor supper Corn bread & cold beef without salt." He had marched one day on just one and a half crackers.[23]

2011), 59. For more information on the problems between the treasury department and the war department regarding soldier pay, see Goff, *Confederate Supply*, 89–90.

22 Harvey Davis, "Harvey Davis's Unpublished Civil War diary," in Francis Dedmond, ed., *Appalachian Journal* (Summer 1986), 393; Allen & Bohannon, *Campaigning with "Old Stonewall,"* 184; *OR* 21, 1016–17.

23 Spencer Welch, *A Confederate Surgeon's Letters to his Wife* (New York, 1911), 36; Henry McCrea, *Red Dirt and Isinglass* (n.p., 1992), 376; Blackford & Blackford, *Letters from Lee's Army*, 138–139; Susan Lee, *Memoirs of William Nelson Pendleton* (Harrisonburg, PA, 1991), 236–37; Hubbs, *Voices from Company D*, 122, 123.

While the ensuing battle of Fredericksburg did little to interrupt the trickle of provisions coming into the army, there was little food for the victorious Confederate army encamped on the Rappahannock River. "For two days, we have been without a mouthful of meat and but a short allowance of bread," penned one South Carolinian. Confederate soldiers were just as hungry after their victory as they had been before. A member of the 5th Alabama believed, "Our rations are outrageously short now." On December 16, Northrop finally ordered provisions from stockpiles in Charlotte and Atlanta. However, transportation issues slowed the arrival of foodstuffs. Lee's army was consuming 1,000 head of cattle a week, with only 4,500 cattle close by and an additional 4,000 cattle 250 miles away. There were several plans to increase supplies. Agents in Europe were authorized to purchase foodstuffs and ship them overseas. Trade began between the lines. Northrop continued to argue for the power to impress items from the farmers.[24]

Transportation presented one problem with procuring food for the ANV during the winter of 1862–63. Not only were rolling stock and lines wearing out, but certain commanders, including Lee, kept railroad cars in reserve just in case they had to redeploy quickly. Northrop was critical of Lee for withholding rolling stock, for continuing to issue full rations of beef instead of the reduced rations prescribed by the commissary's office, and for refusing to use necks and shanks of cattle. Lee wanted to appeal to the citizens to send supplies for his army, but Northrop vetoed the idea. "No cars from Richmond yesterday," Lee noted in a letter home on February 23. "I fear our short rations for men & horses will have to be curtailed." Lee and Northrop quarreled through the winter months. Lee wanted more of the food stockpiled by Northrop in Richmond sent to provision his army. Northrop wanted Lee to detail men, horses, and wagons across Virginia to gather staples for commissary stores in Richmond. Northrop sent Lt. Col. James Crenshaw to meet with Lee on January 9, yet Lee was with Stuart, planning a response to Federal movements. Crenshaw met with one of Lee's staff, then with Lee's chief quartermaster and commissary officers, before returning to Richmond. On January 13, Lee wrote to Seddon about having some cavalry that could help, but no wagons. Wagons were in short supply throughout the army in Virginia. A staff officer in Colquitt's brigade complained that his brigade had only thirty-seven wagons, six of which were broken down. The brigade had only one foraging wagon, needed five more, and was short horses and mules. In contrast, their Federal

---

24 Wyckoff, *The Civil War Letters of Alexander McNeill*, 178–79; Hubbs, *Voices from Company D*, 127; Goff, *Confederate Supply*, 80; *OR* Series 4, 2, 192–193. Moore argues that there was food nearby, but farmers kept it hidden because Confederate money was worthless. *Confederate Commissary General*, 186–187.

counterparts had one wagon for every forty men. One Confederate division-level commissary officer noted that the roads were so wretched that winter they had to resort to hauling flour on pack horses. The flour had to be repackaged, from barrels to sacks, and he estimated that the loss between repackaging and bad barrels was no less than 28 barrels between December and April.[25]

Lee was genuinely concerned that the Federals might renew attempts at Fredericksburg. He needed his army well-provisioned if they had to assume combat operations. Nevertheless, Northrop enacted another ration reduction in mid-January, which Lee decried to his superiors on January 24, 1863. At the same time, Lee ordered Maj. Gen. William Jones, stationed in the Shenandoah Valley, to send men into neighboring counties to collect foodstuffs. In a February 5 letter, Lee outlined the steps taken to secure provisions in the Shenandoah Valley, writing that there was no beef but some bacon. Lee again wrote on February 11, stating that he had sent wagons into the areas between the Rappahannock and Pamunkey Rivers to collect food. Lee even offered to send men to repair the railroad in East Tennessee, attempting to get rations to his men.[26]

To help alleviate the strain, Lee sent portions of Longstreet's command to the Norfolk area in mid-February. This reduced the troops along the Rappahannock by twenty percent. Longstreet's mission was to block Federal buildup in the area, protect the Weldon Railroad, and gather supplies from Southside Virginia and eastern North Carolina. He impressed every wheeled vehicle he could find, along with oxen and horses, and began harvesting as soon as practical. Enough bacon was gathered to feed Lee's army for two months. Officers paid local citizens, but commissary agents from Richmond arrived soon after, paying more for bacon and forcing Longstreet to offer more. Not all locals cooperated. Some were Unionist in their feelings, selling to the Federals not far away.[27]

Despite the work of Longstreet, the pleading with Commissary General Northrop, and the dispatching of men to gather foodstuffs, Lee's soldiers remained hungry. A member of the 18th North Carolina Troops told his family in January not to worry. "You kneed not think that the government will allow us to starve or go necked, although we get scarce sometimes." A South Carolinian recalled

25 *OR* 51, pt. 2, 675; Clifford Dowdey & Louis Manarin, eds., *Wartime Papers of R. E. Lee* (New York, 1961), 407; Joseph Glatthaar, *General Lee's Army* (New York, 2008), 212; Thomas Ballard, CMSR, M331, Roll 0014, RG109, NA; Crenshaw's report can be found in *OR* 21, 1088–1091. Northrop's biographer writes that he was "flabbergasted" at Lee's "refusal to help acquire the outlying food." Yet Crenshaw wrote that Lee had offered some cavalry to help gather wheat in the Shenandoah Valley. Moore, *Confederate Commissary General*, 197.

26 *OR* 25, pt. 2, 598, 612; 51, pt. 2, 676.

27 Steven Cornier, *The Siege of Suffolk* (Lynchburg, VA, 1989), 175–179.

eating his day's allotment of rations all at once. "Slim, very slim," he penned. Half a loaf of bread was better than no loaf at all. A newspaper correspondent noted in February that the roads were impassable. He believed sleds might be better to use instead of wagons. Brigadier General James H. Lane's soldiers built a corduroy road from their camp to the depot to aid in hauling supplies. The method also worked for the 4th Virginia, whose members wrote of laying pine poles on the roads, covering them with brush. A member of the 2nd South Carolina told family at home that "Every thing is very scarce in camp and the surrounding country. It is hard living now as I have ever experienced—I never hungered for beef as badly before. A morsel of old cow would taste as good as 'ginger bread.'" Things were little improved by mid-March when a member of the 39th Battalion Virginia Cavalry recorded fasting after eating his rations all at once. Lee asked for the return of full rations in late March in preparation for the spring campaign.[28]

Reduced rations had a weighty effect on the soldiers. "You wanted to know something about what I thought of the war's closen," an Alabama soldier told his family on March 21, 1863. "Although starvation it seems like is stairing us in the face & a great many think that we will have to give it up on that account but they will never give it up as long as they can get as much as three buiscuits to the man A day. Yet I still hope that it will close soon. I have not given over to dispair." A Tar Heel soldier wrote of seeing a newspaper piece describing Federals believing that they had one general who could whip the Confederates: "ginrel Starvation they say they want to starve us to death." He assured his loved ones that they were "fareing splendid at this time." There was still hope for many in Virginia. Save for Antietam, there were many decisive victories the previous year. While a few men did absent themselves from their commands and head for home, the vast majority held out hope for victory.[29]

Soldiers went to great lengths to supplement their meager rations. Letters poured home, asking loved ones to send food. Hundreds of boxes came from much of the South, transported first into Richmond, and then distributed to the ranks as time and resources permitted. Those who hailed from nearby communities saw family members, slaves, and hired locals drive wagons into their camps loaded with boxes. Others sought out local homes, often buying from those willing to

28 M. A. Hancock, ed., *Four Brothers in Gray* (Sparta, NC, 2013), 164; Benson, *Berry Benson's Civil War Book*, 36; E. M. Munson, ed., *Confederate Incognito* (Jefferson, NC, 2013), 93; Hubbs, *Voices from Company D*, 147; John Roper, ed., *Repairing the "March of Mars": The Civil War Diaries of John Samuel Apperson, Hospital Steward in the Stonewall Brigade* (Macon, GA, 2001), 383–384; Everson & Simpson, *Far, Far from Home*, 195; Jessup, *The Painful News I Have to Write*, 135; *OR* 25, pt. 2, 687.

29 Wood & Jackson, "*Kiss Sweet Little Lillah for me,*" 30–31; John Hatley & Linda Huffman, eds., *Letters of William F. Wagner* (Wendell, NC, 1983), 48.

share. A South Carolina soldier wrote of getting permission to forage across the river, finding two cabbages, milk, bread, and butter. Some soldiers were more resourceful. An Alabama soldier noted catching more than a half dozen squirrels one morning while others sold fish they had caught. One reporter observed two soldiers carrying a barrel of ginger cakes between them on a pole from the depot to camp to sell to their comrades. "Many soldiers make hundreds of dollars in the year in the cake and apple business," he determined. Some Tar Heel soldiers bought a gallon of brandy for $75. After each had taken a stiff drink, they sold the balance for $96. The Confederate government tried to crack down on soldiers selling food to one another. In November 1862, General Order No. 127 noted that complaints had reached army headquarters of such "great evil" and "unworthy practice[s]." Only official army sutlers or civilians had permission to trade or sell to the soldiers and officers. If a soldier was caught, then he was to be arrested and brought to trial.[30]

Other soldiers did visit the sutlers set up near camp or at one of the railroad depots. Sutlers were civilian vendors operating with the approval of army commanders. They appeared in camps on the heels of the first regiments. They often bought foodstuffs and other commodities in bulk and sold to soldiers at exorbitant prices. One member of the 17th Virginia Infantry recalled after the war that the regimental sutler once cleared $6,000 in one day. The arrival of the sutler's wagon was often greeted with joy by many soldiers. "Immediately after reveille," wrote a member of the 5th Alabama in January, "the boys, having found out that Ellison, the Sutler, had come with a load of goods, hastened up to his wagons & bought a number of sugar cakes & ginger cakes which all hands pitched into, & I ate a good many before getting up. Our mess . . . invested $3 each in cakes principally & some apples." This particular regiment, at least in January 1863, had two sutlers.[31]

Regulations stipulated only one sutler per regiment. Many soldiers complained of the sutlers' prices. George Stilwell, 53rd Georgia, grumbled that he could not eat "old fat bacon." The two choices were to do without or purchase something. He could buy beef sausage for $1.50, sweet potatoes for .50 a pound, and cowpeas for .75 a quart. Prices fluctuated with availability. At the same time, many thought their messmates "recklessly extravagant" for blowing through $20 in less than a week on candy, apples, cakes, sugar, and molasses. Many sutlers sold prohibited whiskey

30 Benson, *Berry Benson's Civil War Book*, 58; Hubbs, *Voices from Company D*, 136; Munson, *Confederate Incognito*, 96; Hatley & Huffman, *Letters of William F. Wagner*, 44; *OR* 19, pt. 2, 722.

31 William Glasgow, *Northern Virginia's Own* (Alexander, VA, 1989), 111; Hubbs, *Voices from Company D*, 131.

Private James W. McCulloch, 7th Georgia Infantry Regiment, holding a wooden canteen. *Library of Congress*

on the side. Returning to the 5th Alabama, a member noted that one sutler intoxicated half the regiment. At the end of April, the hospital steward of the 4th Virginia recorded that the provost had confiscated one local sutler's establishment. A search revealed twenty gallons of liquor hidden in sacks of rice and corn. The liquor was sent to the hospital. Sutlers could open the door to foods not normally found at home. A Virginia artilleryman noted an "old negro man" who came to camp weekly with a wagonload of oysters. "Our custom was to buy anything to eat that came along," he recalled. When a fellow soldier from the mountains was asked about selling some recently purchased oysters, he replied, "No, we are not afraid to tackle anything, and we've made up our minds to eat what we've got on hand, if it takes the hair off."[32]

When spring came, concerns of scurvy brought orders for regiments to send out details every morning from every company to procure vegetables such as wild onions, poke sprouts, sassafras buds, and watercress. An Alabama soldier went three or four miles with others from his company to a large field covered in onions. After picking a haversack full, they returned to camp and breakfasted on fresh shad and herring. A Georgia soldier, wanting vegetables, found only wild onions near his camp: "We fry them and they eat finely." Many soldiers ventured to the rivers, streams, and creeks near the camp to fish. Brigadier General William D. Pender noted eating shad and herring on April 1. A soldier in the 28th North Carolina Troops reported that his men were catching hundreds of shad every day, an observation confirmed by Lafayette McLaws: "[O]ur men not only fish in the river but seine it, catching hundreds of fish." Abner Peace, 23rd North Carolina, told his father that his regiment was sending out details of men to catch fish. An Alabama

32 Hubbs, *Voices from Company D*, 138–139; Wyckoff, *The Civil War Letters of Alexander McNeill*, 202; Roper, *Repairing the "March of Mars,"* 399; Edward Moore, *The Story of a Cannoneer under Stonewall Jackson* (Lynchburg, VA, 1910), 166–167.

soldier stated the commissary was supplying nets, while a soldier in the 21st Georgia Infantry recorded that the brigades of Dole and Colquitt had established fisheries near their camps. Of course, their attempts were not always successful. In mid-April, a member of the 4th Virginia chronicled an unsuccessful attempt at fishing and seine hauling due to rough water. Richmond newspapers noted a Federal raid toward the end of April, breaking up the Confederate fishing operations near Port Royal. In that aspect, they were successful, capturing several wagons, horses, mules, and soldiers. The movement of Federals, including two brigades and a pontoon bridge, was a diversion. The Federal commander was attempting to draw the focus away from troops he was shifting to the Confederate left.[33]

Those rations of fresh fish and wild onions prepared the troops for the spring campaign with a rich diet. On April 27, Federal soldiers crossed the Rappahannock River above Confederate camps. They planned to force the ANV out of the Fredericksburg defenses. Their flanking columns stalled around Chancellorsville and were eventually forced back across the river. Part of the plan included releasing Federal cavalry in the Confederate rear, destroying the Richmond, Fredericksburg & Potomac and the Virginia Central Railroads. While a few bridges and depots were burnt, Federal cavalry failed to destroy the more critical bridges north of Hanover Junction. Breaks in the lines slowed provisions and munitions going into the army and the flow of wounded from the Chancellorsville battlefield into Richmond hospitals, but it was a minor disruption. On May 11, the surgeon of the 21st Georgia noted that "Our dead are all buried, our wounded all cared for and sent off, and fishery reestablished, so if the yankees will let us alone, we will have a good time again."[34]

Almost everyone wrote home in May that rations had increased and that they were getting more to eat. "I hate to say so much about eating but I must tell you how I am fairing. Our ration per day is as follows 1 ¼ lbs flour ½ lbs Bacon a mess of Beef Rice Peas soap and sugar We buy soda at 5 dollars per lb. . . . I go fishing just when I pleas and ketch almost as many as I want. I had this morning for Breakfast pancakes sweetened with sugar preceeded by fried ham and good soda

33 Welch, *A Confederate Surgeon's Letters*, 47; Moseley, *The Stilwell Letters*, 145; Peace, *To Tranquillity*, 131–132; Hubbs, *Voices from Company D*, 154, 158; Hassler, *One of Lee's Best Men*, 216; Allen Speer, ed., *"Voices from Cemetery Hill": The Civil War Diary, Reports, and Letters of Colonel William Henry Asbury Speer* (Johnson City, TN, 1997), 96; John Oeffinger, ed., *A Soldier's Generals* (Chapel Hill, NC, 2002), 175; Roper, *Repairing the "March of Mars,"* 419; *Richmond Enquirer*, April 28, 1863; OR 25, pt. 2, 234.

34 McGarity, "Letters of a Confederate Surgeon, McGarity," 1:106. Goff notes after surveying correspondence in the *Official Records*, the battle of Chancellorsville was not "affected by supply factors." *Confederate Supply*, 186.

In the spring of 1863, Confederate soldiers not only fished, but seine hauled, much like the people in this image. *Harper's Weekly*

Biscuits. For dinner the same with the addition of the best kind of Beef stake and Rice custard. All we draw is of the best quality," wrote one Tar Heel from Hanover Junction. From a camp near Fredericksburg, a Georgia soldier wrote of still receiving "old rank pickle beef and bacon." They picked and ate poke and "other weeds. I don't like it much," he confessed. There was a change in commissaries within regiments in May. Congress, for unclear reasons, abolished the position of the regimental assistant commissary of subsistence, turning those responsibilities over to the assistant quartermasters or commissary sergeants. Several hundreds of men who lost their positions overnight became brigade commissaries. Others were simply dropped. Regimental commissary sergeants were appointed by the regimental commander and were responsible for receiving and issuing rations. Men were also detailed out of the ranks to help in the brigade commissary and quartermaster departments. In January 1863, fifteen men from the regiments in Mahone's brigade were so assigned. Later in September, the number increased to thirty-five men.[35]

35 Peace, *To Tranquillity*, 142; Moseley, *The Stilwell Letters*, 165. Robert E. L. Krick speculates that the smaller size of regiments by mid-war, and the need to "centralize supply gathering and transportation in the interest of efficiency," are two reasons. *Staff Officers in Gray* (Chapel Hill, NC, 2003), 31. For more information on commissary sergeants, see August Kautz, *Customs of Service*

By mid-June 1863, most of Lee's Army marched toward Gettysburg. Left behind in the defenses of Richmond and at Chaffin's Bluff and Drewry's Bluff were almost 17,000 men under the command of Maj. Gen. Arnold Elzey. They continued receiving supplies from Richmond while the remainder of the Confederate army battled in Pennsylvania. Confederate soldiers returning to Virginia were battered, shell-shocked, and hungry. It was early August before the veterans of the Gettysburg campaign could report with Dr. Abner McGarity, 44th Georgia Infantry: "Our rations are better today than they have been in some time. We have been getting nothing but beef and flour. Today we get our usual rations with the addition of bacon and sugar." McGarity had been picking blackberries and making pies.[36]

While Gettysburg was a serious loss for the Confederacy, the overall campaign provisioned the Confederate army in the East through the next several months. The amount of foodstuffs sent back from Pennsylvania and Maryland is unclear, but the wagon train included an estimated forty-five miles of impressed stores, almost 30,000 head of cattle, 25,000 head of sheep, and thousands of hogs. "We . . . enjoyed better rations than we ever got again," recalled artillery chief E. Porter Alexander after the war. Most soldiers agreed. Rations were issued with regularity. "Beef, bacon and flour, and sometimes sugar and potatoes," wrote one South Carolinian in mid-August. Another soldier recalled being issued peas. The army was encamped around Orange Court House, and the area had plenty to offer. Sutlers returned to sell watermelons, apples, salt, ground peas or "goobers," ginger cakes, and Confederate coffee. Local people were willing to sell to Confederate soldiers. Another South Carolinian wrote that a regimental lieutenant went out foraging, returning with chickens, Irish potatoes, and green apples. "[W]e had some glorious chicken stew," he recalled. Boxes began to arrive from home, and those with camp servants sent them to procure additional foodstuffs. An officer in the 5th Alabama wrote of his servant returning from Richmond with cantaloupes, apples, peaches, and pears. As August slipped into September and the army recovered, time allowed for officer socials and picnics, as noted by Col. David Lang, 8th Florida Infantry. A member of the 8th Alabama wrote of gathering corn from the same field as the Federals, while a Tar Heel recorded his brigade commissary officer loaning his men a cow. "With very little feeding she gives seven pints twice a day—which is quite a sufficing for table use, allowing us besides to churn twice

(Philadelphia, PA, 1864), 152–164; William Mahone Papers, Box 174, DU. On several occasions, there were special requisitions for candles for the subsistence department "as they are compelled to receive & issue rations in open air at night."

36 *OR* 27, pt. 3, 1065–1067; McGarity, "Letters of a Confederate Surgeon, McGarity," 2:169.

a week. Last Saturday we made a fine saucefull of butter and tomorrow will churn again." Some soldiers improvised in their dairy endeavors; as one member of the 53rd North Carolina Troops recalled at the end of July: "Hugh Sample and myself were out on a forage and milked a cow in his hat, the only thing we had."[37]

Lee and Northrop continued to spar in the months following Gettysburg. Northrop sent two letters to Lee at the end of July. Since there was a limited supply of meat in reserve, Northrop, who had been unsuccessful at curtailing rations prior to Gettysburg, demanded an even harder reduction. Each man would receive only one-quarter of a pound of meat when stationary and one-third of a pound on campaign, halving Northrop's previous restrictions. Furthermore, Northrop demanded 400 wagons detached from Lee's army to assist in the Virginia harvest, adding to the Richmond stockpiles. Lee responded that ration reductions had to extend to every Confederate force in the field. Lee agreed to supply some wagons to assist commissary agents in gathering grain. However, the wagons were to remain under the control of his quartermasters and not Northrop's agents.[38]

Northrop had two new tools at his disposal: impressment and tax-in-kind. The Impressment Act passed the Confederate Congress on March 26, 1863. Boards of commissioners were appointed to mediate disputes between impressment agents and farmers and set goods prices. Prices the government paid to civilians were often 50 percent below market value. Farmers received Confederate script or a certificate allowing later payment. Those near Confederate armies or railroads suffered more at the hands of impressment agents than their more isolated neighbors. Many complained, often noting that impressed foodstuffs were observed rotting at railroad depots, waiting on transportation. Tax-in-kind became law in April 1863. Farmers could keep a certain amount of their harvest for self-consumption. Ten percent of the remainder, destined for the market, had to be given to the government. The list of goods included tobacco, rye, wheat, oats, rice, corn, sugar, potatoes, fodder, cotton, wool, bacon, and pork. Both policies caused major dissention with the civilian population. Protest letters flew to politicians, and many farmers tried to cheat the government. Jacob Hildebrand, from Augusta County, Virginia, wrote

37 Kent Brown, *Retreat from Gettysburg* (Chapel Hill, NC, 2005), 388–389; E. P. Alexander, "Longstreet at Knoxville," in Robert Johnson & Clarence Buel, eds., *Battles & Leaders*, 4 vols. (New York, 1888), 3:745; Moseley, *The Stilwell Letters*, 203; Robert Park, "Diary of Capt. R. E. Park," *SHSP*, (1898), 26:23; Welch, *A Confederate Surgeon's Letters*, 75; Everson & Simpson, *Far, Far from Home*, 272–3; Hubbs, *Voices from Company D*, 197; David Lang, "Civil War Letters of Colonel David Lang," in Bertram Groene, ed., *The Florida Historical Quarterly* (Jan. 1976), 359; Wood & Jackson, *"Kiss Sweet Little Lillah for me,"* 48; Bradley Foley, ed., *Letters Home: The Civil War Correspondence of Lieutenant Colonel Alexander C. McAlister, 46th North Carolina Regiment* (n.p., 2013), 95; L. Leon, *Diary of A Tar Heel Confederate Soldier* (Charlotte, NC, 1913), 43.

38 *OR* 29, pt. 2,625; 51, pt. 2, 738.

Corporal John Agee Booker, 21st Virginia Infantry Regiment, wears a tin drum canteen with his name inscribed on it. *Library of Congress*

of getting up at 3:00 a.m. before the impressment officer arrived, hiding twenty-five bushels of corn. Of the remaining twenty-five bushels, the government agent took fifteen.[39]

In September, portions of Longstreet's corps were sent to Georgia to bolster Confederate forces in the Army of Tennessee. They did not return until April 1864. A few minor campaigns occurred in the fall of 1863, Mine Run and Bristoe Station, but the troops returned to their camps near Orange Court House. In November, Northrop submitted a report to the War Department. He was honest in his assessment, writing that in twelve months, "there will not be enough meat in the country for the people and the armies of the Confederate States." There might be enough wheat to produce bread for soldiers but getting it to Virginia over the existing rail lines was next to impossible. Whiskey was also needed, but only Georgia and Alabama had surplus grain, and Georgia had shut down distilleries. The only hope lay in foreign foodstuffs, and shipbuilding had delayed the shipment of purchased items. One consolation was a shipment of coffee that arrived from overseas. It is believed that this shipment was meant for public sale to raise funds to purchase domestic commodities. However, some soldiers wrote of getting coffee rations in January 1864. Thomas Lupton, 39th Battalion Virginia Cavalry, stated that they had not only fresh beef, flour, salt, and sugar, but "coffee[,] real coffee, none of your confederate compounds."[40]

Soldiers sought diversions during the winter months. After the war, one member of the 13th Virginia Infantry recalled soldiers taking their rifles out of

---

39 Glenn Toalson, ed., *No Soap, No Pay, Diarrhea, Dysentery & Desertion: A Composite Diary of the Last 16 Months of the Confederacy from 1864 to 1865* (n.p., 2006), 66.

40 *OR* Series 4, 2, 968–972, Robert Driver, Jr. & Kevin Ruffner, *1st Battalion, Virginia Infantry* (Lynchburg, VA, 1996), 62.

camp and hunting squirrels. "For two or three days, there was wafted up to us stationed on the mountain's summit a sound of firing like that of a small skirmish." Officers soon stopped such actions, counting cartridges before paying the soldiers and charging them twenty-five cents for every missing round. A 12th Alabama officer told his guard detail to arrest any man leaving or entering camp with a gun "without my written permission. . . . Though barefoot they are hungry." That night, eight men were arrested and confined to the guardhouse. As punishment, they were ordered to build a causeway around the guardhouse for the sentries. Another Alabama officer noted a soldier passing back and forth in front of the guard house with a skillet on his head "for stealing one I suppose." One Tar Heel brigade commander was ordered to search his camp for a missing hog. "[O]ne of the captains was accosted by one of the men whose tent he was searching and laughingly told that he was inspecting the wrong tent; may be he could find something about the old black sow at *the head of the street*, where he understood they didn't get enough to eat. It is a good joke for the men, and the officers take it very gracefully." There were still opportunities to gather foodstuffs from people near the army encampments. One of Longstreet's staff officers ordered a box of tobacco to use for trading. For one plug of tobacco, he could receive "one gallon of sorghum molasses, a turkey, three chickens or three dozen eggs, etc." Others turned to the woods. A soldier in the 18th North Carolina described buying a few items, looking for wild onions, and fishing "a good part of our time-that is a vary good traid—mutch like whare you live, we generally have fisherman's luck—a wet ass and a hungry gut."[41]

Coffee rations continued through April 1864. "I will tell you what we had for breakfast this morning. It consisted of bread and coffee sweetened with sugar, none of your rye or corn or confederate coffee, but *sure enough coffee*, and we actually drew it in rations," wrote a member of the 5th Florida Infantry on April 1. Overall, rations themselves were slowing, dwindling through the winter months. In January, an Alabama soldier bemoaned that they only had meat once every three days and only enough for a meal. A Virginia cavalryman complained in February that they were only receiving one-quarter of a pound of meat every five days. "It is gratifying to see how cheerfully they bear it too rarely complaining—but laughing and joking over it all and wondering how much less a man [can] learn to live on." The 9th Virginia Cavalry was sent home in January. It was easier for family

41 Walbrook Swank, *Raw Pork and Hardtack* (Shippensburg, PA, 1996), 62–63; Parks, "Diary of Capt. R. E. Park," *SHSP* 26:29–30; Hubbs, *Voices from Company D*, 213; James Lane, "Glimpses of Army Life in 1864," *SHSP*, (1890), 18:409; Blackford & Blackford, *Letters from Lee's Army*, 235; Hancock, *Four Brothers in Gray*, 256. Goff notes that the Ordnance Department limited each soldier to three rounds, instead of forty, when not in the face of the enemy. *Confederate Supply*, 140.

members to feed both horses and men than to let either starve. The 55th Virginia, when they returned to their camps near Orange Court House, found few rations. The officers sent the regimental wagons into Essex County to supplement their meager foodstuffs. Some soldiers feasted on honey, ham, pies, biscuits, apples, stewed peaches, and peach butter.[42]

Writing after the war, a band member for James Lane's brigade recalled rations coming once every twenty-four hours. "One man drew rations for his company— the company was divided into squads of from 5 to 10 men. The ration was cut up into as many pieces as the mess contained, as near equal as possible. Then one was blindfolded, or turned his back, while another called out, "who gets this?" pointing to a ration. The answer came, "John Smith," and again, who gets this? and so on until all had been served." This system was undoubtedly witnessed in many camps across the Richmond-Petersburg front. A Virginia soldier recalled soaking hardtack, or crackers, before frying them in bacon grease. Once finished, the mess's frying pan was set outside for the camp dog to lick clean.[43]

The feud between Lee and Northrop continued. In January 1864, Lee regretted that the beef supply was "nearly exhausted," yet did not believe that he had the power to impress food from the public. Part of Lee's concern came from the ranks. One of his staff officers recalled a letter from a soldier, asking the general if he knew how little food they were receiving. Lee did not respond to the soldier but, on January 22, issued a general order, stating he regretted the temporary reduction of rations and that he was doing everything to increase them. On the same day, Lee wrote to Secretary of War James Seddon. "Short rations are having a bad effect upon the men, both morally and physically. Desertions to the enemy are becoming more frequent, and the men cannot continue healthy and vigorous if confined to this spare diet for any length of time. Unless there is a change, I fear the army cannot be kept together." While Lee had written to various officials in the past regarding food, this was his most poignant missive to date. Lee complained that current army regulations allowed commissaries to sell food to army officers. That should be rescinded, Lee believed. Davis wrote to Northrop concerning Lee's plight, and Northrop ordered 90,000 rations sent from Wilmington, but again, they took time to arrive. Secretary Seddon authorized the purchase of meat for

---

42 John S. Ledford, "A Florida Soldier: in the Army of Northern Virginia: The Hosford Letters," in Knox Mellon, Jr., ed., *Florida Historical Quarterly* (Jan. 1968), 270; Hubbs, *Voices from Company D*, 210; R. L. T. Beale, *History of the Ninth Virginia Cavalry* (Richmond, VA, 1899), 108; Edward Williams, ed., *Rebel Brothers* (College Station, TX, 1995), 187; Richard O'Sullivan, *55th Virginia Infantry* (Lynchburg, VA, 1989), 66.

43 O. J. Lehman, "Reminiscences of the War Between the States, 1862 to 1865," *The Union Republican*, October 19, 1922; Toalson, *No Soap, No Pay*, 94–95.

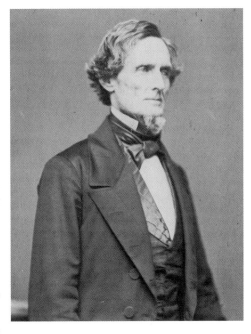

Jefferson Davis struggled to find someone to head the Commissary department, and then struggled to understand why it was not managed well. *Library of Congress*

the ANV at any price. Stealing was becoming a major problem as well. One commissary official complained that every train was robbed of eight to fifteen hundred pounds of meat. A few days later, Lee complained to Davis that 5,000 pounds of bacon, equal to 20,000 rations, were missing. "If railroad agents will take no care of the safety of Government freight, Government agents had better be sent with each train of provision," the commanding general wrote.[44]

Lee again broached the idea of trading between the lines. He wrote Secretary Seddon on February 6, noting that meat might be obtained by trading cotton and tobacco with civilians who lived in Virginia border counties. The exchange rate in the New Market area was estimated at one pound of cotton for two pounds of bacon. Trading between the lines was nothing new. Soldiers on picket often met between the lines, swapping Confederate tobacco for Yankee coffee. While officers discouraged fraternization, this small-scale trading continued. Another type of trading was conducted along the Chesapeake Bay, with many independent smugglers who sold their wares to Richmond's civilian market. These entrepreneurs often used small boats to sail down the bay. By the fall of 1862, the Federal navy was working hard to shut these down, often capturing the boats or supplies once they were deposited on shore. One account from November 1862 stated that ten men were captured, along with whiskey, tea, shoes, and calico. A bigger haul was made in early April 1863. Among the items seized were boots intended for Jefferson Davis and two embroidered nightgowns for Varina Davis, and hundreds of pounds

---

44 J. William Jones, *Life and Letters of Robert E. Lee* (New York, 1906), 320; Frederick Maurice, *An Aide-de-Camp of Lee* (Boston, 1927), xxiii–xxiv; Dowdey & Manarin, *The Wartime Papers of R. E. Lee*, 660; Samuel Pickens, 5th Alabama, related what is probably the same story regarding the letter sent to Lee, except in his diary, the letter was accompanied by a small piece of bacon. Pickens believed the letter came from a soldier in Battle's brigade. Hubbs, *Voices from Company D*, 213.

Pickets often met between the lines to exchange tobacco for coffee or newspapers. *Library of Congress*

of bacon, pork, wheat, corn, beans, and oats. Prisoners, horses, and mules were captured, two ferries were demolished, and a smuggling schooner was burned. Reports of the captures of smugglers continued through the end of 1864.[45]

Eventually, the Confederate government entered the illegal trade. Smuggling flourished whenever commercial cities like New Orleans and Nashville were captured. While the Federal government only traded with loyal citizens, goods often made their way into Confederate hands. In the Norfolk area and northeastern North Carolina, citizens bought cotton from the Confederate government, then took the cotton through the lines to sell, returning with salt, sugar, and miscellaneous supplies. The salt was used to cure pork, which was sold to the Confederate government. There was a route running from Norfolk, through the Dismal Swamp Canal to the Albemarle Sound, and up the Chowan River to one of the various points where supplies were unloaded and taken by wagons to the Weldon Railroad. In 1864, 50 bales of cotton were swapped for 10,000 pounds of bacon, sugar, coffee, molasses, and codfish, quickly traveling to Lee's army. Northrop and his agents were intimately involved in this trading. He wrote after the war that these men operated "by my authority alone . . . this became a very large business. Nearly 30 little agencies around Virginia were trading yams and

45 *OR* 33, 1181; *Evening Courier and Republic*, Dec. 1, 1862; *Brooklyn Evening Star*, April 4, 1863; *Buffalo Courier*, Nov. 14, 1864; *New York Times*, Nov. 6, 1862.

tobacco for bacon, and on the Blackwater, in North Carolina, 1500-2000 bales of cotton were traded every month. The Secretary of War officially knew nothing about these latter arrangements, but they supplied Lee with meat."[46]

In February 1864, there was another policy change. Following the old US Army custom, officers were not issued rations but given an allowance to purchase rations from the commissary. These officers could purchase an extra ration for their camp servants, slaves, or themselves. On February 17, the regulation changed: officers drew the same rations as privates, with no opportunity to purchase extra. An officer in the 39th Battalion Virginia Cavalry had a hired boy to help with cooking, getting wood, and other camp chores. Now, the mess of six only drew rations for five. They were getting by on their small rations, but it "is true there is no danger of our eating too much," the officer wrote home. Samuel Walkup, colonel of the 48th North Carolina Troops, noted in a letter that the new regulation went into effect on March 24. After explaining to his wife the quantities of corn meal, bacon, rice, molasses, and coffee officers received, Lt. Col. Alexander McAlister, 46th North Carolina Troops, told his wife to fix the same amount and have it suffice for her and their daughter, for twenty-four hours. General Lane went so far as to write Lee, asking him if the officers' servants could be listed as laundresses. The answer was no unless the servant was a laundress for all the men.[47]

Lee wrote again to the secretary of war on April 12, encouraging preparation for the upcoming campaign. Lee was most anxious regarding the collection and safe storage of foodstuffs. In Lee's opinion, the railroads should provide exclusively for the army. On April 11, headquarters ordered commissaries to keep seven days' worth of rations on hand and send excess baggage to the rear. Missives continued to fly between Seddon, Davis, and Northrop regarding food. Seddon proposed seizing the railroads, prompting railroad men to promise daily shipments of 10,000 bushels of corn to Virginia. The Confederate treasury department fell further behind on paying Subsistence Department requisitions. Questions arose over how Northrop worked with suppliers, namely the flour company of Haxall, Crenshaw & Company, leading to supply disruptions. Northrop also quarreled with Gen. Braxton Bragg, Davis's new military advisor, who tried issuing orders to

46 Ludwell Johnson, "Contraband Trade During the Civil War," *The Mississippi Valley Historical Review* (March 1963), 642; Moore, *Confederate Commissary General*, 242. See also Goff, *Confederate Supply*, 166–167, 224, 250. Leigh writes that "Grant was trying to cut off Lee's supplies from the Confederacy when Lee's provender was almost entirely furnished from Yankee sources." Philip Leigh, *Trading with the Enemy: The Covert Economy during the American Civil War* (Yardley, PA, 2014), 99.

47 Driver & Ruffner, *1st Batt. VA Inf.*, 66–67; Walkup Diary, 68, Walkup Papers, SHC; Foley, *Letters Home*, 198–199; James Lane, "Glimpses of Army Life in 1864," *SHSP*, 18:409.

the bureau chiefs, although they technically answered only to the secretary of war. Northrop then quarreled with Davis himself over the flour company.[48]

The Federals splashed across the Rapidan River in early May, initiating the Overland campaign. The campaign lasted into mid-June, resulting in several large battles, and at times, disrupted supplies for Confederate forces. Federal cavalry struck the depot at Beaver Dam Station, on the Virginia Central Railroad, on May 9. Two trains were sitting on sidings, loaded with commissary stores that Lee had requested. After taking as much food as they could carry, the Federals torched the rest, destroying an estimated 1,500,000 Confederate rations. On May 10, a call went out to all subsistence officers in the field in Virginia: "Impress freely if necessary. Give receipts for these supplies, to be paid for in cash or to be returned hereafter in kind, at the option of the party. . . . Act with promptness, as the exigency is great." Northrop reported that he still had almost a million rations in Richmond, Lynchburg, Gordonsville, and Hanover Junction. However, a million rations would not last long given the number of men. Simultaneously, Lee's army lost thousands of men killed and captured. While Lee was successfully parrying the Federals' attempts to wedge between Richmond and the ANV, they moved closer to Richmond with each drive. War Department clerk Jones noted on May 29 that wagon trains of provisions were on Broad Street, waiting for the commissary wagons of various brigades to arrive for reloading before returning to the front.[49]

Northrop increased the food ration for Lee's men in early June. Lee requested a whiskey ration, but there was insufficient whiskey, so sugar and coffee were substituted. When Gen. Robert Ransom, whose troops were idle in the trenches around Richmond, heard that Lee's men enjoyed increased rations, he complained to Gen. Cooper, resulting in reduced rations for Lee's men who had been fighting the Federals for more than a month. Bragg likewise found a discrepancy. Lee's men were getting sugar and coffee, while those soldiers manning defensive works were not. Northrop had to issue these items to other soldiers as well. There were thousands of soldiers stationed between Richmond and Petersburg, entrenched at places like Drewry's Bluff. One staff officer noted these men had seen little service and had constructed "nice houses [with] little gardens around them." The meddling by Ransom and Bragg constituted a great disservice to Lee's soldiers.[50]

---

48 While it is unclear just who began questioning the deal with Haxall, Crenshaw & Company, Moore suggests that it was Bragg. *Confederate Commissary General*, 252–258.

49 Stephen Starr, *The Union Cavalry in the Civil War* (Baton Rouge, 1979), 2:100; Earl Miers, ed., *A Rebel War Clerk's Diary* (New York, 1958), 384. Confederates placed the number of rations lost at Beaver Dam Station at 915,000 of meat and 504,000 of bread. *OR* 33, 1277; 51, pt. 2:909–910.

50 *OR* 36, pt. 3, 898; Blackford & Blackford, *Letters from Lee's Army*, 258.

For the bulk of Lee's army, the war changed in mid-June. On June 15, the siege Lee had feared commenced with an attempt to capture Petersburg. The attack failed, and for the next nine months, the Federals launched nine different attempts to punch holes in the Confederate defenses or cut supply lines into Petersburg. Most Confederate foodstuffs came through the lines or the port of Wilmington, and meat was in short supply through June. From Petersburg on June 19, a Tar Heel soldier wrote of getting bread, sugar, and coffee, "yet Bacon is a little short." At the end of the month, a South Carolina cavalryman noted that his rations consisted of coffee, sugar, rice, and vegetables.[51]

In July, Lee sent a force of 15,000 men under Jubal Early into the Shenandoah Valley, driving to the outskirts of Washington, D.C., before falling back into the lower Shenandoah due to a lack of numbers. Lee continued to split his remaining defenders between the works east of Richmond and Petersburg. Often, brigades moved back and forth across the James and Appomattox Rivers, attempting to foil Federal attempts to capture Confederate defenses. Eventually, those defense works stretched over thirty miles. Petersburg was a strategic rail hub, with five different railroads converging in the Cockade City. While some of the lines lost their importance in the first year of the war, others, such as the Weldon Railroad and the South Side Railroad, were vital as the conflict continued. The Weldon Railroad ran south into North Carolina, connecting the port at Wilmington. At the same time, the South Side Railroad linked to Lynchburg, the upper Shenandoah Valley, and, thanks to the recently completed Piedmont Railroad, Greensboro, North Carolina. These railroads supplied Lee's beleaguered army.

In August, a Federal push cut the Weldon Railroad below Petersburg. Supplies were unloaded eighteen miles further south and brought by wagon up the Boydton Plank Road into Petersburg. Over the same months, Confederate forces lost much of the Shenandoah Valley. The first campaign lasted from May through June, resulting in the battles of New Market, Piedmont, and the recapture of Lynchburg. Federal forces followed Early's Confederates back into the Shenandoah Valley in July. A new Federal campaign was launched in August, resulting in nearly a dozen battles and skirmishes. The Federals torched many farms and supplies, destroying foodstuffs earmarked for the ANV in the Richmond-Petersburg area.

Feeding those remaining men in the trenches around Petersburg was challenging. Soldiers seem to have received food in two different ways. A member of the 53rd Georgia Infantry wrote of groups of men detailed by officers to prepare

51 Stuart Wright, ed., *The Confederate Letters of Benjamin H. Freeman* (Hicksville, NY, 1974), 44; William G. Hinson, "The Diary of William G. Hinson during the War of Secession," in Joseph Waring, ed., *The South Carolina Historical Magazine* (Jan. 1974), 19.

A captured Confederate camp near Petersburg, June 24, 1864. *AHEC*

food at the rear and bring it to those manning the works. W. A. Day, 49th North Carolina Troops, recalled being rotated out of the lines near Petersburg and sent to a "wagon yard to wash and rest." They were allowed visits to the city, supplementing their issued rations. "We bought rations at the market-house, cooked and ate and had a fine time generally," Day wrote. That evening, they rotated back into the trenches. Reaction to foodstuffs was mixed in July. A member of the 5th Virginia Cavalry, stationed along the Jerusalem Plank Road, thought they were "living quite well now," receiving "Flour, Meal, bacon, occasionally Sugar, Coffee, & beans." Brigadier General William N. Pendleton complained that his ration was only half what he needed, costing him $100 a month extra to purchase eatables. "But to beat the Yankees and gain our independence I would submit to vastly more," he told those back home.[52]

By early August, mutton was issued to some soldiers, while others could pick blackberries. Overall, the food was meager. An inspector found Benning's

---

52 Timothy Morgan to his wife and children, July 1, 1864, Morgan Papers, Petersburg National Battlefield; John L. G. Wood to father, July 20, 1864, Georgia Division of Archives & History; W. A. Day, *A True History of Company I, 49th North Carolina Troops* (Newton, NC, 1893), 81; Lee, *Memoirs of William Nelson Pendleton*, 354.

brigade in poor health, stemming from cooking methods. "The meat is usually boiled to nothing except the fiber and the bread is cooked in the most indegestable manner. . . . No vegetables are now issued," he found. By mid-August, foodstuffs captured by Early's men in Maryland were reaching the main army. One 44th North Carolina Troops member wrote of eating beef, sugar, coffee, peas, flour, and cornbread, all captured and sent to the Petersburg-Richmond front. A staff officer from Field's Division noted the same at the end of August. He considered Jubal Early "our efficient commissary."[53]

In September, Northrop complained to new Treasury Secretary George Trenholm that money to purchase foodstuffs was exhausted, and he owed $30 million. Even worse, reports by mid-month stated that commissary agents had collected only enough food for the upcoming week. People refused to sell, afraid that the government could not reimburse them. An inspector for Pickett's division in the field complained that hucksters from Richmond were set up at Chester Station, selling to sick men and men in camps. These peddlers were driven off, but he permitted "several well recommended providers" to set up near the trenches to sell vegetables and fruits at reasonable rates. Confederate cavalry helped alleviate some of the stress regarding rations. Between September 14 and 19, Gen. Wade Hampton led 3,000 troopers on a 100-mile raid behind Union lines, capturing over 2,600 cattle. "We draw very good rations now. We get some good Yankee beef and some bacon and good flour," a member of the 45th Georgia Infantry wrote home at the end of the month. The beef sustained the army for about a month. A member of the 13th South Carolina Infantry noted on October 23 that Hampton's beef had just about run out.[54]

"We are eating new beautiful onions from Nassau," Charles Blackford wrote in June 1864. Blackford served as assistant judge advocate on Longstreet's Corps' staff and had just come through the battles comprising part of the Overland campaign. Blackford's letter home about the onions is a little more revealing concerning provisions in the ANV in the spring and summer of 1864. While Blackford was not sure if those onions had been raised in Connecticut, he knew they had been shipped through the blockade and into the port of Wilmington. "With our onions we have bacon cured in Ohio and shipped to Nassau to be sent to us by blockade

53 Sarah Chapman, ed., *Bright and Gloomy Days: The Civil War Correspondence of Captain Charles Frederick Bahnson, A Moravian Confederate* (Knoxville, TN, 2003), 129; Wright, *The Confederate Letters of Benjamin H. Freeman*, 49–50, 52; Inspection Report, Benning's Brigade, M935, Reel 10, NA; Richard Corbin, ed., *Letters of a Confederate Officer to His Family in Europe During the Last Year of the War of Secession* (New York, 1913), 62.

54 *OR* Series 4, 3, 622–623; Inspection report, Pickett's Division, M935, Reel 10, NA; McCrea, *Red Dirt and Isinglass*, 514; Welch, *A Confederate Surgeon*, 110–111.

Confederate General Wade Hampton led a cavalry raid in September 1864, capturing over 2,000 badly needed Federal cows. *Harper's Weekly*

---

runners." By 1864, most foodstuffs for the army in Virginia came from Nassau on blockade runners and into the port at Wilmington.[55]

Only a few days after the firing on Fort Sumter, Lincoln declared a blockade of Southern ports. While the blockade was ineffectual at first, by the end of 1861, more than 260 warships were on duty, and over 100 more were under construction. The blockade comprised part of the grand strategy of Lt. Gen. Winfield Scott, the aged senior General of the United States army whose Anaconda Plan had the North blockading Southern ports along the East and Gulf Coast and sending an army down the Mississippi River to New Orleans. Cut off from commerce and foreign assistance, the South would ultimately languish and die. An estimated five out of six blockade runners slipped past the net of ships. However, the Union navy eventually captured enough Southern ports to slow the flow of commerce. The loss of both ports and food-laden ships proved detrimental to the Confederacy's existence.[56]

By November 1862, Commissary General Northrop realized he could not procure enough food to provision the army, and soon Confederate European agents began purchasing subsistence for shipping overseas. Large ocean-going vessels, often slow and susceptible to seizure, could seldom clear sand bars at most Southern ports. Instead, they made for the Bahamas. There, smaller steam-powered ships were reloaded. In Europe, much of the responsibility for purchasing foodstuffs fell on Capt. William G. Crenshaw. An artillery officer and pre-war merchant, Crenshaw had many responsibilities, from purchasing supplies to

---

55 Blackford & Blackford, *Letters from Lee's Army*, 252.

56 *Wilmington Daily Herald*, Feb. 15, 1860; *The Charleston Daily Courier*, April 9, 1860, Nov. 8, 1860; Frank Owsley, *King Cotton Diplomacy* (Tuscaloosa, AL, 2008), 229–230.

In October 1864, the USS *Eolus* captured the blockade runner *Hope* off the coast of Wilmington. *Harper's Weekly*

purchasing or building vessels. By April 1863, Crenshaw had placed an order for 5,000 tons of meat for the Commissary Department.[57]

Blockade-running stopped in the summer of 1863, partially due to the Federal build-up in Charleston and the Yellow Fever epidemic in Wilmington. Some three million pounds of meat, which Crenshaw had sent to Bermuda, simply sat on docks, rotting away. At the same time, ship captains willing to run the blockade often left food in port, substituting more lucrative products.[58]

By the spring of 1864, the subsistence bureau began to get regular food shipments. Once in Wilmington, supplies were loaded onto the Wilmington & Weldon Railroad cars and transported north toward Virginia. Soldiers knew of the overseas sources. Surgeon William Taylor noted after the war that they were fed on the "fat of the land, it was the land of Nassau." As the Federals continued to push west of Petersburg, supplying troops in the trenches was difficult. Once the railroads were cut, the provisions had to be unloaded and placed into wagons to circumnavigate Federal positions.[59]

Moxley Sorrel, who had served on Longstreet's staff before being promoted to brigadier general and assigned a brigade under William Mahone, found the rations in the fall of 1864 to be

57 Stephen Wise, *Lifeline of the Confederacy* (Columbia, SC, 1998), 91, 103.

58 Goff, *Confederate Supply*, 153. Wise wrote that "After June 1863, the steamers coming into Wilmington represented the single most important elements in the Confederate supply system." *Lifeline of the Confederacy*, 129.

59 William Taylor, "Experiences of a Confederate Surgeon," *Transactions of the College of Physicians of Philadelphia* (1906), 100.

execrable, really unfit. Some bacon from Nassau was coming through the blockade, and it would not be incredible for the blockading fleet to allow it to come through in hope of poisoning us. A third of a pound of this stuff and some corn-meal was often the full extent of the daily ration. . . . Sometimes we got better allowances of wheat flour, and then General Mahone took a notion to improve on it by baking. The brigade commissaries were ordered to set up ovens—plenty of bricks and material lying about—and issue the flour baked in good loaves. There is, too, a slight gain in weight in baking. But the men would [have] none of such food, it was too light and wholesome. Their stomachs wanted the flour stirred with grease in a skillet and cooked solid and hard. When a chunk was eaten it stayed with the soldier and kept his appetite partly appeased. But these new-fangled loaves—so easily digested! Hunger came again, almost before finishing one of them. Not so for Johnny Reb was this thing; he wanted, like Tommy Atkins, 'some bulk in his inside,' and one fine morning Mahone's ovens were found completely demolished. The soldiers took again to their old-time toothsome and staying morsels out of the skillet.[60]

While there was meat coming through the blockade, it was never enough. It was estimated that in the last six months of 1864, 3.5 million pounds of meat came through the ports of Wilmington and Charleston, but it took time to unload it from ships, then onto trains to make the journey toward Petersburg, to be unloaded and continued by wagons into the city. A few soldiers enjoyed the imported meat. One brigadier general thought it better than Confederate beef, making an excellent hash. It was "cooked, prepared and canned in London. The soldiers call it '*The London Times*.'" Whether they preferred it or not, meat from overseas was often the only choice. The Shenandoah Valley was wrecked, providing little. Food trading between the lines and boxes from home were sustaining the army. From New Market, a Virginia soldier complained about half rations in November: "we have had very rough times out here." It was the same from a camp near Richmond for a South Carolina soldier: "We are having hard living here now. We usually get cornbread and that is miserable stuff for a soldier," he wrote at the end of the month. A member of the 53rd Virginia Infantry recalled two deer that ran through his lines, the picket post out front, and into the no-man's land between the armies. Both sides fired, and the deer went down. The opposing sides agreed to divide the meat, and a few Confederates ate venison that evening. There were public attempts to help feed the troops. Richmond citizens decided to feed the army a grand New Year's Day meal. When the meal finally arrived, a few soldiers ate well, but most found little. "This has been a day of disappointment. Our expected dinner was delayed until patience was exhausted, and then when it came it was of such meagre

---

60 G. Moxley Sorrel, *Recollections of A Confederate Staff Officer* (New York, 1905), 281.

dimensions that we concluded to give our portion to the other companies of the battalion," recalled a member of the Richmond Howitzers.[61]

Almost every letter home grumbled about sparse rations, like David Parker in the 54th North Carolina, who observed those around him in the trenches and carefully weighed his options. He did not want to "run away" but was tempted. "If they had not given me more to eat I do not know what I should of done though I do not expect to run away while I can help it for it never was my notion to away. You know that I all ways was opposed to it but hunger will make men do that they do not want to do. So long as Jefferson Davis does feed me as he is at this time I will stay with him." Thousands were less dedicated. Lee's army was dissolving before his eyes. Lane's brigade of North Carolina regiments had seven desertions in January, 122 in February, and 51 in March. "At last . . . [we] got so hungry that the site of a well fed yankee troop was too much," one Tar Heel wrote. Between January 10 and March 28, Lee's army lost at least 5,928 men to desertion. Some went toward home, others into the Federal lines. Lee fully recognized the problem. He complained in a letter on January 11 that the country had been swept clear of provisions. Heavy rains also wiped out portions of the Piedmont Railroad from Danville to Greensboro. Lee appealed to farmers in the area for "breadstuffs, meats (fresh or salted), and molasses." In an even worse catastrophe, Fort Fisher, protecting the port of Wilmington, fell to a combined Federal naval and army attack on January 15, 1865, closing the Cape Fear River to blockade runners. Rear Admiral David Porter, in his post-action report, advised his superiors in Washington, D.C., that he had found "immense quantities of provisions, stores, and clothing [that had] come through this port into rebeldom." All of it was English. A telegraph from Robert E. Lee had been found, advising the commander in the area that "if Forts Fisher and Caswell were not held he would have to evacuate Richmond." Porter thought that Lee might have already been forced from the Confederate capital by the time he wrote his report. But when it came to the port of Wilmington, "No more will ever come this way."[62]

---

61 Lane, "Glimpses of Army Life in 1864," *SHSP*, 18:420; Toalson, *No Soap, No Pay*, 66, 254; Wyckoff, *The Civil War Letters of Alexander McNeill*, 523; Toalson, *No Soap, No Pay*, 286; Harry Townsend, "Townsend's Diary," *SHSP*, (1898), 34:99.

62 *War of the Rebellion: A Compilation of the Official Records of the Union and Confederate Navies* (Washington, 1892), 11:619, 620. Frank Vandiver noted that by the end of December 1864, a total of 8.6 million pounds of meat had been delivered to Sothern ports. *Confederate Blockade Running Through Bermuda* (Austin, TX, 1947), xxix; Henry, *Pen in Hand*, 136; Hardy, *General Lee's Immortals*, 336; Pen Pittard, *Alexander's Confederates* (n.p., n.d.), 65; John Horn, *The Petersburg Campaign* (Pennsylvania, 1993), 217; Jones, *Life and Letters of Robert Edward Lee*, 348–349. Mark Weitz writes that 103,400 Confederates deserted during the war, from all Confederate armies. *More Damning than Slaughter* (Charlottesville, VA, 2005), ix.

Long-overdue changes began in early 1865. Samuel Ruth, superintendent of the Richmond, Fredericksburg & Potomac Railroad, was arrested for treason in late January. A member of the Richmond Unionist underground, Ruth not only facilitated the delivery of information to Federal generals but also delayed shipments of supplies to troops in the field. His arrest was short-lived as informants were unreliable when questioned. Lee sent a note to the secretary of war stating that his men, in line of battle enduring hail and rain, had not received a mouthful of meat in three days. This was followed by a second letter on January 27, blaming the lack of supplies on Northrop, writing that "with proper energy, intelligence, and experience on the part of the Commissary Department a great deal more could be accomplished." Shortly after, Northrop was forced to submit his resignation. He was replaced by Brig. Gen. Isaac St. John. Before his appointment, St. John had risen through the ranks, from a private to serving on the staff of Magruder as a captain of engineers, to the commander of the Confederate Nitre and Mining Bureau. Like Lee, St. John appealed to the general public for foodstuffs and worked on building a reserve. By early April 1865, he had accumulated 300,000 meat rations in Richmond, 180,000 in Lynchburg, 2,000,000 in Danville, and 1,500,000 in Greensboro.[63]

Soldiers reported scarce rations through February 1865. An 18th Georgia Infantry member told his family they were all well but "hungry as wolves." An Alabama soldier described guards posted around wagons with cooking utensils and officer's baggage. The next day, he wrote of members of his brigade trying to steal corn from a nearby mill, only to be caught by local civilians. One soldier was wounded in the face by "small shot," while the others dove into the mill pond to escape. A commissary officer in Kershaw's division told an inspector that standing orders in Longstreet's corps dictated one day's rations on hand at a time. "[I]t is unsafe to keep them . . . the troops having taken by armed force supplies" from the commissary officers. It is unclear just how many groups of soldiers were raiding their commissaries. A Tar Heel noted in January that 200 men from Mahone's division raided the commissary train of Bushrod Johnson's division and wrote that members of Rodes's division attacked the government mills in Petersburg, "depriving the needy soldiers of fifty sacks of corn meal."[64]

---

63 *Richmond Whig*, Jan. 26, 1865; Ernest Furgurson, *Ashes of Glory: Richmond at War* (New York, 1996), 294–297; Moore, *Confederate Commissary General*, 275–277; *OR* 46, pt. 2, 1211–1126; Goff, *Confederate Supply*, 234.

64 William Starr Basinger Papers, SHC; Hubbs, *Voices from Company D*, 356, 357; Capt. R. N. Lowrance, Chief of Subsistence, Kershaw/I Corps, Endorsement, March 1, 1865, to Maj. E. L. Costin, Asst. Adjt. & Insp. Gen., Kershaw/I Corps, Feb. 28, 1865, Inspection Reports, NA, microcopy M935, roll 15, NA; Noah Collins, Papers, 1861–1865, NC Archives, 68–69.

Rations improved by mid-March. There were whiskey rations, more meat, and bread. A 3rd North Carolina Cavalry trooper believed that troops in Petersburg were "faring sumptuously" and had "stopped deserting." Another Tar Heel echoed those thoughts, writing that rations were improved and "the soldiers are in better spirits." Much of this progress was due to the work of St. John. Many soldiers realized that with spring coming, active campaigning would begin. But all were aware of the reality that the Confederacy of 1865 was not the same as it had been the year previous. Confederate forces retained a fraction of the territory they once held. Atlanta, Savannah, Charleston, and Wilmington were all in Union hands, while the Breadbasket of the Confederacy—the Shenandoah Valley—was wrecked by Union campaigns the previous year. Thousands had deserted, to home or the Federals. "But I was talking about hunger," a 12th Virginia Infantry member chronicled on March 30, "I have seen veterans of three full years who have faced death incessantly who believe in the southern cause as sincerely as I do, finally be conquered by gnawing hunger and desert to the enemy in the hopes of a full meal. I hate the idea, but I won't criticize. I have a queer feeling that if we have to evacuate Petersburg it will be on account of the man born in that very city—Winfield Scott—who planned the 'Anaconda Scheme' to strangle the south, to cut off all food and supplies by a blockage of our coast."[65]

Three days later, Petersburg and Richmond fell, beginning the final campaign of the ANV.

---

65 Hubbs, *Voices from Company D*, 358; Edmund Jones to father, March 14, 1865, Edmund Walter Jones Papers, SHC; R. S. Webb to Dear Wife, March 23, 1865, Webb Family Papers, SHC; Whitehorne diary, March 31, 1865, SHC.

Chapter 2

"If I live, I shall want a big box of provisions"

Food from Home

W alter Battle, private in the 4th North Carolina, had already seen much of the war. After enlisting in June 1861, he endured a flurry of campaigns and battles, and while well fed at times, he was often hungry. In January 1864, his regiment was encamped near Orange Court House. A community member had brought several boxes from Wilson County to Battle's company. "You can't tell how I prize that middling of meat. It came in the very nick of time. I had just finished the ham and sausages which you sent by Nixson. The things which you have sent me will last me several weeks; with what I draw will give me just as much as I want by mixing rations," he wrote home. Besides a furlough home, a box of provisions was one of the most coveted items during the war.[1]

As more troops poured into Virginia, the Confederate commissary department struggled to feed them. Over time, rations were reduced, and opportunities to purchase or forage for food gradually disappeared. Any available food was often too costly for the common soldier. Requesting food from home was a viable option. Those boxes supplemented dismal rations and helped connect the war-weary soldier to the family left behind.

No sooner had troops arrived in Northern Virginia than eatables began to arrive from home. A soldier from the 5th Alabama wrote from near Union Mills at the end of July that a recently arrived box contained "Hams, eggs, butter, preserves, biscuit, light bread and two bottles of good whiskey." From a camp near Manassas Junction, a soldier in the 27th Virginia Infantry received a box with "ketchup,

1 Laura Battle, ed., *Forget-me-nots of the Civil War* (St. Louis, MO, 1909), 105.

pies, cake, apples, pickles and . . . wine." A Hampton's Legion member from South Carolina wrote of brandy, sardines, crackers, French mustard, and pickles. Another Virginia soldier received peaches, grapes, and apples. Brigadier General Lafayette McLaws thanked the folks at home for oranges and sausages. All of this was before the end of 1861. Railroads were still in good shape, and the Federals controlled very little of the Southern home front.[2]

Boxes continued to flow into the army throughout 1862 and 1863. Letters home served as personal supply lines. Besides thanking the people at home for the food and other supplies, soldiers requested specific items. Chaplains, generals, regimental and company grade officers, down to privates, asked their loved ones to supplement their corn meal, beef, and bacon. A Catholic chaplain asked those of his order back in Louisiana to send white wine and brandy or whiskey. The former was used during mass, while the latter was to ward off diarrhea and camp diseases. Colonel William D. Pender asked for butter, hams, preserves, pickles, lard, coffee or tea, and sugar. He was writing in September 1861 from Northern Virginia. Four 45th Georgia members asked for a combined box in November 1863. While Marion Fitzpatrick was concerned about the scarcities at home, he asked his wife to help cover part of the cost of constructing the box. Anything sent should not be prone to spoil, "a little more pepper and some soap" were Fitzpatrick's requests. A month later, a Tar Heel soldier asked for "Sumthing more to eat . . . beens & cabetch and one possum & apeace of pork." A trend developed in the letters passing back and forth: Requests were sent once the army went into winter quarters, along with letters of thanks for items received in the spring and summer months.[3]

The geography of the Confederacy drastically changed in the war's third year. There had been losses, such as the Mississippi River and most of Tennessee, but 1864 brought the war to everyone in Virginia. The Shenandoah Valley was stripped bare by Federal forces, and the siege of Petersburg slowly cut rail lines from the south that fed soldiers and civilians. Boxes continued arriving in the camps until active campaigning began in May. In June, a 45th North Carolina member confessed that getting boxes from Richmond to their position at Gaines Mill was impossible. Anything coming out of Richmond was limited to military necessities. As the armies settled around Petersburg, they could still get boxes

2 Hubbs, *Voices from Company D*, 28; Turner, *My Dear Emma*, 40; Moffett, *Letters of General James Conner*, 56; Dayton, *The Diary of a Confederate Soldier*, 23; Oeffinger, *A Soldier's General*, 125.

3 Cornelius Buckley, ed., *A Frenchman, A Chaplain* (Chicago, IL, 1981), 87; Hassler, *One of Lee's Best Men*, 55–56; McCrae, *Red Dirt and Isinglass*, 441; Louisa Emmons, ed., *Tales from a Civil War Plantation* (n.p., 2014), 142.

from the Carolinas. From Culpeper in September, Brig. Gen. James Conner asked family in South Carolina to send a box each month composed of rice, grits, or cowpeas. In October, another South Carolinian wrote that it was taking two weeks for a box to arrive.[4]

Boxes were still trickling in during the first three months of 1865, mainly for North Carolina soldiers and those whose Virginia families were not burned out. Sherman's march across South Carolina tore up many railroads. "We had the biggest dinner Friday you ever saw in camp. Had Joe's golbler nicely stuffed, and baked besides boiled ham, turnips, etc.," Private William Carr, 43rd North Carolina Troops, told his family back home in January. Carr wrote again in mid-February about receiving another box. "We have plenty to eat and gave away a good deal and have nearly half the raw meat yet. . . . It is not a good plan to have too much on hand at a time. We have to move too often." Toward the end of March, soldiers were still writing home for boxes, "as rashions is tolerable scerce," a 6th North Carolina soldier confessed. An unknown number of care packages sitting at depots were undoubtedly lost in the evacuation of Petersburg and Richmond.[5]

Most foodstuffs from home were packaged in wooden boxes, although barrels or simple bags were sometimes used. Inside were crocks, glass jars, or even tinware. Writing in November 1861, a 9th Alabama Infantry soldier thanked his wife for sending some items in tin buckets, which he found "very acceptable, the Bucket its self will be quite an acquisition to my cooking vessels." A South Carolina officer thought he had received a keg of liquor but discovered pickles inside. A member of the 11th Georgia Infantry wanted his items shipped in the smallest possible box "so it will be as little trouble as possible to Handle." He later added that he wanted pickles cut up small and placed in jugs. "Thay dont do well in jares to ship this fair." One South Carolina soldier thanked his wife for the small bags of peaches, pepper, garlic, and coffee. A Tar Heel soldier instructed his wife to label the outside of the box. Another Tar Heel wanted eggs, instructing his wife to pack them securely in sawdust.[6]

4 Ellen Frontis, ed., *Letters Home to Baughn Mountain* (n.p., 1979), 59; Moffett, *Letters of General James Conner*, 154; Welch, *A Confederate Surgeon's Letters*, 111.

5 Robert Aycock & Elsie, eds., *The Civil War Letters of W. D. Carr* (n.p., n.d.), 65, 66; Iobst & Manarin, *The Bloody Sixth*, 254.

6 Carter, *Welcome the Hour of Conflict*, 101; Moffett, *Letters of General James Conner*, 77; James Thompson, "A Georgia Boy with 'Stonewall' Jackson: The Letters of James Thomas Thompson," in Aurelia Austin, ed., *The Virginia Magazine of History & Biography* (July 1962), 321, 327; Joyce, "A Collection of Confederate Letters," Madison-Mayodan Public Library; James Amick to dear wife, Apr. 10, 1862, James Joshua Amick Papers, USC; Chapman, *Bright and Gloomy Days*, 43.

People at home were often left in dire straits as they attempted to supplement the food of the soldiers at the front. *Harper's Weekly*

James Edmondson, 27th Virginia, wrote of a fellow soldier arriving with a haversack of food from Edmonson's friend back in Staunton. In February 1865, a Botetourt County farmer wrote his son in the 11th Virginia Infantry about a box on the way with turkeys, chickens, ham, butter, cake, pies, potatoes, dried fruit, lard to fry chickens, and other delectables. To protect the box from thieves, the farmer wrapped hickory strips around it "so that there would be a little trouble to get in." Concerning a box sent to Robert E. Lee in April 1863, the General promised to try to return the jars Mary had sent with foodstuffs. Likewise, Lt. Col. Alexander McAlister, 46th North Carolina, promised to return the glass bottles to his family back home.[7]

Quite possibly, the most heart-touching letter regarding the arrival of food came from William T. Jackson, a private in the 8th Alabama Infantry. The regiment

7 Turner, *My Dear Emma*, 83; Toalson, *No Soap, No Pay*, 324–325; Dowdey & Manarin, *The Wartime Papers of R. E. Lee*, 437; Foley, *Letters Home*, 82. An Alabama newspaper asked local people to make boxes for soldiers, noting that the supply in "town is completely exhausted." *Democratic Watchtower*, Sep. 18, 1861.

was camped near Orange Court House on May 1, 1864, on the verge of the battle of the Wilderness and Overland campaign. Jackson wrote home to his wife:

> [B]ut let me tell you in all the things you have ever sent me has nothing ever struck me so deep as that old worn out sack that you sent that dried fruit in which was made of your old dress. It was dark when Low got in that night & as soon as he come I gathered the sack he had them in & ran to the fire to see what all he had. I ran my hand in to sack & behold the first thing I saw was A piece of your old dress. My dear my feelings were indiscriable. I felt like I was thunder struck & as the briney tear ran down my cheek I had to hide my face to keep that were arround me from knowing it. It brought your memory to me afresh. I could almost see you with my natural eyes in my imagination. The thought ran through my mind in A moment how many days I had seen you ware it & how many hours of pleasure I had enjoyed with you in them days & how many times I had threw my arms arround your lovely neck & kiss you with that same old dress on. . . . Little did you think when you were fixing up that sack to send them things in that it would ever cause A tear to fall from my eye.[8]

Transporting foodstuffs from communities across the South to soldiers in Virginia always proved challenging. A family or community member could haul a wagonload of boxes if regiments were nearby. This was usually limited to regiments from Virginia or upper North Carolina. Jim Humbles, a free man of color living in Lexington, was hired to haul boxes by the parents of the young men in the Liberty Hall Volunteers. A 12th Virginia soldier recalled that the agent for transporting supplies for the city of Petersburg arrived right before Christmas in 1862 with a wagonload of goods. According to Westwood, the soldiers gathered around the wagon, "listening for their names to be called out as box after box made some fellow's heart glad. I was enjoying the good luck of the boys when a box was called out for me. I was surprised and delighted, on opening the box, which was filled with all kinds of good things." Charles Blackford, serving on Longstreet's staff, noted in February 1863 that "old John F. Tilden" came every two or three weeks to deliver boxes and packages to soldiers. The process was often more laborious for those from further south. A soldier going home on furlough could take charge of several boxes on his return and help shepherd them through various railroad depots and train changes.[9]

---

8 Wood & Jackson, *"Kiss Sweet Little Lillah for me,"* 60.

9 W. G. Bean, *The Liberty Hall Volunteers* (Charlottesville, VA, 1964), 158, n14; "Westwood A. Todd Reminiscences of the Civil War," 79; Blackford & Blackford, *Letters from Lee's Army*, 167.

The *Edgefield Advertiser* announced in March 1863 that the chaplain of the 12th South Carolina Infantry was returning to Virginia in April and that any boxes should be sent to the "Central Association" in Columbia. In January 1864, an advertisement appeared in the *Western Democrat,* announcing that Abraham Torrence, 37th North Carolina, was at home on leave, and that anyone who had boxes for his company could take them to Torrence, or deliver them to the railroad for him to see them through. Later in 1864, a 2nd Battalion North Carolina Infantry soldier wrote of shepherding 58 boxes from home into Richmond, where he deposited them at the North Carolina Depot. He had sent a telegram, presumably inquiring about a wagon to pick up the boxes but had not heard anything and was planning to head to camp the next day to make arrangements.[10]

The process of moving these boxes was complicated. There was always the option of sending a box using the Southern Express Company. Many, like Col. William D. Pender, in November 1861, found this option too expensive. Prices escalated as the war progressed. It was much cheaper to send boxes via the railroad at freight prices. However, boxes sent as freight were not guaranteed to arrive at camp. A traveler wrote of seeing a huge pile of "soldier's boxes," near the depot in Wilmington. Soldiers arriving on the train from the deeper South were told that there was not room for the box full of provisions on the next train, but their boxes were being sent on the following train. *"And that is the last he ever sees of his box,"* the correspondent recorded. Marion Fitzpatrick was home in Georgia in January 1863 and returned to the army with several boxes containing food and clothing. "I carried my box in the car with me a portion of the way, but at some places they would not let me pass with it and then I had to put it on the baggage car," he wrote home from camp at Guiney's Station. "I had to get a passport in Petersburg before I could get on the cars. . . . When I got off the cars in Richmond, the guards halted me. I told them my furlough was not out and I had a box of clothing to take to my company. They told me to pass and go where I pleased." Fitzpatrick left his boxes at the American hotel, failed at getting his ration money as the office was closed, but succeeded in getting a passport. He slept that night on the hotel floor and then got the boxes onto the train the following day. Not everyone was as fortunate as Fitzpatrick. Some 23rd North Carolina soldiers started to the depot with boxes in March 1863, only to find the railroad too crowded. They took their boxes back home. Lieutenant Colonel William Morris had the same problem. He sent his box home and instructed his wife to contact the families who had sent along items for

---

10 *Edgefield Advertiser*, Mar. 25, 1863; *Western Democrat*, Jan. 12, 1864; Chapman, *Bright and Gloomy Days*, 115.

other soldiers. If they could not be found, then he wished the items to be sold, and the cash returned to the families.[11]

At several points along the route, boxes could be opened and searched for "contraband," usually alcohol. A newspaper correspondent traveling with several boxes noted they were being searched at the depot in Weldon, North Carolina. He also mentioned that there was no place to store boxes, so they simply sat in the open, waiting their turn. A surgeon in the 3rd North Carolina State Troops complained in December 1863 that boxes were frequently robbed of their contents. A 12th North Carolina State Troops member, writing after the war, was blunter. While stationed near Fredericksburg in the winter of 1862–1863, he looked forward to "an occasional box from loved ones at home, when that box could thread the intricacies of transportation then in vogue, and escape the ravages of hungry employes [sic]." The railroad employees were not the only culprits. Charles Blackford, serving on Longstreet's staff, noted in January 1863 that to send packages to Hamilton's Crossing Station was "to give them away, as every box sent there is pillaged by the men placed as guards over them." Many boxes were simply stolen outright.

Another 12th North Carolina soldier wrote that he had three boxes in tow at Weldon. He took his own and put it on the next train, leaving the other two in the care "of a man who offered to watch them till he got back. When he got back, the man, boxes, and all were gone." In his diary, John Cowin, 5th Alabama, recorded that his aunt had shipped him "a box of Chickens, about fifty," in August 1861, while the regiment was stationed in Fluvanna County, Virginia. Not having agents to watch over the chickens, Cowin lamented that soldiers "stole every one. We grieve more for the chickens than any thing else, for Chickens does fine in the army." Cowin's aunt tried to ship chickens again a month later, and when the wagon returned from the depot, it came with the coop in which the chickens were shipped, "but 'nary' chicken." Additionally, a box containing pies was torn open, and half of the pies were gone. "There are some terrible scoundrels in the army, men who would steal a dime from dead persons eye and then kick him because it was not a quarter," Cowin lamented. The larceny of boxes and contents did not improve as the war progressed. In January 1864, a Tar Heel noted that all

11 *Southern Confederacy*, Feb. 9, 1862; Hassler, *One of Lee's Best Men*, 102; McCrea, *Red Dirt and Isinglass*, 393; Leonidas Torrence, "The Road to Gettysburg: The Diary and Letters of Leonidas Torrence of the Gaston Guards," in Haskell Monroe, ed., *North Carolina Historical Review* (Oct. 1959), 503; William G. Morris to Deare Companion, Mar. 4, 1863, Morris Letters, SHC. The *Atlanta Appeal* once claimed there was no greater public service in the South than the Southern Express Company. See Dudley Johnson, "The Southern Express Company," *The Georgia Historical Quarterly* (Summer 1972), 34.

boxes deposited at warehouses were robbed. The commanders of both Steuart's and Battle's brigades sent armed guards to depots to escort the boxes back to their respective camps.[12]

The loss of boxes could produce hard feelings among messmates. No better illustration can be found than in a letter from a member of the 26th North Carolina Troops, written in October 1862 from Petersburg:

> I hapen with bad luck with my boxes. I loste them. I fetch them on to Raleigh and then had to put them on a mail trane, and Couden go an it my Self. I had to go on a nother train, but Collete and Fleming was on the train that the boxes were on, and that Said tha wouls have them taken Cair of when the got to wldon, but the never look fore them when tha got their. And when I got their, I Coulden fine them, and I thought tha had taken them on, but tha haden and So I hante Seen them.

> Tha woulden lete mee go back to get them, and I tride to git that damd Fleming to go after them, and he woulden go. I tole him I would pay all exspense if he would go, and he woulden at tall, and a damber Shit ass than him never was than him, and that damd bill is. And he hante worth hells room. He lays in his tente all day. You Cante see him oute of his tente with oute he goes to the docter. I wante you to tell bob that I Said he might go to hell and bee god damd, and the nex thing I aske him to doo he will doo it for mee. I wouden doo a thing fer him to Sav him from hell.[13]

Some of those boxes that did arrive took so long that their contents were spoiled. Thomas Rollins, while in Northern Virginia after First Manassas, received a box from home and invited his messmates to join him in a feast. As they gathered, the lid was pried off. "It would have done you good to see them scatter—such a scent as arose from the box," a fellow soldier wrote. Soldiers mentioned spoiled bread and moldy cakes in August and October 1861, March and April 1863, and February, May, and August 1864. A box full of broken vessels or ruined food was a blow to morale. Soldiers were angry in some instances. "I abused him for not eating the contents before they spoiled," Sandie Pendleton wrote in August 1861. When soldiers received boxes with spoiled items, they salvaged what they could. A

---

12 Munson, *Confederate Incognito*, 163; Donald Koonce, ed., *Doctor to the Front* (Knoxville, TN, 2000), 130; Walter Clark, ed., *Histories of Several Regiments*, 5 vols. (Raleigh, NC, 1901), 2:116; Blackford & Blackford, *Letters from Lee's Army*, 156; George W. Davis, Rebecca Pitchford Davis Letters, SHC; Hubbs, *Voices from Company D*, 34–35, 43–44; Chapman, *Bright and Gloomy Days*, 105; Earl Hess, *In the Trenches at Petersburg* (Chapel Hill, NC, 2009), 220. Wiley notes that in another case, 55 live fowl were shipped from Mecklenburg County to Jamestown in Oct. 1861. *The Life of Johnny Reb*, 99.

13 William S. Setzer, "Your Neighbor Boys That Fell in Defense of their Country: The William A. Setzer Letters," Locke W. Smith, Jr., & Greg Mast, eds., *Company Front* (2015), 38.

45th Georgia soldier wrote from Harrisonburg in February 1864 that the potatoes and cakes were rotten, while the "butter is sound, but taste pretty rank. . . . I am going to work it over and see if I can't get some of the old smell from it."[14]

Several different states established depots in Richmond. The North Carolina Depot, at 228 Main Street, was up and running by July 1862. "All Packages and Boxes sent to Regiments by Express or Freight can be found at the N.C. Depot," the advertisement ran. Claiborne Watkins was the agent. Announcements for the South Carolina depot began to appear in September. Robert Barnwell, Jr., supervised the facility located at 81 Main Street. Depot staff promised to protect trunks and boxes left in their care. The North Carolina Depot advertised in the *Richmond Dispatch* in March 1863, listing the boxes and packages awaiting collection. They had 200 on hand, with five additional "mess chests" for various Tar Heel companies. Brigadier General James Conner reported in October 1864 that Kershaw's old brigade, which Conner temporarily commanded in the Shenandoah Valley, had 200 boxes waiting in the South Carolina depot.[15]

Individual states set up collection points to help move boxes from families to soldiers. In South Carolina, Rev. John Bachman was instrumental in getting boxes to soldiers and hospitals. In November 1862, the aged minister wrote to Thomas Ruffin that he had become an agent "for receiving and distributing funds, food, etc.," to various hospitals. "I am personally interested in the Army of Virginia. I signified my willingness to receive contributions for hospitals there, and finally resolved to take on the car-load of provisions and clothing I had collected." Bachman distributed that load of provisions in hospitals between Lynchburg and Winchester. An appeal was issued by Bachman in August 1863 to the farmers and planters in South Carolina, "in behalf of our suffering soldiers." He asked for donations of poultry, bacon, lard, butter, eggs, cowpeas, brandies, wines, cordials, sweet potatoes, and other vegetables from those living along the Greenville or Charlotte railroads. Citizens responded generously to Bachman's appeal. A month later, he listed dozens of contributions from citizens and ladies aid societies. These included a barrel with six shoulders and three hams, several coops of chickens, one gourd of lard, flour, rye, potatoes, eggs, bacon, and other items. In South Carolina, the Central Association was established in October 1862. These various

---

14 Bean, *The Liberty Hall Volunteers*, 23; W. G. Bean, *Stonewall's Man: Sandie Pendleton* (Charlottesville, VA, 1964), 47; McCrea, *Red Dirt and Isinglass*, 459.

15 *Richmond Dispatch*, Jul. 15, 1862, Sep. 2, 1862, Mar. 3, 1863. There was also a Mississippi Depot in Manassas in Sep. 1861. *Richmond Dispatch*, Sep. 18, 1861; Moffett, *Letters of General James Conner*, 157. An 1863 Richmond directory listed Alabama, Georgia, Mississippi, North Carolina, South Carolina, and Virginia Depots. *The Stranger's Guide and Official Directory for the City of Richmond* (Richmond, VA, 1863), 26.

organizations also worked to get boxes from home to the men in the armies in Virginia and Georgia. In October 1864, they advertised that railroad cars were dispatched every Wednesday. "It is again requested that boxes be properly secured by wooden straps; and that molasses jugs and bottles be excluded from the boxes." In April 1864, under the direction of Surgeon General Edward Warren, North Carolina designated 12 deposit sites across the state where boxes for soldiers or prisoners of war were forwarded to the troops in Virginia. In a post-war letter, Warren wrote of establishing these points and forwarding the collected items at regular times.[16]

Physically collecting the boxes was challenging. Many soldiers lamented that their boxes were so close yet unreachable. From near Fairfax Court House in October 1861, a soldier in the 5th Alabama complained that boxes remained at Manassas due to their sheer number. A member of the 7th Georgia Infantry, writing in February 1862, found the roads a wreck. In December 1863, several boxes for the 2nd Battalion North Carolina Troops languished at Orange Court House. Captain Charles Bahnson tried to procure a wagon to retrieve them but was denied by General Robert Rodes. Bahnson sent a member of his company, Cyrus Chadwick, "who ran the blockade successfully, and returned late this evening with the package." In December 1864, James Lane wrote to give thanks for several boxes that arrived at Christmas time, although sometimes the boxes had to remain at the depot for a day or two "for want of transportation." Lane sent his own headquarters wagon to the depot to collect boxes for his men.[17]

Some soldiers received items to sell in their boxes from home. Andrew McCoy, 25th Virginia Infantry, while in camp near Orange Court House in January 1864, received a barrel containing seven cheeses, which his mother wanted him to sell. "I will try to sell them to the best advantage," McCoy wrote, promising to send the money home at the first chance.[18]

With tens of thousands of men leaving their farms to join the Confederate armies, it fell upon women, children, and men too young, old, or unfit for duty to manage large and small farms. In antebellum years, men primarily tended the farms, working in the fields during planting and harvest. Now those men were

16 C. L. Haskell, *John Bachman, the Pastor of St. Luke's Lutheran Church* (n. p., 1888), 364–365; *Edgefield Advertiser*, Aug. 12, 1863; *Charleston Courier*, Sep. 15, 1863; *Charleston Mercury*, Oct. 29, 1862, Oct. 15, 1864; *Asheville News*, Apr. 21, 1864; Edward Warren, *A Doctor's Experiences in Three Continents* (Baltimore, 1885), 309.

17 Hubbs, *Voices from Company D*, 59; Parks & Baker, "I am Writing on My Canteen," *Company Front*, 12; Chapman, *Bright and Gloomy Days*, 100; Lane, "Glimpse of Army Life," *SHSP*, 18:420.

18 Andrew McCoy to Miss M. E. McCoy, Jan. 16, 1864, McCoy Letters, Virginia Military Institute.

gone, encamped on fields far away. Most believed that the war's duration would be short. Men who enlisted in the spring expected to be home in time for the fall harvest. As harvest time approached, many realized the contest would be a prolonged one. "How queer the times, the women can't count on the men at all to help them," lamented Grace Elmore of South Carolina in 1865.[19]

William G. Morris told his wife in North Carolina to manage things the best she could; he later advised her to "Save all the Grain" possible, ask neighbors about salt in September 1862, and sell cattle and wheat two months later. Morris inquired about the condition of hogs and the family pork supply, offering guidance about assistance: "Tell Randle to doo the Best he can for Me this Summer he can Manage the farm as Well as I can[.]" Morris first mentions receiving a box from home in April 1863. "Not One of the Eggs broken," he reported. Later he wrote of stockpiling salt and keeping enough corn to fatten the hogs. Morris was captured on the third day of the battle of Gettysburg, spending the balance of the war as a prisoner at Johnson's Island. His short letters home, brought south through the "Dixie Mail," no longer contained farm advice.[20]

Families struggled to send food to the front. There were droughts, flooding, and unusual cold snaps. In addition, the war itself slowly crept across the South. By 1863, much of Tennessee, the Mississippi River Valley, and coastal areas in North Carolina, South Carolina, Georgia, and Florida, were under Federal control. Other areas, such as the Southern Appalachian areas of Western North Carolina, Southwest Virginia, and Eastern Tennessee, were engaged in guerilla wars pitting neighbor against neighbor and citizens against both armies. Watauga County, North Carolina, one of those mountain communities, sent three companies to the ANV. Leah Adams Dougherty later recalled, "I was called out of bed any hour of the night to cook and pack a knapsack with three-day rations for my soldier brothers, and for men who were on furlough or returning to the front." From 1863 on, Watauga County was frequently traversed by those hiding from the army in the hollers and caves or trying to reach Union lines in East Tennessee. Locals became quite adept at hiding food. Sally Brown, whose husband was in a prisoner-of-war camp in Maryland, pulled the siding from her house, "crammed meat, grain, and dried food such as beans, dried fruits and vegetables between the walls, then nailed the boards back in place." Next, she put good seed potatoes in

---

19 Grace Elmore Diary, Feb. 11, 1865, South Carolina Library.

20 William Morris to Deare Family, Sep. 25, 1862; Oct. 4, 1862; Oct. 11, 1862; Dec. 4, 1862; Dec. 25, 1862; Mar. 29, 1862; Apr. 15, 1863; Apr. 19, 1863; Morris letters, *SHC*. Randle appears to be a local slave, but not owned by Morris, as Morris adds that he is willing to purchase Randle if Randle is so inclined.

the potato hole, covered them with straw, and raked bad potatoes on top. When the Federals finally arrived, they found only rotten potatoes and no meat. Often such encounters could prove deadly. In neighboring Ashe County, Isaac Wilson, a former lieutenant in the 37th North Carolina and now a recruiting officer, was bushwhacked as he plowed his field, dying several hours later.[21]

Citizens sought to protect food supplies when large armies were nearby. In Lexington, the Prestons, hearing that Federal cavalry were approaching, hid their valuables and moved a large amount of bacon and flour into the surrounding mountains. When the Federals arrived, they broke into the smokehouse, taking everything, then "seized the newly churned butter" from the cellar. They later took the china, "a firkin of lard . . . a keg of molasses," and the breakfast then being cooked. "My children were crying for something to eat; I had nothing to give them but crackers," Margaret Preston wrote. In Fauquier County, not far from Washington, D.C., invading armies frequently passed through the streets of Warrenton and surrounding communities. Fanny Carter Scott wrote in 1862 of Federal soldiers stealing cattle, corn, and poultry, walking into a kitchen, demanding dinner, and then not paying. "Scarcely anyone ploughing, fences pulled down, fields many of them in commons, stores closed, no one traveling about, the public roads deserted; a few travelers on old, broken-down steeds that no one would care to possess himself of," she chronicled in her diary. Even Federal officers noted the depredations. As the Army of the Potomac moved into Fauquier County following the Battle of Gettysburg, a Federal provost marshal saw that "Officers & men are turned thieves and robbers—The whole country is full of Stragglers & the Officers all permit it and say nothing." A few days later, he wrote that a detail he sent out captured ten men from a Federal cavalry regiment who were out robbing, telling their captors that they were operating under the provost marshal's authority.[22]

Early in the war, civilians often contributed voluntarily, supplying food from their pantries and gardens. As volunteers prepared to march off to war, citizens prepared community picnics in their honor. Volunteers left town with rations in homemade haversacks slung over their shoulders. Those traveling by rail to the seat of war in Virginia might find communities offering laden tables. A 4th South Carolina Infantry soldier, moving between Wilmington and Richmond in June 1861, noted his company was "treated to all we could get and drink (and that was

21 Bud Altmayer, *A Family History of Watauga County* (Boone, NC, 1994), 12, 98–99; Sandra Ballard & Leila Weinstein, *Neighbor to Neighbor* (Boone, NC, 2007), 96–129.

22 Elizabeth Allan, *The Life and Letters of Margaret Junkin Preston* (Boston, 1903), 186, 189, 190; Eugene Scheel, *The Civil War in Fauquier County* (Warrington, VA, 1985), 30, 60.

considerable) at every place we stopped at." The soldier went on to tell how his
captain telegraphed ahead to Petersburg, asking that a dinner be prepared, with all
the company members promising to pay the captain later. They found the dinner
ready on their arrival. "I don't know that I ever saw men so near eating their worth
of their money before in my life," the South Carolinian wrote. As they left, the
soldiers crammed the leftovers into their pockets for later.[23]

Ladies aid societies sprang up across the South, attempting to keep the war
a community event by supporting the local men in service. These more formal
organizations had officers and regularly met in homes, churches, or local businesses
to sew clothing, make bandages, and package food for men in the army or state
hospitals in Virginia. The Ladies' Relief Association of Fairfield, South Carolina,
made regular contributions throughout the war. One shipment to the hospital in
Charlottesville contained port wine, blackberry wine, plum cordial, cherry cordial,
and damson plum cordial. To one local Confederate company, the Association sent
several boxes, including cordials, coffee, sage, sugar, rice, salt, breads, cakes, biscuits,
tea, flour, cloves, nutmeg, wine, peaches, jelly, and mustard, along with culinary
accessories, including plates, knives, forks, spoons, teakettles, and a tin coffee pot.
Many of these groups, such as the Keswick Aid Society of Alamance County,
Virginia, chose a focus: the sick and wounded in the hospitals in Charlottesville.
Besides soliciting donations or providing items from their cupboards, some groups
raised funds through various means. The "Amateur Minstrels" of the 3rd Alabama
Infantry put on a concert on behalf of the Ladies' Soldiers' Aid Society in Norfolk
in September 1861. One young lady in Caroline County raised chickens, sold
them, and gave the $5 profit to her local aid society, purchasing materials for
clothing. In February 1862, Harry Macarthy, "the Arkansas Comedian," gave a
concert in Richmond on behalf of the Ladies' Soldiers' Aid Society, the proceeds
of which were given to the sick and wounded in area hospitals. In June 1862,
the Ladies' Soldiers' Aid Society members in Rockbridge County opened their
homes to 100 wounded soldiers, promising to feed and care for them. In July,
the Richmond group advertised that they were looking to buy six cows for the
hospital. Many of these groups continued working throughout the war years, but
as resources evaporated, they were able to contribute less and less.[24]

23 James Faust, *The Fighting Fifteenth Alabama Infantry* (Jefferson, NC, 2015), 7; David McGee,
"Home and Friends," *North Carolina Historical Review* (Oct. 1997), 371; J. W. Reid, *History of the
Fourth Regiment of S.C. Volunteers* (Dayton, OH, 1975), 10.

24 Sally Taylor & Sallie Conner, *South Carolina Women in the Confederacy* (Columbia, SC, 1903),
21–25, 44–45; *Richmond Dispatch*, Jul. 25, 1861, Sep. 11, 1861, Feb. 11, 1862, Jul. 23, 1862;
Richmond Enquirer, Nov. 1, 1861, Jun. 6, 1862. A list generated after the war enumerated 100 ladies'

Churches often urged their parishioners to contribute with prayers and material contributions. The pastor of the Presbyterian Church in Lenoir, North Carolina, reminded those in attendance of the words of Jesus in Matthew: "for I was hungry and you gave me food, I was thirsty and you gave me drink." When Southern independence looked bleak, a pastor in the same community preached from the book of Ruth, reminding listeners that the way to escape famine and despair was by trusting in God. In Georgia, Roman Catholic Bishop Elliott instructed the clergymen within his diocese to collect clothing, medicines, and nourishment for their state's sick and wounded soldiers. In May 1862, the Ladies Aid Society in Richmond asked pastors "to take up a collection in their respective churches, as funds are getting low." Churches frequently appeared in those long lists of contributors in various newspapers. In one account in Richmond in August 1862, the congregation of Sugar Church in Mecklenburg County, North Carolina, donated crackers, lint, and bandages.[25]

Food shortages hit across the South, and letters flew to elected officials. In December 1862, Kenneth Rayner wrote that eastern North Carolina was "at the mercy of the enemy," and citizens were frequently robbed of crops and livestock. It was no better in Wilmington in January 1863. A citizen wrote to North Carolina treasurer Jonathan Worth that Confederate forces protecting the port of Wilmington frequently seized foodstuffs and confiscated wagons and carts. Consequently, farmers had quit bringing items into the city. "We are almost starved out," was the writer's opinion. From Appomattox County in April 1864, a citizen wrote Secretary of War James Seddon about "suffering much for corn," and the families of local soldiers depended on the government to send aid. In Rockingham County in November 1864, army agents had been "foraging, impressing, and hauling off a portion of the scanty subsistence left, until our people are almost reduced to beggary," two citizens wrote to the Honorable John Baldwin. The wealthiest families seldom felt the pinch of need, especially those outside the cities.[26]

Letters from home often described hard times. One wife in Augusta County wrote her husband in the 52nd Virginia Infantry in February 1862 that since her

---

aid societies in South Carolina alone. See also William Blair, *Virginia's Private War: Feeding Body and Soul in the Confederacy, 1861–1865* (New York, 1998), 37–38.

25 McGee, "Home and Friends," 372, 384; T. Conn Bryan, "The Churches of Georgia During the Civil War," *The Georgia Historical Quarterly* (Dec. 1949), 288; *Richmond Dispatch*, May 10, 1862, Aug. 6, 1862.

26 Lynda Crist, et al., eds., *Papers of Jefferson Davis* (Baton Rouge, 1995), 8:369, 536; J. G. Hamilton, *The Correspondence of Jonathan Worth*, 2 vols. (Raleigh, NC, 1909), 1:277; *OR* Series 4, 3, 285, 845. Mary Massey argues that Davis was disturbed every so often by the requests for help, but never "took any positive stand on any definite program." *Ersatz in the Confederacy* (Columbia, SC, 1993), 33.

father had sold his horse, she had to rent both a horse and wagon to haul anything. "You don't know what hard times I have here about wood," she confessed. A couple of family members had hauled some, but once that supply was exhausted, "I don't know what I will do." A woman in rural Tennessee chastised the "gay ladies of our fashionable cities" regarding how little they knew of the real war. "Many a woman who never before held a plough is now seen in the corn-field. . . . Many a Ruth as of old, is seen to-day, binding and gleaning in the wheat-fields. . . . [A]t every farmhouse and cottage, the regular sound of the loom, as the shuttle flies to and fro, with the whirl of the spinning-wheel, is heard." Citizens slowly tightened their belts and did without. Margaret Preston, in Lexington, Virginia, noted in April 1863 that her family was surviving on "soldiers' rations in regard to meat." Once a day, members of the household received "a quarter of a pound apiece for the whites," while their slaves received "a half a pound." She noted that her husband gave the government "every pound of bacon he can spare, after putting his family on short allowance." In Winchester in May 1864, one woman recorded that Federals had again assumed control of her town. There was such an immense number of soldiers that sutlers had arrived. "Almost everyone is out of groceries and will buy all that is possible," she noted in her diary.[27]

Tax-in-kind and impressment hit local communities hard. In March 1864, Burke County, North Carolina, in the Appalachian foothills, submitted its tax-in-kind receipt. Thirty-six men and women had paid a tithe of 672 bushels of corn, 111 bushels of wheat, 23 bushels of oats, 34 bushels of rye, 1,550 pounds of cured hay, 1,035 pounds of cured fodder, 24 pounds of wool, two bushels of peas, and 2,407 pounds of bacon. As these items were turned over to Confederate officials, artillerymen from James Longstreet swept into western North Carolina, impressing food and fodder for artillery horses. Letters flew from communities to Governor Vance and from the governor to officials in Richmond. Calvin Cowles, a Wilkes County farmer, wrote to Vance that Longstreet's men had "come down through McDowell, Burke & Caldwell [Counties] & have nearly consumed all the grain they could pick up. . . . What are poor day laborers to do for bread when every crib in the land is depleted to the lowest possible standard. . . . I see a dark day ahead for the poor sons of toil and in fact for us all unless some unforeseen good luck should happen." Vance wrote to Confederate Secretary of War Seddon on March 26 that Longstreet's men caused "inconvenience and perhaps some suffering." In a more scathing letter on April 11, Vance complained that many had lost their

27 Mary Dedrick to Dear Henry, Feb. 1, 1862, Henry Dedrick Letters, VMI; *The Charleston Daily Courier*, Jul. 24, 1863; Allan, *The Life and Letters of Margaret Junkin Preston*, 162; Toalson, *No Soap, No Pay*, 104.

crops between Tories, deserters, and Longstreet's men, robbing and eating out the countryside. Once Longstreet's men left, local farms "will be altogether wretched, and hundreds will go to the enemy for protection and bread."[28]

Eventually, widespread food shortages were felt across the Confederacy. Droughts, floods, and shortened growing seasons hurt people at home. Farmers tried to increase the production of wheat and oats but were struck with rust, a fungal disease. The blockades of Southern ports also cut off imported goods and a collapsing transportation system. What supplies were available went to the military first. In some instances, Confederate soldiers raided local farms, causing resentment toward soldiers who were supposed to protect citizens. Newspapers and government officials urged Southerners to grow more food crops and less cotton. By 1863, Davis himself was urging people to substitute food crops and livestock for cotton and tobacco. He encouraged planting crops near railroads, rivers, and canals to alleviate the strain on the South's crumbling infrastructure. Like Davis, who offered limited suggestions regarding the food crisis, the Confederate Congress shifted much of the problem to the states for redress. North Carolina and Georgia each purchased blockade runners, bringing munitions of war, coffee, liquors, and medicines. Governor Zebulon Vance advocated for the establishment of depots where food could be stored, then sold to the poor at cost. Most counties had a committee to distribute aid to soldiers' families, using funds received by the state. In Georgia, Governor Joseph Brown fought many of the same problems as Vance, namely a starving populace. Brown halted shipments of salt outside the state, closed distilleries that used grain better suited for feeding people and animals, and, when frost hit the northern counties in late summer 1863, led state lawmakers to purchase 97,500 bushels of corn for distribution.[29]

Despite government intervention, at least on the state level, there were still famished wives, mothers, and children. At times, they did more than write their representatives in state capitals or Richmond. In more than a dozen cases, they took to the streets to voice their displeasure and fill empty stomachs. Some of these insurrections were small. In January 1863, fifty dissidents raided salt stores

28 Calvin Cowles to Zebulon Vance, Apr. 4, 1864, Cowles Papers, NCDAH: Zebulon Vance to James Seddon, Mar. 26, 1864; Zebulon Vance to James Seddon, Apr. 11, 1864, Joe Mobley, *The Papers of Zebulon Baird Vance* (Raleigh, NC, 2013), 160, 170.

29 Massey, *Ersatz in the Confederacy*, 34; Paul Escott, "Joseph E. Brown, Jefferson Davis, and the Problem of Poverty in the Confederacy," *The Georgia Historical Quarterly* (Spring 1977), 59–71. A few natural disasters that befell the Confederacy included droughts in Texas, 1861, and southern Alabama in 1862; the Mississippi River flooded in 1861 and 1862; and the Appomattox River in 1864. See Massey, *Ersatz in the Confederacy*, 29; Robert Krick, *Civil War Weather in Virginia* (Tuscaloosa, AL, 2007).

in the western North Carolina hamlet of Marshall. A year later, in neighboring Yancey County, a group of women raided commissary stores in Burnsville. In the piedmont North Carolina town of Salisbury, a group of women calling themselves "Soldiers' Wives" raided merchants and a Confederate depot, taking twenty-three barrels of flour, two sacks of salt, half a barrel of molasses, and twenty dollars. Simultaneously, in Atlanta, twenty women stormed stores, "seizing bacon, meal, and vegetables, paying such prices as they thought proper." Local police broke up the demonstration.

There were other raids: Savannah, Georgia; Barnwell, South Carolina; Waco, Texas; and Petersburg, Virginia. The most notable of these raids was in Richmond, Virginia, on April 1–2, 1863. A local woman gathered others to protest the food crisis. Richmond's population had more than doubled in two years of war, and the combination of government workers, soldiers, and refugees strained local markets. Speculators drove up prices. When the government attempted to institute price controls, farmers stopped bringing produce to market. In early March, the secretary of war ordered the seizure of every barrel of flour in Richmond for the army's use. On April 2, a group gathered on Capitol Square, wielding clubs, hatches, knives, and pistols. John Jones, a government clerk, was told by a "young woman, seemingly emaciated . . . that they were going to find something to eat." A few women went to see the governor, who told them to go home. Disgruntled, the group, now numbering close to 1,000, including some men, headed into the heart of the city, robbing merchants and government storehouses. The mayor arrived, attempting to disperse the mob, to no avail. President Davis heard the commotion and came, attempting to defuse the situation. Finally, the mayor called out the public guard, which arrived with loaded muskets. Davis gave the masses five minutes to disperse before the guard opened fire. Slowly they left, and Davis did not fire upon his citizens. Rumors gripped the city for the next few days of other uprisings. The city council met soon after to set about reforming poor relief.[30]

The multitude of boxes, barrels, and sacks of foodstuffs might seem an inconsequential fragment of the war. Quite the opposite is true. When the Confederate army in Virginia struggled to provide more than bacon and cornmeal, boxes arrived containing all sorts of meat, dried or preserved fruits and vegetables, and sweets. These added not only diversity, which was doubtless good for morale, but in the winter months, could keep a soldier's immune system strong and perhaps thwart scurvy. A parcel from home kept the soldier in touch with his

30 R. Douglas Hurt, *Agriculture and the Confederacy* (Chapel Hill, NC, 2015), 130, 200; Andrew Smith, *Starving the South* (New York, 2011), 50; Stephen Ash, *Rebel Richmond: Life and Death in the Confederate Capital* (Chapel Hill, NC, 2019), 193–199; Furgurson, *Ashes of Glory*, 193–196.

There were many food riots across the South as foodstuffs began to dwindle. *Frank Leslie's Illustrated Newspaper*

loved ones back on farms across the South. Those packets reminded the soldier why he was fighting, keeping the war in perspective. Of course, when raiders or Federal soldiers came, robbing families of all their provisions, a letter from home might also lead a soldier, unable to secure a furlough, to absent himself without leave to aid his family. Lastly, these parcels connected the people back home to the war effort. They were growing, harvesting, and preparing items for their soldier boys at the front.

The war was not felt just in Virginia, along the Rappahannock, or the trenches below Petersburg, but also in regions that did not experience large-scale battles, from the foothills of western North Carolina to the lowlands of South Carolina. These emissaries from home were critical to the war. The ripples of each package's creation, journey, and delivery formed a complex pattern that touched the soldiers and families back home and transportation facilities across the South.

Chapter 3

"[T]he mess kettles of many a weary soldier"

Food on Campaign and in Battle

Walter Lenoir had seen little of the war when he was elected company captain in July 1862. Lenoir accompanied his brother while forming a company for the 25th North Carolina Troops. He then became a lieutenant in another company which was a part of the 58th North Carolina Troops, before finally accepting the position in the 37th North Carolina. His first campaign came in August 1862, as Stonewall Jackson began maneuvering against Federals under Maj. Gen. John Pope. "We were often without cooking utensils to prepare our rations," Lenoir wrote about the time of the battle of Cedar Mountain. The "men would make their flour into dough, on oil cloths, and bake it into cakes at the bivouac fired on pieces of staves, around sticks, etc. The beef and bacon they would roast on sticks, but generally preferred to eat the bacon raw. I learned to eat fat bacon raw, and to like it. The beef roasted on sticks and the hard and dry army crackers which I generally used for bread, were so delicious to my taste after the fierce appetite gained by hard marching that I never enjoyed eating so much." Lenoir's observations were echoed by many in the ranks.[1]

Supplying soldiers on campaigns or engaging in battle presented a new set of obstacles. Three- or four-days' worth of rations were all soldiers could typically carry. Wagon trains, following every brigade or division with mess equipment, often trailed far behind the men. Rations were often sparse unless a captured Federal depot was nearby. Then soldiers frequently ate themselves sick. They became ill from the green corn and apples found along roads. Many soldiers resorted to

1 Thomas Hickerson, *Echoes of Happy Valley* (Chapel Hill, 1962), 83.

raiding haversacks of dead Federals. Seldom did caloric intake from issued rations or foraged foodstuffs match the exertions demanded by a soldier on campaign.

New troops traveling to the war in Virginia usually struggled during their first campaign. When Hampton's Legion set out from South Carolina by train in June 1861, ham and hard biscuits were distributed, leaving men famished and thirsty. At one stop on a siding, they spotted three women and shouted for water. One elderly woman sent for her slaves and, using buckets, supplied the men on the cars. Water "was always the first thing the men called for as the cars stopped," an officer recalled. When the 5th Alabama arrived in Richmond, men were turned loose on the city to find something to eat. "Soldiers are looked upon in Richmond as suspicious persons, not to be trusted," one soldier wrote. They found nothing and returned to camp. Some Alabamians discovered their camping grounds belonged to a Pennsylvania Unionist and helped themselves to his milk and butter. Finally, the writer heard of a "free old negro" willing to sell food to soldiers. They walked a mile to his house to buy dinner. Soldiers from other states were not alone in meeting hard times procuring food. A member of the 2nd Virginia Cavalry, moving through Amherst Courthouse, found no provisions for "men or beast, and there was no disposition on the part of the inhabitants to show us hospitality or to relieve our wants except for money." That is not to say that local people did not turn out when soldiers passed. One member of Hampton's Legion who begged for water noted that the ladies in Greensboro, North Carolina, distributed food as they passed through the city.[2]

Moving to Manassas in preparation for battle was the first challenge for the army. A soldier in the 9th Alabama recalled scarce rations, as the wagon train had moved ahead while the infantry awaited transportation. They had to depend on the local population, and as the 4th Virginia Infantry moved via the railroad, local people threw buttered biscuits and sliced ham into the train. Many soldiers noted a dearth of foodstuffs and water during the battle. At the same time, spoils of war were left behind by retreating Federals. A member of Stuart's staff saw "barrels of sugar, crackers, ground coffee . . . cooking utensils, in fact everything." A South Carolinian wrote of filling wagons with pork, beans, and crackers. E. Porter Alexander, in his official report, documented coffee mills, barrels of commissary stores, 1,650 camp cooking utensils, 2,700 camp mess utensils, and scales to weigh

---

2 Moffett, *Letters of General James Conner*, 32; Hubbs, *Voices from Company D*, 6–7; Blackford & Blackford, *Letters from Lee's Army*, 9.

Soldiers were often loaded up with food as they began their journey across the South to Virginia.
Battles and Leaders

foodstuffs. These items undoubtedly helped supply the Confederate army gathered around the plains of Manassas.[3]

Several small skirmishes and a handful of minor battles occurred in Virginia during the next eleven months. The most trying in terms of sustenance were those in western Virginia, such as Robert E. Lee's campaign in Northwest Virginia in the fall of 1861 and Stonewall Jackson's Romney campaign in January 1862. Copious rain and poor roads hampered Lee's plans to beat a Federal force and provision his troops. Jackson's men managed to capture some supplies from the Federals but were often hungry and cold. "We had a most disagreeable time at Romney," remembered one Virginia artilleryman. While his men were quartered in a church, they had to cook in the adjoining graveyard. Another artilleryman wrote that wagons were often far behind the rapidly moving troops due to road conditions. The retreat from Manassas to the Fredericksburg area in March 1862 also brought some minor

---

3 John Barrett, ed., *Yankee Rebel: The Civil War Journal of Edmund DeWitt Patterson* (Knoxville, TN, 2004), 7; Roper, *Repairing the "March of Mars,"* 113; Trout, *With Pen & Saber*, 20–21; Everson & Simpson, *Far, Far from Home*, 37; OR 2, 571.

This idealized woodcut shows Federals attempting to load supplies as their army retreated from Manassas. Confederate forces captured tons of supplies from frantically retreating Union forces. *Harper's Weekly*

discomfort. A member of the 21st Georgia, already carrying two haversacks, was forced to leave behind his butter and most of his mess's cooking utensils.[4]

The Peninsula campaign in the spring of 1862 varied with respect to the provisioning of troops. Soldiers in the trenches at Yorktown, according to a member of the 14th Louisiana Infantry, were for a time obliged to live on pickled pork and "hard biscuits." Later, they established a cooking area in the rear. Supplies ran short when Johnston retreated up the Peninsula, much to the consternation of his men. "We half to march 3 days on one days pervision," wrote a member of the 7th South Carolina. However, rations for those troops soon arrived from Richmond. Jackson and Richard Ewell were active in the Shenandoah Valley in May. In a missive to one Confederate brigade commander en route to join those troops, General Ewell reported flour was abundant, but there was no salt, recommending that a subsistence officer be sent ahead to purchase additional foodstuffs not brought by the men. "The road to glory cannot be followed with much baggage," Ewell posturized. The state of rations was poor in many areas. One of Stuart's staff officers complained that while they were in the rear of the army, the only way they survived

4 J. William Jones, *Personal Reminiscences of General Robert E. Lee* (New York, 1875), 384; Jessup, *The Painful News I Have to Write*, 76; Monroe Cockrell, *Gunner with Stonewall: Reminiscences of William Thomas Poage* (Wilmington, NC, 1987), 17; Williams, *Rebel Brothers*, 42–43; Allen & Bohannon, "Campaigning with 'Old Stonewall,'" 79.

was "by plundering and stealing and many a home has been made desolate by the approach of Stuart's Cavalry. The standing order is impress everything that may fall into the enemy's hands. And thus we march with the wailing of women and children constantly ringing in our ears." One of Jackson's staff officers recalled members of Ashby's cavalry, after driving the Federals, stopping to plunder Federal wagons, giving "themselves up, in their hunger . . . [and] reduced in numbers that they were virtually inefficient." Even Jackson was seen to dismount and remove hardtack from an overturned wagon.[5]

Battles frequently brought disruptions to supplies, but Confederate soldiers with Lee during the Seven Days found plenty to curb their appetites. Moving through the recently abandoned camp of an Illinois cavalry regiment, a Texan discovered a cup of rice and ham. The rice was too warm to tuck away in his haversack, so the soldier sat down and consumed it. A member of the 15th Georgia saw that the Federals had attempted to destroy commissary stores as they retreated, but did a poor job, as they found "unbroached boxes of crackers, barrels of meat, rice, Irish potatoes, &c., &c., in great numbers. Coffee parched and ground was poured on the ground and in ponds of water, but large quantities have been found uninjured, and much has been used by our own soldiers." When Confederate cavalry captured the Federal supply base at White House, Heros von Borcke found among the flames hundreds of boxes of oranges and lemons, with barrels of sugar, salted fish, and eggs. This gave the Confederates "a repast as we had not enjoyed for many months."[6]

August 1862 was a real test for the commissary department. On August 6, Lee ordered three wagons from every regiment reassigned to haul subsistence stores. This reduced the baggage hauled by every regiment setting out on campaign. Part of Jackson's command took the railroad northwest to Gordonsville. Wagon trains bearing cooking equipment were left to follow on local roads. One officer in the 34th North Carolina Troops recounted "making up wheat dough on poplar bark without grease or salt and baking it before the fire on an oak chip." Captain Nicholas Gibbon served as assistant commissary of subsistence for the 28th North

5 Robert H. Miller, "Letters of Lieutenant Robert H. Miller," in Forrest Conner, ed., *The Virginia Magazine of History & Biography* (January 1962), 81; Jones, *The Boys of Diamond Hill*, 39; OR 12, 3, 890; Trout, *With Pen & Saber*, 68; Henry Kyd Douglas, *I Rode with Stonewall* (Chapel Hill, NC, 1940), 54–55. Browning & Silver contend that part of Jackson's poor performance during the Seven Days was due to lack of rations. *An Environmental History of the Civil War* (Chapel Hill, NC, 2020), 74.

6 J. B. Polley, ed., *A Soldier's Letters to Charming Nellie* (New York, 1908), 52–53; Ivy W. Duggan Diary, UGA, 63; Heros von Borcke, *Memoirs of the Confederate War*, 2 vols (New York), 1:66–67. John Tucker, 5th Alabama, chronicled several times in his diary of bringing commissary stores to his regiment during the campaign. Hubbs, *Voices from Company D*, 94.

On going into camp after a march, soldiers had to build a fire, roll out their dough, and gather water for a meal. *Battles and Leaders*

Carolina in August when Branch's brigade commissary, Daniel Carraway, became the acting commissary on A. P. Hill's staff. Gibbon's diary is an excellent source for the role of a brigade commissary on campaign from August 5 through December 1862. As the wagon train traveled from Gordonsville to Madison Courthouse, Gibbon was responsible for driving a herd of cattle along with the wagons. Upon arriving at the brigade's camp after dark, Gibbon had to construct a fence to corral the cattle and roust up a guard before he could retire. Early the following day, some cattle were slaughtered and issued to the men. "In all the marches from Gordonsville through Maryland to Bunker Hill, Virginia, Maj. Gen. A. P. Hill's Division [wagons] moved together," he recorded. Following the battle of Cedar Mountain, the men were forbidden to have fires, so Gibbon issued "hard bread." As the brigade marched to the rear the next morning, Gibbon issued fresh beef. This was common in other commands, as a Virginia artilleryman wrote of cooking a piece of fresh beef, without salt, and eating it with hard crackers on August 11.[7]

---

7   General Order 101, August 6, 1862, General Orders, Army of Northern Virginia, RG109, M921, NA; Michael Taylor, ed., *Cry is War, War, War: The Civil War Correspondence of Lts. Burwell Thomas Cotton and George Job Nuntley, 34th Regiment North Carolina Troops* (Dayton, OH, 1994), 95; Gibbon, Diary, 16–17, UNC-Charlotte; Jones, *The Spirits of Bad Men Made Perfect*, 105.

Gibbon's wagon train continued to follow the army around Virginia. On August 24, before Jackson's men stepped off for Manassas, Gibbon wrote of issuing the soldiers fresh beef and flour. It was almost a week before he caught back up to Branch's brigade. Jackson's wagon train, at least his commissaries, joined Longstreet's wagoneers as Jackson moved toward Manassas Junction. The Federal supply depot at Manassas Junction fell to the hungry Confederates on August 26. After the war, one member of the 13th Virginia recalled that there were "sulter's stores of choice liquors, fruits, and delicacies; great quantities of sugar and coffee; carloads of meat and flour; and a profusion of everything included in the rations of well-fed soldiers." A member of the 55th Virginia wrote of entering Manassas Junction with green corn-stuffed haversacks and leaving with "French mustard . . . sardines, canned meats and fruit, and desiccasted vegetables." What was not consumed or carted away was burned. One staff officer with Jackson believed that Federal Gen. John Pope was a better commissary than Gen. Nathaniel Banks.[8]

Around midnight, following Longstreet's successful attack on August 30, Gibbon was ordered to move toward the field. After a narrow escape in the darkness, he finally found the brigade early the next day. Jackson's men were well fed for a couple of days by stores captured at Manassas Junction. A soldier in the 13th Virginia recalled taking a piece of pickled pork and hardtack from his haversack, scraping part of the raw pork onto the cracker, and eating it. He considered it one of the "most delicious and satisfying meals I ever ate." Slowly the wagon train followed the Confederates advancing toward Ox Hill. Yet, they could not come up as the fighting subsided that evening, so soldiers set out to find food. One member of the 40th Virginia Infantry, looking for sustenance, stumbled upon a group of Federal soldiers seeking a wounded officer. Another "found a haversack strapped to a man who would never use his teeth again." Inside were crackers and coffee mixed with sugar. Quickly, the soldier had a fire going and "soon had a pint of steaming beverage." Harvey Davis, an enlisted man in the 1st North Carolina Cavalry, chronicled in his diary of raiding a farmer's field for corn, and then on September 3, being out of rations. They had given their rations to wounded Federals, then resorted to stealing corn and slaughtering cattle with their sabers, "as we were too near the enemy to shoot, but having no salt the beef went begging."[9]

8 Gibbon, Diary, 17–18, UNC-Charlotte; Swank, *Raw Pork and Hardtack*, 31; O'Sullivan, *55th Virginia Infantry*, 34; Douglas, *I Rode with Stonewall*, 136. It is plausible that had Jackson's commissary wagons been close by to load captured supplies, straggling during the Maryland campaign might not have been as bad.

9 Gibbon, Diary, 18, UNC-Charlotte; Swank, *Raw Pork and Hardtack*, 34; Wayland Dunaway, *Reminiscences of a Rebel* (New York, 1913), 45–47; Davis, "Harvey Davis's Unpublished Civil War Diary," 391.

Soldiers captured an abundance of supplies at Manassas Depot. Due to a lack of wagons, they were only able to take what could be eaten or carried. *Battles and Leaders*

With the Federal capital and thousands of soldiers just a few miles away, Lee realized he could not stay in his current position. He was too far from the railroad, and the surrounding countryside could not support his army. There was a rail line from Richmond to Fairfax Station, but the bridges over the Bull Run, Rappahannock, and Rapidan had been destroyed. Lee moved his army to Loudoun County, setting in motion a movement north of the Potomac River. Much of his logic was tied to provisioning his army. Once in Maryland, Lee wrote on September 4 that he believed he could "obtain supplies to advantage." That same day, orders were issued authorizing quartermasters and commissaries to purchase supplies on behalf of the army and forming a provost guard which was charged with arresting stragglers and placing rear guards behind each brigade to prevent the men from leaving the ranks to forage independently. Lee also ordered a further reduction of wagons.[10]

10 *OR* 19, pt. 2, 590, 592. Visiting the Washington, D.C., area after the war, Lee pointed to the Federal works, stating "I could not tell my men to take that fort when they had had nothing to eat for three days." Robert Lee, Jr., *The Recollections and Letters of General Lee* (New York, 1904), 416.

Lee's army was in motion by September 5. Nicholas Gibbon's wagon train and beef herd followed the infantry and artillery over the Potomac River although foodstuffs were in short supply. When Jackson ordered Brig. Gen. Lawrence Branch to prepare two days' provisions on September 6, Branch responded that he had nothing to cook. Jackson ordered him to send men into a nearby cornfield to procure roasting ears. General Pender complained that his men, living on green corn, were being used up. "Jackson would kill up any army the way he marches and the bad management in the subsistence Dept." One of Longstreet's aides, Moxley Sorrel, recalled that the countryside was beautiful and rich, "but we were constantly hungry." Straggling was caused "by want of food." Corn was plentiful, but soldiers, parching the corn with a little salt, soon developed "bad attacks of diarrhea." Many soldiers wandered the countryside, begging or buying from Marylanders. One Virginia artillery captain wrote of visiting a Dutch farmhouse for "first rate meals." While not pro-Confederate, the family "took our Confederate money and gave us the best they had." Several Confederates noted little plundering as the army moved around western Maryland. A soldier in Gregg's brigade recalled thousands of troops passing by orchards laden with apples and taking none. Yet a quartermaster in Micah Jenkins's brigade noted some civilians objecting to Confederate money, "which necessitates us to adopt the rather stringent measures of taking the desired articles by force, which process is popularly known in the army by the name of 'pressing.'" Others sent their cooks and camp servants into the surrounding countryside to glean "chickens, butter, flour, etc.," recalled a member of Kershaw's brigade.[11]

For some Confederates, the captures of Williamsport and Martinsburg helped, as the Federal garrisons had beaten a hasty retreat to Harpers Ferry. One artilleryman recalled drawing corn and crackers, while a Virginia infantryman wrote of receiving captured flour. In Hagerstown on September 12, Longstreet's men captured 1,500 barrels of flour, a fraction of what was necessary. An excellent prize for Jackson's command came on September 15 when the Federal garrison at Harpers Ferry surrendered. "We boys were turned loose on these good things and you may be sure we availed ourselves," recalled a member of the 7th North Carolina State Troops. Other troops, such as McLaw's Division, were less fortunate.

---

11 Gibbon, Diary, 18, UNC-Charlotte; Branch to wife, in James Lane, "History of Lane's brigade," *SHSP* (January 1907), 10:243; Hasler, *One of Lee's Best Men*, 173; Sorrel, *Recollections of A Confederate Staff Officer*, 109–110; Cockrell, *Gunner With Stonewall*, 42; J. F. J. Caldwell, *The History of a Brigade of South Carolinians* (Philadelphia, PA, 1866), 69; Sarah Carroll, ed., *Lifeline to Home from John William McLure* (Greenville, SC, 1990), 110–111; D. Augustus Dickert, *History of Kershaw's Brigade* (Wilmington, NC, 1990), 151–152.

When they finally arrived, the provisions were picked clean, and they headed to Sharpsburg hungry. Soon, Jackson's divisions, save A. P. Hill's, were on their way.[12]

Longstreet's wagon train, possibly with the reserve train of the army, was ordered from Hagerstown to Williamsport on the evening of September 14. His troops spent the day fighting at South Mountain, attempting to protect strategic passes. Lee then concentrated his forces east of Sharpsburg, along Antietam Creek. General John Bell Hood set out to find his divisional wagon train in the dark, but the wagons did not arrive until 5:30 a.m. on September 17, carrying only flour. After preparing a dough, Hood's Texans had just wrapped it around their ramrods or placed it on boards and rocks to bake when Federals pitched into Confederate lines. The fighting was fierce on the Confederate left in the West Woods and around the Dunkard Church, but the lines held. In the center, Confederates were driven out of the Sunken Road, but the Federals failed to follow up their success. On the Confederate right, Federals managed to cross Antietam Creek, moving toward Sharpsburg, when A. P. Hill's division arrived late in the day, attacking their flank, and driving them back. Considered the single bloodiest day of combat during the war, the battle was a draw. The wagon train of Jackson's command had followed behind the men, and as night set, there was a call for the wagons. Jedediah Hotchkiss, on Jackson's staff, wrote in his journal that Jackson ordered "cooking utensils and provisions" sent to the troops after the battle. The 48th Virginia Infantry moved near Hauser's Farm, where they drew bacon. Captain Thomas Ballard, commissary for Lawton's division, recalled orders to take one day's rations across the Potomac River that night and deposit them about two miles from the brigade. "Some of the troops being in line it could not all be issued before night, the wagons having been previously ordered to the Virginia side of the river," he complained.[13]

Lee's army was stationary throughout September 18, then pulled out under cover of darkness. Long columns of wagons came first, followed by the infantry and artillery, and finally, a cavalry screen. The torrents of rain turned the roads to sludge, and troops struggled to re-cross the Potomac River. One Tar Heel cavalryman wrote that Wade Hampton permitted his colonel to forage for bacon. Before the commissary could return, the colonel found several "fat hogs" eating corn earmarked for the regiment's horses. Orders were given to kill the hogs

---

12 Jones, *The Spirits of Bad Men Made Perfect*, 124; *OR* 19, pt. 2, 605; O'Sullivan, *55th Virginia Infantry*, 38; Austin Jones, *The Capture of Harpers Ferry* (n.p., 1922), 2. For more on McLaw's division, see Joseph Harsh, *Taken at the Flood* (Kent, OH, 1999), 557, n45.

13 *The Charleston Daily Courier*, Sep. 29, 1862; Archie McDonald, ed., *Make Me a Map of the Valley* (Dallas, TX, 1973), 82; John Chapla, *48th Virginia Infantry* (Lynchburg, VA, 1989), 40; Thomas Ballard, CMSR, M331, Roll 0014, RG109, NA.

using rocks and sabers because of their proximity to the enemy. Unsatisfied, the colonel took his pistol and began dispatching the hogs. "Orders were given to press pots," wash kettles were secured, the hogs skinned, and cooking commenced. By September 21, the Confederate army was across the Potomac River and encamped around Bunker Hill. The campaign was a disaster. The lower Shenandoah Valley was clear of Federals, as was most of Virginia, but active campaigning since August had taken its toll. According to E. Porter Alexander, writing many years after the war, "in the matter of shoes, clothing, and food the army was . . . probably worse off during this brief campaign than it had ever been before or ever was again. . . . For rations, we were indebted mostly to the fields of roasting ears, and to the apple orchards. Such diet does not compare with bacon and hardtack for long marches, and, before the campaign was over, the straggling from all causes assumed great proportions." While Lee's army did not rival the Federals in Maryland, better food could have increased his ranks and combat effectiveness.[14]

The battles of Fredericksburg and Chancellorsville were not extended campaigns comparable to Antietam or Gettysburg. Confederate forces were in Fredericksburg several days before the Federals launched their attack across the Rappahannock River. Before the battle, supplies from Richmond were already limited. After intense fighting on December 13, Federal forces broke through the Confederate right. Before being stopped by a piece of hardtack in his haversack, a ball punctured the canteen of a 37th North Carolina officer posted along the railroad cut. A counterattack drove the Federals back, restoring the line. On the Confederate left, several unsuccessful attacks on Marye's Heights produced thousands of Federal casualties. While stragglers in battle were common, there seemed to be more accounts of men trying to avoid the battle at Fredericksburg than in previous engagements. A soldier in the 1st Battalion Virginia Infantry, serving as provost, noted many were turned back toward their regiment for lacking passes to cook in camp. A 48th North Carolina officer wrote of slightly wounded men, "many of them receiving only mere scratches or bruises not unfitting them for duty & leaving the field in consequence & never returning during the fight & many not until the next day, having gone back 4 miles where our wagons, tents, sick, cooks & barefooted men were left." There was some scavenging among the dead, and

14 Davis, "Harvey Davis's Unpublished Civil War Diary," 393; E. P. Alexander, *Military Memoirs of a Confederate* (New York, 1907), 223. Most historians agree that there were thousands of stragglers during the Maryland campaign. An estimated 10,000 men rejoined the army on the night of the battle, with 5,000–6,000 more back at Winchester. Despite the claim by Beringer that "no Confederate army lost a major engagement because of the lack of army, munitions, or other essential supplies," the loss of 16,000 or more men at Sharpsburg due to a lack of "essential supplies," hampered Lee during the battle. *Why the South Lost the Civil War* (Athens, GA, 1986), 9; D. Scott Hartwig, *To Antietam Creek* (Baltimore, MD, 2012), 636–637; Harsh, *Taken at the Flood*, 468.

Originally captioned "Rations from the Stalk," the image depicts how many Confederates found food as they marched along. *Battles and Leaders*

one soldier from the 21st Georgia picked up coffee from a dead Federal afterward. With the Federals returning to their side of the river, the Confederates encamped in the surrounding area for the winter.[15]

Fishing around Confederate camps near Fredericksburg ended in late April 1863 as Federal soldiers attempted to flank Confederate forces. Lee countered, dividing his army three times. Jackson's maneuvers on May 2 were a resounding success, caving in the Federal flank. The May 2 attack found Federal soldiers fixing dinner, and many hungry Confederates paused for a moment to snatch food as they chased the fleeing Federals. A member of the 55th Virginia recalled "dipping real coffee from the boilers and blowing and drinking it as they move[d] along." It was always tricky to provision troops on the firing line. The 5th Alabama was near some trenches that evening when a corporal arrived with rations. Before he could distribute them, the Federals began shelling the position, forcing the Alabamians to take shelter. As the fire slackened, a man headed for the rations, drawing for two or three men near his position. Over the next few days, the Confederates drove the Federals back across the river, but with costly loses, including Stonewall Jackson. While Federal cavalry cut the railroad to Richmond, many Federal rations were strewn about, as eight days' worth had been issued before the campaign. Several Confederates wrote of picking up coffee, sugar, desiccated vegetables, meat, salt, and crackers.[16]

15 William Morris to Dear Companion, Dec. 18, 1862, Morris Papers, SHC; Driver, *1st Batt. VA Inf.*, 33; S.H. Walkup diary, Walkup Papers, SHC; Allen & Bohannon, *"Campaigning with 'Old Stonewall,'"* 197.

16 Koonce, *Doctor to the Front*, 74; O'Sullivan, *55th Virginia Infantry*, 47; Hubbs, *Voices from Company D*, 163; Moseley, *The Stilwell Letters*, 154, 156; Jones, *The Boys of Diamond Hill*, 91; W. G. Bean, ed., *"A House Divided," The Virginia Magazine of History & Biography* (October 1951), 413–414. A member of the 5th Alabama commented on the eight days' rations carried by the Federals. See Hubbs, *Voices from Company D*, 160.

Lee reorganized his army into three corps following Jackson's death. First Corps was commanded by James Longstreet; Second Corps, Richard Ewell; and Third Corps, A. P. Hill. Virginia had been stripped of foodstuffs by both armies for months. British military observer Col. Arthur Freemantle noted in June 1863 that large parts of the state were "now completely cleaned out. It is almost uncultivated, and no animals are grazing where there used to be hundreds." Pushing north again, across the Potomac River, was a strategy intended to force the Federals to follow, allowing central Virginia farmers to plant new crops. Furthermore, Maryland and Pennsylvania could not only supply the Confederates with foodstuffs, but also with horses, fodder, horseshoes, and other much-needed items. A victory on Northern soil might bring in outside recognition or empower Northern Copperhead Democrats tired of the strife.[17]

By early June, Lee had portions of his army in motion. Hill's corps stayed behind in Fredericksburg, ensuring the Federals did not cross the river and strike for Richmond, while Longstreet and Ewell's corps headed toward Winchester. Federal garrisons, such as those at Martinsburg and Winchester, fell. After the Confederates captured Berryville, a soldier in the 53rd North Carolina wrote that the birds had flown, but did not take their nest. "Their camp, with all their cooking utensils, quartermaster and commissary stores, were all left in our hands. They were evidently cooking a meal, for plenty of pots full of eatables were still on the fire when we got into their camp. We ate up all we could find, and filled our haversacks and pushed on." Hill's corps followed on June 14. Along the route, local citizens did what they could for the moving masses. Passing through Millwood, one Alabama soldier recalled two "glorious young ladies" with cold water. A few days later, there was a lady distributing buttered bread and buttermilk at Smithfield. By June 22, portions of Ewell's corps crossed the Potomac River. A soldier in the 18th North Carolina wrote of seeing a herd of 700 "fine cattle" pass toward the rear.[18]

Longstreet's and Hill's corps were near Chambersburg, Pennsylvania, by June 24, while Ewell's divisions were moving toward Carlisle and York. The soldiers found foodstuffs everywhere. From Chambersburg, a Virginia soldier wrote that chickens along their route "filled the mess kettles of many a weary soldier." This was echoed by an Alabama soldier, who noted that as soon as his troops stacked arms in the streets of Chambersburg, "the men were off by scores to the neighboring houses & brought back a great many hens & milk, butter, etc. . . . The people gave everything to the soldiers as they said our money would do them no good."

---

17 Arthur Freemantle, *Three Months in the Southern States: April, June 1863* (Mobile, AL, 1864), 178.

18 Leon, *Diary of a Tar Heel*, 31; Hubbs, *Voices from Company D*, 177, 178; Hancock, *Four Brothers in Gray*, 210.

General Ewell prohibited his men from forcing Confederate money on the civilian population, instead requiring they use Federal currency. From Shippensburg, one soldier wrote that chickens soon disappeared from the barn near where they were encamped. "Some few were paid for by men who happened to have a little US currency," implying that those who could not follow orders stole the chickens. Lee issued two orders concerning foraging while on campaigns. The first came June 21, setting forth proper foraging procedures. Goods had to be bought at fair market value, and private property was to be respected. The second order came on June 27. The war was not being waged on civilians, and any soldier caught abusing private property would be arrested and punished.[19]

There were undoubtedly many soldiers who abided by Lee's dictums. A soldier in the 2nd Florida Infantry wrote that some of Lee's generals were attempting to enforce his new orders. However, many felt like a soldier in the 9th Alabama: Stealing chickens was not half as bad as the atrocities committed by Federal soldiers in Southern states. Pender wrote on June 28 that the men behaved well in Maryland, but it was hard to restrain them once they crossed the Pennsylvania line. While they took poultry and hogs, some did pay for them, in Confederate script, but his troops "have done nothing like the Yankees do in our country." However, on June 28, from Chambersburg, a member of the 3rd South Carolina Infantry noted that "most of our soldiers seem to harbor a terrific spirit of revenge and steal and pillage in the most sinful manner. They take poultry, hogs, vegetables, fruit, honey, and any and every thing they can lay their hands upon. Last night Wofford's Brig[ade] of this div[ision] stole so much that they could not carry what rations they drew from the commissary." Most officers turned a blind eye to the foraging by individual soldiers. In one instance, several South Carolina soldiers had descended on a farm, taking all the fowl they could. General Lee, when confronted by the lady of the house, simply touched the brim of his hat, telling her good morning, and rode on.[20]

Orders were conveyed to the quartermasters and commissaries in the army, who collected to supply troops in the field and to send the surfeit back to Virginia. On June 21, General Order No. 27 directed these officers to "make requisitions" on civilians and local authorities for supplies. Going rates were promised to those who complied. Those who resisted or attempted to hide items had them seized. Medical,

19 Roper, *Repairing the "March of Mars,"* 474; Hubbs, *Voices from Company D*, 180, 181; Peace, *To Tranquillity*, 147; *OR* 27, pt. 3, 912–922.

20 Francis P. Fleming "Francis P. Fleming in the War for Southern Independence," in Edward Williamson, ed., *The Florida Historical Quarterly* (Oct. 1949), 145–46; Barrett, *Yankee Rebel*, 111; Hassler, *One of Lee's Best Men*, 253; Everson & Simpson, *Far, Far from Home*, 251, 262.

ordnance, quartermaster, and subsistence officers moved across the landscape, up to forty-five miles from the main army, acquiring items. In Chambersburg, Pennsylvania, on June 24, Early's chief commissary demanded from the town "50,000 lbs bread; 100 sack salt; 30 barrels molasses; 500 barrels flour; 25 barrels vinegar; 25 barrels beans; 30 barrels dried fruit; 25 barrels sauerkraut; 25 barrels potatoes; 11,000 lbs coffee; 10,000 lbs sugar; 100,000 lbs hard bread." Some went straight to the army, while the majority went to Winchester. Colonel Freemantle recalled seeing "great quantities of horses, mules, wagons, beef and other necessities" headed south as the army moved north. According to speculations, Lee's men seized between 45,000 and 50,000 head of cattle, around 35,000 head of sheep, and thousands of hogs, plus untold quantities of flour, corn, oats, coffee, and other items.[21]

Lee concentrated parts of his army near Cashtown, protecting the Cumberland Valley passes, while his army foraged to the west and north. He had planned to move Longstreet's and Hill's corps towards Harrisburg on June 29, yet intelligence convinced him the Federal army was on the march. Instead of moving north, Lee ordered his dispersed army to consolidate at Gettysburg. By July 1, portions of Ewell's and Hill's corps had reached Gettysburg, driving the Federals beyond the town to a series of hills to the south and east. For the next two days, Lee attempted to dislodge the enemy, only to fail on July 3.[22]

Gettysburg, like most battles, brought a disruption to the soldiers' food supply. Setting off toward town on June 30, a member of the 26th North Carolina band recalled short rations, and thanks to a previous sweep by the commissary department, nothing remained locally. A member of the 2nd South Carolina recalled bedding down on the evening of July 1 with nothing to cook and no fires. A Virginia artillery officer arriving in camp found his servant with haversacks full of rations, taken from dead Federals in the Railroad Cut. "By 8 o'clock my mess were all filled with real coffee and other substantials, thankful to God in a double sense, for the death of the Yankees." In the rear of each division, often two or three miles behind the lines, were the division hospitals and wagon parks where live animals were penned, awaiting distribution to the front lines. Tar Heel bandsman Julius Lineback recalled being sent to the front on the evening of July 1 to play for the troops. "As we went to the regiment, we were in the midst of an immense train

21 *OR* 27, pt. 3, 912–13; Jacob Hoke, *The Great Invasion of 1863* (Dayton, OH, 1887), 139; Freemantle, *Three Months*, 186. For more description of how the ANV acquired items, and what was sent back, see Brown, *Retreat from Gettysburg*, 22–34.

22 The idea of a movement to Harrisburg on June 29 comes from an 1875 letter from J. S. D. Cullen to James Longstreet. See James Longstreet, *From Manassas to Appomattox* (Philadelphia, 1896), 383.

of wagons, cattle, etc. pushing forward to feed the exhausted and hungry army in front." However, some divisions were not in place, or regimental or brigade commissary officers were unaware of camps' and regiments' precise locations. Many soldiers awakened July 2 with little in their haversacks. An assistant surgeon in the 3rd North Carolina set up at an abandoned farmhouse, finding a springhouse with milk and cream, which he purchased. Later that day, the house was ransacked by soldiers from a Louisiana regiment. "They took a hive of bees in the open day between two of them, marching straight through a bivouac of men, the infuriated bees flying in every direction. After the bees had quit the hive, the plunderers sat down and destroyed the honey." Writing after the war, a member of the Stonewall brigade recalled that on the second day of the battle, he and his comrades were "rather short of rations." They visited neighboring farmhouses, finding barrels of flour, a smokehouse full of bacon, and springhouses with milk, butter, and apple butter. They built fires in one farmhouse's stove and commenced baking bread and cooking meat and chickens. "We told the boys in the regiment about it, and some of them came over and cooked rations and carried them back for others." Also writing years later, a member of the 17th Georgia Infantry recalled finding a barrel of brandy while traveling to the battlefield. Those who filled their canteens regretted the lack of water as the day grew warmer, eventually drinking out of a muddy puddle in a ditch. On the morning of July 3, Moxley Sorrel, on Longstreet's staff, found an abandoned farmhouse full of food and breakfasted on bread and apple butter. A Union private, captured on July 3, noted passing "long lines of negro cooks baking corn pone for rebel soldiers at the front." One of those cooks might have been "Uncle John Price," who brought provisions to one company of the 4th Texas Infantry on the Confederate right, laying the food on a flat rock. The Texans were still under fire. The lieutenant of the company yelled from behind a rock to Cpl. Val Giles: "Sergeant Norris always issued the rations to the men but poor Mose is dead now and you must take his place. I appoint you second sergeant of company B. Divide the rations into fourteen equal parts and have the men crawl up and get them." Under fire from the Federals, Giles crawled "up to the camp kettle of boiled roasting ears and meal sack of ironclad biscuits that Uncle John had brought in and began dividing the grub and laying it on top of a big flat rock." With minie balls flying around, Giles finished dividing the food, and the remaining members of the company crawled toward the makeshift lunch counter.[23]

23 Harry Hall, *A Johnny Reb Band from Salem* (Raleigh, NC, 2006), 45; John Coxe, "The Battle of Gettysburg," *CV* (Sep. 1913), 21:433; Julius Lineback Diary, Jul. 3, 1863, Lineback Papers, SHC; Coupland R. Page, "Revelations of a Confederate Artillery Staff Officer: Coupland R. Page's

After the assault failed on the afternoon of July 3, Lee contracted his lines along Seminary and Oak Ridges, inviting the Federals to attack. One Tar Heel wrote that they were ordered on July 4 to cook two days' worth of rations. The reserve wagon train, loaded with equipment and foodstuffs, headed for Virginia. Under cover of darkness, Confederate infantry and artillery pulled out, with the rain enveloping the moving columns. By July 6, rations were running low. Men in the 5th Alabama drew nothing during the day as they trudged along. They did happen upon some beef bones left by Ramseur's brigade, which they boiled. That night, their "cooking detail" arrived with half a day's worth of rations, and someone managed to acquire three chickens for their dinner. The lack of foodstuffs was not limited to rank and file. The same day, Ewell sent out a staff officer with members of his courier company to forage. They broke down the door of a smokehouse and took enough to feed the corps for one day. The officer confessed that he had never been "so abused in his life as by the old woman" who owned the bacon.[24]

Confederates began arriving at Falling Waters, Maryland, on July 7, discovering that Federal cavalry had destroyed the pontoon bridge and recent rains swelled the Potomac River. Lee was trapped. He ordered entrenchments dug and began constructing a new bridge while a ferry boat moved the wounded. Some Confederates were able to forage the surrounding countryside. One of Longstreet's staff members wrote of a big kettle with corn, potatoes, chickens, and other vegetables on the evening of July 7. That was not the consensus across the army. "I was soaking wet . . . without meat and with little bread, and have been for some time," wrote a member of the 4th Texas on July 9. Assistant Surgeon Thomas Wood, 3rd North Carolina, noted that only ordnance wagons were allowed from the south side of the river. Their enterprising brigade commissary officer found an ordnance wagon, loaded it with rations, and crossed the river. Other commands remained hungry. "We are out of rations-some of our men have not had bread in 48 hours. Our foraging in the country is cut off," an officer in the 28th North Carolina noted in a letter home on July 13. Lee was finally able to get his army across the river on the evening of July 13, and the Gettysburg campaign came to an end.[25]

Reminiscences of the Battle of Gettysburg," in Thomas Elmore, ed., *Gettysburg Magazine* (Jan. 2016), 71–72; Koonce, *Doctor to the Front*, 106; John Casler, ed., *Four Years in the Stonewall Brigade* (Columbia, SC, 2005), 176; *Tipton Gazette*, June 6, 1912; Sorrel, *Recollections of A Confederate Staff Officer*, 179; Pettijohn, *Gettysburg and Libby Prison*, 6–7; *American Statesman*, Jul. 5, 1908.

24 Lawrence Lohr, ed., *The Mauney Brothers* (Kings Mountain, NC, 2013), 47; Hubbs, *Voices from Company D*, 185–186; Terry Jones, ed., *Campbell Brown's Civil War* (Baton Rouge, LA, 2001), 226.

25 Gary Gallagher, ed., *Fighting for the Confederacy: The Personal Recollections of General Edward Porter Alexander* (Chapel Hill, NC, 1989), 270; John West, *A Texan in Search of a Fight: Being the*

Confederate artillerymen taking a break during the battle of Gettysburg. *Battles and Leaders*

While Gettysburg was a Confederate defeat, the campaign achieved some of Lee's goals. The Federal army left Virginia, and Lee supplied his army in enemy territory. They had lived off the land and secured supplies to ensure their survival for months. "We have plenty of beef and bread to eat. We gathered up thousands of beeves in Pennsylvania—enough to feed our army until cold weather," a member of the 13th South Carolina wrote from camp at Bunker Hill. The gathered provisions allowed Lee to remain idle while sending a portion of Longstreet's command to Georgia in September. There were minor campaigns, such as Bristoe Station in October and Mine Run in late November and early December, but the ANV did not undertake another serious campaign for almost a year.[26]

The Bristoe campaign lasted several weeks, with cavalry battles at Auburn and Buckland and infantry fighting at Bristoe Station and Rappahannock Station. A member of the 4th North Carolina wrote on October 18 of capturing crackers

---

Diary and Letters of a Private Soldier in Hood's Texas Brigade (Waco, TX, 1901), 88; Speer, *"Voices from Cemetery Hill,"* 109. Wood wrote that ordnance wagons were painted black. Koonce, *Doctor to the Front*, 108.

26 Welch, *A Confederate Surgeon's Letters*, 60.

from a Federal camp, and then being ordered to cook three days' rations, without cooking utensils. The soldiers kneaded their dough on gum blankets and placed it on barrel staves or wrapped it around ramrods to cook before the fire. "I think it is the sweetest bread that I ever ate. I think there must be something in the appetite also," he concluded. Ingenuity in the ranks was evident, as some Tar Heels broiled their beef "on griddle irons made of telegraph wire. I think I was the first in our regiment to make one; since then nearly every man has one along with him. Colonel Grimes detailed a blacksmith and sent him to me to get mine to make him one like it. He said it was the most useful thing he had seen. We cook bread on them also." The Mine Run campaign, an attempt to turn the right flank of Lee's forces, was fought in the intense cold in late December 1863. There was little fighting and even fewer mentions of foodstuffs in letters home.[27]

Campaigning in the spring of 1864 got underway on May 4, as the Federal army crossed the Rapidan River, planning to force the Confederates into the open where they could be beaten. Lee caught the Federals in the Wilderness. While the battle was raging on May 7, a cooking detail was organized in the 5th Alabama, and Henry Beck took detailed men back to the wagon train, where they cooked through the evening. The next morning, these rations were delivered to the regiment, and the wagons were sent further to the rear. Presumably, other regiments did likewise. Lee successfully stymied the Federal advance. Unlike previous encounters when the Federals skulked back across the river, they moved east this time, attempting to get between Lee and the Confederate capital once again. Lee pulled his men out of their field works, barely beating the Federals to the crossroads at Spotsylvania Court House. A member of the 52nd Virginia wrote that many men gave out on the march due to heat, "no rations and very little water." Fighting at Spotsylvania Court House was intense. Along with the rain, soldiers had to scrounge or go hungry. A member of McGowan's Sharpshooter Battalion made soup with a turtle he found. David Holt, 16th Mississippi, wrote that it was raining too hard to make a fire on the night of May 11. Instead, he ate wet corn pone and uncooked bacon before wrapping himself in his blanket in a puddle. In other commands, such as the brigades of Battle and Lane, rations seemed to make their way to the front.[28]

Unable to sustain any type of breakthrough in Confederate lines, the Federals slid east again on May 22, and the two sides battled again around North Anna River between May 23 and 26. Rations continued to travel to the front. Henry

27 Lee, *Forget-me-nots of the Civil War*, 96–97.

28 Hubbs, *Voices from Company D*, 261, 262, 268; Alexander Stewart Coffman, "Civil War Diary of Alexander Stewart Coffman," in Ralph Coffman, ed., *Augusta Historical Bulletin* (Fall 1992), 18; Toalson, *No Soap, No Pay*, 114, 115; Speer, "Voices from Cemetery Hill," 133.

Beck, 5th Alabama, served in the commissary department for his regiment. On May 25, he noted rations were drawn from the trains behind the lines, then carried to the front where cooking commenced directly behind the troops in the works. The bigger story during the fight along the North Anna River was the "bilious dysentery" attack that afflicted Robert E. Lee, allowing the Federals to elude his trap. The Federals again slipped out of their improvised trenches, attempting to get between Lee and Richmond. Once more, Lee thwarted their plans. An attack launched at Cold Harbor on June 3 was easily repulsed with severe Federal casualties. The assistant surgeon of the 3rd North Carolina recalled after the war that the food supply was irregular, the opportunities to cook short, and cooking utensils so sparse "that what we had was merely to appease hunger."

Henry Beck struggled to find his regiment through the early morning hours of June 2. He decided to return to the brigade wagon train about daybreak, unsuccessful in his search. "We will get plenty when we are still. I get more meat than I want but not quite enough bread, plenty good coffee and sugar. Sometimes peas or rice. While the army is moving or fighting so much we cannot get as much as we want. We ought to expect it," deduced a member of the 45th North Carolina on June 12 from camp near Gaines Mill. Some regiments saw raw food being delivered to the men in the trenches. "We had to cook in the trench. Often a bullet would skip over the top of the parapet and fling sand into the frying pan. One time I had to cook a small lot of beans over 3 times, and wash them between cooking," recalled a member of the 16th Mississippi on June 12.[29]

Following a defeat at Cold Harbor, the Federals slipped across the James River, laying siege to the city of Petersburg. For nine months, there were numerous attempts to crack the Confederate defenses and cut supply lines, slowly starving out Confederate defenders. Nevertheless, Federal attacks against Lee's army were not the only battles in Virginia. There was a move against Richmond from Bermuda Hundred and another up the Shenandoah Valley. Known as the "Breadbox of the Confederacy," the Shenandoah Valley supplied the Confederate army with foodstuffs. While the war had ravaged some northern Virginia counties, the area was still agriculturally rich. The first Federal attempt to push south was defeated on May 15 at New Market. A new campaign to capture Lynchburg began in early June. The valley was primarily held by Confederate cavalry, and on June 6, Lee ordered Maj. Gen. John C. Breckinridge from the lines along the Chickahominy River to the area. Breckinridge's force contained about 5,000 troops, plus the 4,000 cavalry already in the area. Six days later, Lee ordered Jubal Early to take his

---

29 Hubbs, *Voices from Company D*, 278; Koonce, *Doctor to the Front*, 144; Stone, *Letters Home to Baughn Mountain*, 51; Toalson, *No Soap, No Pay*, 149.

corps, about twenty-five percent of the ANV, to the valley and assume command. Federal forces tore through the Shenandoah Valley. Stanton, with its commissary stores, was sacked on June 8 and Lexington on June 11. The Federals were turned back after fighting at Lynchburg on June 18, and Early's Confederates followed for a couple of days. His men were hungry. "We got one day's rations in the night. Most of the men were without rations yesterday," a soldier in the 52nd Virginia wrote on June 20. "Been almost without rations; hard marching, and nothing to eat," brigade commander Bryan Grimes noted the next day. On June 22, the men drew rations for two days, which they promptly ate, and then tried to forage for additional food, according to an Alabama soldier, but could find only cherries. Early soon put his corps in motion. Lee urged Early to move toward Washington, D.C., hoping to pull some of the reinforcements recently sent to bolster the Federal army outside Richmond back toward the Federal capital.

Portions of Early's Confederates moved through Lexington on June 25. "The good people along the route gave to us of their scanty stores and added greatly to our former monotonous diet of dried beef and tallow biscuits." One Tar Heel told Early that the "tallow struck to the roof his mouth, so that he expected to have to build a fire on the top of his head to melt it out." The lack of rations slowed Early's advance. Foodstuffs were coming via the railroad from Waynesboro. Staff officer Campbell Brown complained that had Jackson's old operating procedure been followed, with three days rations being issued at once, the advancing columns could have gotten an earlier start each day. Instead, the soldiers were up half the night cooking or forced to await supply trains.[30]

Early continued to press down the valley, passing through Mount Jackson, New Market, Woodstock, Strasburg, and Winchester. Federal soldiers evacuated Martinsburg on July 2 and Harpers Ferry on July 4. While the Federals removed 160 railroad cars of equipment before being pushed out of Harper's Ferry, there were still provisions to be captured. A Virginia artilleryman noted that a great deal of "plunder" was left. "Some of our boys went into the town to plunder," a Virginia artilleryman noted. "They got quite a lot of sugar, coffee, hardtack, molasses, etc. John McCorkle went in on a mule . . . to bring out a water bucket of molasses, . . . The Yanks were amusing themselves by throwing among our plundering boys a lot of shell." A Tar Heel thought it "strange to see 'Confeds' with cigars, sugar, coffee, lemons, whiskey and everything which the most fastidious soldier could desire."

30 Coffman, "Civil War Diary of Alexander Stewart Coffman," 21; Gary Gallagher, ed., *Extracts of Letters of Major General Bryan Grimes to his Wife* (Wilmington, NC, 1986), 56; Hubbs, *Voices from Company D*, 294; Koonce, *Doctor to the Front*, 154; Jones, *Campbell Brown's Civil War*, 265; Brett Spaulding, *Last Chance for Victory* (Gettysburg, PA, 2010) 25. Sometime around June 23, Early changed the name from II Corps, ANV, to Army of the Valley District.

A 5th Alabama soldier observed commissary wagons arriving in town to provision the troops but found the men "well supplied with Yankee rations."[31]

The Confederates then moved back into Maryland. At Middletown on July 7, the commander of the 2nd Maryland Cavalry demanded families supply each Confederate trooper with a loaf of bread and a piece of meat. Once provisioned, they moved on. Ransom's division arrived next, demanding 8,000 rations in two hours, which the citizens also provided. When Confederate forces entered Frederick on July 9, they demanded a ransom of $200,000 and thousands of pounds of sugar, coffee, salt, and bacon. A mile from Frederick, Confederate forces ran into a makeshift Union force protecting the railroad junction and bridge over the Monocacy River. After a day-long engagement, the Federals retreated. The Confederates continued advancing, and by the afternoon of July 11, arrived on the outskirts of Washington, D.C.. For two days the Confederates tested the defenses around Fort Stevens. Early realized on the second day that he could not capture the Federal capital. Using the dark for cover, he pulled out his command, heading back to Virginia. He reached White's Ford during the early morning hours of July 14, crossing back into Virginia shortly thereafter. Overall, the campaign was a success. They had driven one Federal army out of the Shenandoah Valley, and while Early could not take Washington, Federals were rushed from the Petersburg front to defend the city. Plus, Early's men had been able to gather foodstuffs. One member of the 23rd North Carolina wrote of 12,000–15,000 beeves taken, and "a great many wagons loaded with supplies."[32]

Following their return to Virginia, the Confederates camped near Bunker Hill, while the foraging expeditions continued. Early's army was self-sustaining, wrote a member of the 61st Alabama Infantry, noting that their foodstuffs, flour, beef, sugar, and syrup came from the Federals. Plus, they were sending supplies back to Lee's men. On August 10, a new Federal general, Phil Sheridan, ordered a newly created army of veterans to seek out Early. Federal orders were simple: Leave nothing "to invite the enemy to return. Take all provisions, forage, and stock wanted for the use of your command; such as cannot be consumed, destroy." It took only three days to maneuver Early out of the lower Valley. Confederate reinforcements allowed Early to push the Federals back north slowly. Regimental commissaries scoured the countryside for foodstuffs. One officer wrote after the war that Early planned to "scatter to subsist, and concentrate for battle." On August 14, six men from the 5th Alabama started on an overnight "beef expedition," returning with

---

31 William Runge, ed., *Four Years in the Confederate Artillery* (Chapel Hill, NC, 1961) 85; Koonce, *Doctor to the Front*, 154; Hubbs, *Voices from Company D*, 297–298.

32 Spaulding, *Last Chance for Victory*, 47, 80; Peace, *To Tranquillity*, 211.

five head of cattle. As Confederates moved through Winchester on August 18, they were greeted by war-weary townspeople, still able to give them small quantities of food, cold water, and even milk.[33]

Unfortunately, the Federal directive to leave the land bare was taking its toll. A soldier in Battle's brigade went into camp two miles from Winchester on August 22 and wrote home that he could see "the effects of the last Yankee raid, in the shape of burnt barns, ruined wheat and hay stacks, and all sorts of depredations. We found it very difficult to get anything to eat tonight, the Yankees having carried off every cow, etc. they could get hold of, managed to get some bread & milch by paying one gold dollar for it." The two contending forces eyed each other in the lower Shenandoah Valley for the next few weeks, with Confederate forces near Winchester. The men purchased or impressed wheat locally when they could find it, having it ground at a mill not far away. A Tar Heel Confederate wrote that they had consumed all the fruit north of Strasburg. Confederate reinforcements returned to Petersburg on September 15, leaving Early with his original force.[34]

Active campaigning got underway on September 19 as Federal troops pitched into Confederate forces north of Winchester. The commissary for the 5th Alabama wrote of arriving with rations for his regiment as they prepared to move out. He grabbed a piece of bread and meat and moved with them. After intense fighting all day, the Confederates were forced to retreat south of Winchester, taking up a position on Fisher's Hill, two miles south of Strasburg. Fighting resumed on September 22, and Early was again forced out of his position. The Federals camped at Mount Crawford for a few days, then retraced their steps down the valley, burning barns and mills, and taking thousands of head of livestock. Foodstuff reports for Confederate forces were mixed. Early's men wrote of being hungry September 25–26, capturing Federal beef on September 27, and being fairly well fed on October 8. Once again, reinforcements arrived from Richmond, and Early chased after the Federals. Early successfully routed three Federal divisions in a surprise attack on October 19 at Cedar Creek. As Early paused to reorganize his commands, the Federals counterattacked, driving him from the field.[35]

33 McGarity, "Letters of a Confederate Surgeon, McGarity," 3:249; *OR* 43, pt. 1, 697–698; John Daniel, "General Jubal A. Early," *SHSP* (1894), 318; Hubbs, *Voices from Company D*, 307; Park, "Diary of Robert E. Park," 1:430.

34 Hubbs, *Voices from Company D*, 308; Parks, "Diary of Robert E. Park," 1:434; George W. Davis. to Rebecca Davis, Sep. 16, 1864, Rebecca Pitchford Davis Letters, SHC.

35 Hubbs, *Voices from Company D*, 313; James Garnet, "Diary of James M. Garnet," *SHSP*, 27:10; Burnett, "Letters of Barnett Hardeman Cody" 2:376. U. S. Grant encouraged the Federal commander in the Shenandoah, Phil Sheridan, to keep moving south and continue to wreck the railroad. "Keep

Early's men returned to their camp, not stirring again until November 10. He moved down the Shenandoah, skirmishing with the Federals near Newtown and Cedarville. Unable to provision his small army, Early fell back to New Market. The lack of supplies was evident to many. "I hope that we will not go further in the direction of Winchester as it is clearly impossible to supply our army this far from our supplies. We have already had our bread allowance reduced to 3/4 lb. of flour instead of one pound which was barely enough to sustain life," concluded a 2nd South Carolina soldier on November 12. "Provisions and forage are scarce. Some of our troops have had unground corn issued to them," wrote Maj. Gen. Bryan Grimes at the end of the month. Kershaw's division returned to Petersburg, while part of Early's cavalry command went elsewhere. There were minor battles in the valley as the year slipped away. Early's three divisions of infantry were transferred back to the Petersburg front.[36]

With the loss of the Shenandoah Valley and the ever-tightening blockade, it was only a matter of time. There was not enough food for Lee's army and the civilian population. Another blow came in mid-January with the capture of Fort Fisher, closing the only port supplying the ANV. In late February 1865, Federal cavalry in the valley overwhelmed Confederates in Waynesboro. Upon turning east, they wrecked portions of the Virginia Central Railroad and the James River Canal. Even if foodstuffs could come out of the valley, getting them east to the main Confederate army would have been difficult. On March 31, Confederate forces below Petersburg lost a fight along White Oak Road. Lee ordered men from various points out of the works to Five Forks, attempting to hold the junction and protect the South Side Railroad. The gambit failed, and early on April 2, the Federals attacked all along the Confederate works below Petersburg, punching a hole in the lines near the Boydton Plank Road. Lee's hungry troops fell back to some inner works, and Petersburg and Richmond were abandoned that evening. Lee's army was not prepared for the movement.

Those troops forced to retreat along the South Side Railroad had to rely on the scanty rations in their haversacks as the army was issuing just one day's rations at a time. Troops east of Petersburg or Richmond had a few more hours to prepare. The members of the Richmond Howitzers were told to take as many rations as each man could carry, as transportation was not available. Another artilleryman came upon a "house of commissary supplies" with soldiers helping themselves. They pitched in, taking flour and "fat meat." Many soldiers woke up hungry on April

on and your good work will cause the fall of Richmond," Grant wrote. L. W. V. Kennon, "The Valley Campaign of 1864," *CV* (Dec. 1918), 26:522.

36 Wyckoff, *The Civil War Letters of Alexander McNeill*, 515; Gallagher, *Letters of Bryan Grimes*, 88.

3. Berry Benson, 1st South Carolina Infantry, recalled after the war of sending a soldier to procure meal and meat for his company of sixteen. He returned with two hogs and meal, and later that evening, they borrowed a farmer's wash kettle. The hogs cooked throughout the night "boiled almost to a jelly," much to Benson's dismay. After eating, the men started again toward the west. The 12th Virginia lost most of its cooking utensils, and after being issued corn meal and bacon on April 4, the men were forced to share a frying pan. Sergeant Whitehorne wrote of rumors that the commissaries were out of rations. Members of the 28th North Carolina stumbled across a mill and convinced the owner to let each soldier have a half gallon of meal. A Virginia artilleryman was not as fortunate. The commissary ran out of rations before reaching the Richmond Howitzers. The men were instead issued two ears of corn, originally for the batteries' horses. "Chewing the corn was hard work. It made the jaws ache and the gums and teeth so sore as to cause almost unendurable pain," he recalled.[37]

Amelia Court House was the designated place for the various corps and divisions to converge. Lee had asked that rations be shipped to the community for his troops. Some were on hand, but not enough, and Lee felt compelled to issue an appeal to local farmers and send out commissary wagons, all the while waiting for the rest of his scattered command to gather. Reports on ration amounts are mixed. A sergeant in the 12th Virginia recorded in his diary cooking corn pones on the evening of April 4, while a member of the Richmond Howitzers recalled receiving rations on April 5. After the war, E. Porter Alexander wrote that he sent out "darkies as foragers" who purchased two hens. Alexander instructed the men to pluck the chickens while riding along, and when they stopped for the evening, they "soon had our hens boiling." Many wagons returned near empty. A staff officer under Ewell saw the general give a soldier permission to kill a steer. Later, when a sergeant asked the staff officers for permission to kill a hog, it was granted. The hog was quickly skinned, divided, and eaten raw.[38]

Onward the Confederate army plodded. Lee's strategy was to reach Burkeville, turn south down the Piedmont Railroad, and link up in North Carolina with the Army of Tennessee. The Federal army was also on the move, catching various elements of the Confederate rear guard at Rice's Station, High Bridge, and more

37 W. S. White, "Stray Leaves from a Soldier's Journal." *SHSP*, 11:553; Toalson, *No Soap, No Pay*, 361; Whitehorne diary, n.p.; Benson, *Berry Benson's Civil War Book*, 193–194; Lohr, *The Mauney Brothers*, 70; McCarthy, *Detailed Minutiae of Soldier Life*, 128. Emory Thomas estimates that Lee's army now contained about 30,000 men, 200 cannons, and 1,000 wagons. *Robert E. Lee* (New York, 1995), 356.

38 Whitehorne diary, n.p.; Townsend, "Townsend's Diary," SHSP, 34:103; Gallagher, *Fighting for the Confederacy*, 520–521; Jones, *Campbell Brown's Civil War*, 200.

importantly, Sayler's Creek. "I am suffering from hunger," a soldier in the 7th South Carolina Cavalry confessed in his diary on April 6. A friend had just given him a piece of cornbread. As a member of the 12th Virginia polished off his breakfast, he recorded in his diary that he had eaten everything in his haversack. Things were little better on April 7. There was an attempt to issue rations to the men from commissary wagons at Farmville, but Federal artillery chased them away before every Confederate soldier could pass. One Confederate wrote after the war that a detail was sent to town from the battle line at Farmville, seeking rations. They found a "tierce of bacon" and quickly overpowered the guard, taking the bacon. Members of the regiment's "commissary department" could be seen marching along "with a piece of bacon swung on a pole between them. . . . The battalion passed on, the men cutting slices from their piece of bacon and eagerly devouring them." One Confederate staff officer recalled taking corn from his horse, beating it between rocks, and swallowing it. "The little army was willing to march and fight, but starvation made stragglers of them."[39]

"I am hungry and mad, perfectly reckless, don't care what happens. . . . I have eaten nothing except corn from a farmer's crib last night, since Thursday morning, and I am almost famished," one Virginia soldier confided in his diary on April 8. "I scribble in this diary to take my mind off food." The Confederate losses at Sayler's Creek amounted to almost 9,000. While Lee could not afford to lose any men, he could not properly feed those left. "Had to flank [steal] some turnips (as I was very hungry) & parched some corn for supper," another Virginia soldier wrote. A South Carolina trooper was shocked at what men could endure. Commanding a division under John B. Gordon, Bryan Grimes complained that his men were jaded and lacking food. The stops they were allowed did not give the men enough time to prepare anything, and what cooking utensils they still had were left elsewhere. Some soldiers were more fortunate, such as Cpl. John Porter, Washington Artillery, who, while scouting ahead of his battalion, found a local doctor to feed him. Many roamed the countryside, foraging for provisions. J. F. J. Caldwell, McGowan's brigade, wrote that on the evening on April 8, they bivouacked four or five miles east of Appomattox. "I ate my first meal since noon the preceding day," he wrote shortly after the war.[40]

39 Hinson & Waring, "The Diary of William G. Hinson during the War of Secession," 2:118; Whitehorne diary, n.p.; Dowdey & Manarin, *The Wartime Papers of R. E. Lee*, 936–937; McCarthy, *Detailed Minutiae of Soldier Life*, 143, 146, 147; Douglas, *I Rode with Stonewall*, 331.

40 Whitehorne diary, n.p.; Driver & Ruffner, 1st Batt. VA Inf., 46; Hinson & Waring, "The Diary of William G. Hinson during the War of Secession," 2:119; Gallagher, *Letters of Bryan Grimes*, 113; Porter diary, DU, Apr. 7, 1865. Caldwell, *The History of the Brigade of South Carolinians*, 297. Marvel concludes that "many of Longstreet's men carried rations they would cook that evening." Yet

On April 9, Lee attempted to push through the Federal cavalry west of Appomattox. A member of Poague's artillery battalion recalled rising early. "A cup of coffee (real article), some corn bread and bacon made our mess a tolerable breakfast." An early morning attack pushed aside the Federal cavalry and captured some artillery, but Federal infantry soon filled in the gaps, blocking Lee's escape route. Surrounded, Lee was forced to surrender the ANV. While meeting with Federal generals in the McLean home in Appomattox Court House, Lee made known that he had hungry Federal prisoners and hungry former Confederate soldiers. A Confederate supply train had been captured at Appomattox Station a day earlier. These captured rations were issued to the hungry Confederates. Some Confederates chronicled in their diaries that they were hungry the next three days as the details were arranged for the surrender. Others noted that rations, possibly some of those captured, came through on April 10, and on April 12, a member of the 31st Virginia reported, "The Yanks issued us rations without any limit."[41]

Robert E. Lee wrote his final official report on April 12 to Jefferson Davis before heading to Richmond. He considered "fatal" the twenty hours he had spent seeking subsistence at Amelia Courthouse. All hope of gaining foodstuffs was lost when the Federals moved on the railroad at Burkesville. After the attack on the wagon trains and the losses at Sayler's Creek, there was an attempt to reorganize the army. "But the men depressed by fatigue and hunger . . . threw away their arms, while others followed the wagon trains and embarrassed their progress." After explaining attempts to break through the lines on April 9, Lee concluded his missive: "We had no subsistence for man or horse, and it could not be gathered in the country . . . the men deprived of food and sleep for many days, were worn out and exhausted."[42]

From Big Bethel Church to Appomattox, soldiers battled in Virginia, Maryland, and Pennsylvania for four long years, attempting to win a war with the odds stacked against them. They were often compelled to live off the land, acquiring foodstuffs from fellow citizens and the enemy. Frequently, these captured foodstuffs allowed the army to endure, feeding men on campaigns, or in the case of Gettysburg, allowing the army to survive for months after the campaign ended. Nevertheless, slowly, the Confederates in Virginia lost the war of attrition. Supplies

Caldwell's statement leads one to believe that some of these men were going more than 24 hours between meals. *Lee's Last Retreat* (Chapel Hill, NC, 2002), 144.

41 Cockrell, *Gunner with Stonewall*, 124; *OR* 46, pt. 1, 1109; Hinson & Waring, "The Diary of William G. Hinson during the War of Secession," 2:120; Whitehorne diary, Apr. 10, Apr. 11; Dayton, *The Diary of a Confederate Soldier*, 137.

42 Dowdey & Manarin, *The Wartime Papers of R. E. Lee*, 935–938.

Union soldiers sharing their rations with Confederates after the surrender at Appomattox.
Battles and Leaders

no longer flowed up the railroad from North Carolina, or the Shenandoah Valley to the west. With "no subsistence for man or horse," campaigning for the once seemingly invincible ANV became simply unsustainable.

Chapter 4

"[A]ny delicacies, such as would gratify and be suitable for the sick and wounded"

Food and the Plight of the Sick and Wounded

There was a sick call almost every morning, save when the army was on campaign. Soldiers who were ill but able to line up were presented to the surgeon or his assistant. William H. Taylor, assistant surgeon, 19th Virginia Infantry, recalled the experience from his side of that line. He confessed that in one pocket of his trousers was a ball of blue mass, and there was a ball of opium in the other. He asked each man the same question: "How are your bowels?" If the soldier's bowels were open, he gave a "plug of opium." If closed, he administered "a plug of blue mass," a mercury-based laxative. While the soldiers suffered almost every conceivable malady, the "prevailing diseases were intestinal disorders."[1]

Considering the poor food and polluted water, it is surprising that anyone survived the first year of the war. Almost 750,000 soldiers died during those four years, two-thirds from disease. The inadequate food and tainted water led to cholera, typhoid fever, scurvy, diarrhea, and dysentery. Neither doctors nor generals understood how these diseases were transmitted. Typhoid fever, or "camp fever," was spread through excrement, with poor sanitation and improperly placed latrines leading to contaminated food and water. It started with a fever and general fatigue and often led to diarrhea. Widespread cholera epidemics swept the United States in 1832 and 1849, killing thousands. Like typhoid fever, cholera primarily spreads through feces-contaminated water and food, leading to extreme diarrhea, vomiting, and cramps. The cholera bacteria kept the body from absorbing liquids. Deficiencies in vitamin C caused scurvy. Soldiers who were not eating enough

1 Taylor, "Experiences of a Confederate Surgeon," 100.

vegetables were sluggish, with muscular weakness and depression, developing a sallow complexion and frequently losing their teeth. All these maladies could lead to diarrhea and dysentery, which led to dehydration and death. With limited medicines in the South, doctors turned to the forests and fields for aid. Some used blackberry root and sweet-gum bark for diarrhea and dysentery, while the seeds from watermelons and pumpkins were diuretics.[2]

Acceptance of germ theory was a few years away, but there was some level of comprehension regarding cleanliness. Confederate regulations specified that company commanders were responsible for the cleanliness of their men. A detail of troublemakers was placed under the officer of the day to clean the camp, and cooking utensils had to be kept clean. Latrines were to be dug 150 paces in front for enlisted men and 100 paces in the rear for officers. Hospital structures and tents required "scrupulous cleanliness" and followed prescribed regulations regarding meals and cooking. Despite seemingly countless circulars and orders on cleanliness, the men lived in absolute squalor. Animals were butchered in camps, latrines, when they were actually dug, were often too close to the water supplies, and men whose stomach ailments produced vomiting and diarrhea often did not reach latrines. Disease-causing bacteria were everywhere. Volunteer officers knew as little as anyone else, and the few West Point-trained officers seemed unable to correct problems. Thousands of men became sick. While campaigning in western Virginia, Robert E. Lee complained in a letter to his wife in September 1861: "Our poor sick, I know, suffer much. They bring it on themselves by not doing what they are told. They are worse than children, for the latter can be forced."[3]

Despite the directives in various regulations, there was an apparent disregard for maintaining proper sanitation. Bedford Brown served as the surgeon with the 14th North Carolina Volunteers in the fall of 1861 in the mountains of western Virginia. He estimated 17,000 Confederate soldiers encamped in the area, with no sanitary arrangements. The soldiers were "permitted indiscriminately to use the surface of the earth surrounding the camp for the deposit of the excreta of the sick and the well. The excrementitial matter was washed daily by the copious rains into the springs and foundation" that supplied water to the camps. Before long, 4,000 cases of illness, including "typhoid fever, septic dysentery, and pneumonia,"

---

2 Soldiers and doctors of the period did not always differentiate between the various diseases. Scurvy was more recognizable, but others were similar. Good overviews can be found in Margaret Humphreys, *Marrow of Tragedy* (Baltimore, MD, 2013); H. H. Cunningham, *Doctors in Gray* (Baton Rouge, LA, 1958); and Frank Freemon, *Gangrene and Glory* (Cranbury, NJ, 1998). For more on substitute medicine, see Wyndham Blanton, *Medicine in Virginia in the Nineteenth Century* (Richmond, VA, 1933), 284.

3 *Confederate Regulations* (Richmond, VA, 1863), 9, 10, 55, 59, 236; Lee, *Recollections and Letters*, 46.

Dr. William Gibbs McNeill Whistler served at the Jackson hospital in Richmond before being assigned as the assistant surgeon, 1st South Carolina Infantry (Orr's Rifles), in late 1864.

Library of Congress

with many deaths, racked the Confederates. "We ascertained that the cause of the epidemic was purely excrementitial in character," Brown concluded. A year later, Brown, serving as surgeon of the 43rd North Carolina, found the same conditions around Drewry's Bluff. The area was flat, poorly drained, and "covered with human and animal excreta," which "filtered into the drinking fountains." It only took a week for an "epidemic of typhoid, dysentery, and diarrhea" to develop. With time and work, the conditions at the camp on the James River eventually improved.[4]

Every regiment was supposed to have a surgeon, assistant surgeon, and hospital steward on staff. Added to these were a knapsack bearer who followed the assistant surgeon onto the field during battle, and the Infirmary Corps, thirty detailed men from each regiment who served as stretcher-bearers. Later, the senior surgeon in each brigade served as brigade surgeon. There were also division-, corps-, and army-level surgeons. A brigade hospital wagon hauled stoves and cooking utensils. Regimental-level surgeons were responsible for the cleanliness of the camp and soldiers, while also recommending improvements to the commanding officer. While most of these doctors were professionally educated and had been in practice for years, their experience did little to prepare them for the masses of sick men and the horror of combat injuries.[5]

The early days of the war quickly overwhelmed the small medical staff of each regiment. Between July 1861 and March 1862, the Confederate Army of

4 The 14th North Carolina Volunteers was re-designated the 24th North Carolina Troops. Bedford Brown, "Personal Experiences," *Southern Practitioner* (Nov. 1893), 444–445.

5 Cunningham, *Doctors in Gray*, 114; Koonce, *Doctor to the Front*, 145; J. Julian Chisolm, *A Manual of Military Surgery for the use of Surgeons in the Confederate Army* (Richmond, VA, 1861), 102–106.

Dr. Henry Briscoe served in hospitals in Richmond, Wilmington, and the 26th Virginia Infantry. *Library of Congress*

the Potomac reported 36,572 cases of diarrhea and dysentery. Officers had few resources, with one complaining in May of no house for a hospital at Gloucester Point. An inspector found a general hospital in Harpers Ferry, but few beds. Early on, the sick remained in camp or with local families. In August, one South Carolina soldier in a Culpeper hospital thought that if his food was better, his health could improve. Many died of exposure, he wrote.

Near Manassas, John Hite, 33rd Virginia, was sick in a hospital. He received "a cup of tea or coffee, and two small biscuits for breakfast and supper, and rice for dinner." Hite believed that if he received more food, he might recover faster.[6]

Those left in camp suffered the most. Abner Peace, 23rd North Carolina, stayed to tend up to twenty-four sick men in August 1861 as his regiment moved to a new camp. "So I . . . imagine myself a great cook having cooked the best bread I have eaten since I left home," he wrote his father. Marion Fitzpatrick was detailed to accompany some of the 45th Georgia's sick at the end of May 1862. Near Ashland, he drew five days' rations, hiring some local ladies to cook for his charges. By June 1, he was sick, quartered in some outbuildings two miles northeast of Richmond. He complained that he was "eating too much that is not suitable for a sick man. I have the appetite of a wolf now." A relapse two weeks later brought "diareah and sick stomach," although not "the bloody flux" like his previous ailment. Fitzpatrick wrote that two men from his company had been detailed to draw rations for the sick.[7]

---

6 The Confederate army numbered just 49,394 men those same nine months. *Medical & Surgical History of the War of the Rebellion*, 6 vols. (Washington, D.C., 1870), 2:26; Jones, *The Boys of Diamond Hill*, 21–22; Jessup, *The Painful News I Have to Write*, 30.

7 Peace, *To Tranquillity*, 49; McCrea, *Red Dirt and Isinglass*, 349, 354, 357.

Ambulatory sick soldiers could beg for food from the surrounding families. William Pendleton, chief of artillery, had dysentery in the fall of 1862. He could call at local houses and get "a soft-boiled egg and a little milk." A messmate or relative in the sick man's company might scour the countryside to find better food for the less able. An 8th Alabama soldier did just that in March 1863. Henry Wood was camped in the Fredericksburg area, managing to find butter and a cup of brandy to make a stew for his ill brother, but no chickens. Hordes of sick men, looking for shelter or food to supplement their rations, seriously crippled the production of the agrarian communities. Wood's letter also told his mother that the local people survived on what they raised in their yards: chickens and a cow or two kept close to the farmhouse.[8]

Those lacking transportation or not sick enough to warrant a hospital trip faced a dilemma. The ambulance corps stayed at the regiment's rear when on the move. Those who fell out or were too ill to walk could ride in the ambulances if there were room. John Apperson, a hospital steward with Jackson's men, noted an order from his brigade commander in May 1862 placing the sick, including men with diarrhea and dysentery, in the rear of the column under the care of the assistant surgeon. The sick men were termed Company X, or "Crockett's Battalion," after Joseph Crockett, the assistant surgeon of the 4th Virginia. Whenever Lee was preparing the ANV for a major campaign, such as Gettysburg, orders sent men too sick to accompany the army to a nearby town or hospital.[9]

Many sick soldiers went without food during their sojourns. Ada Bacot, at a hospital in Charlottesville, wrote of a group of South Carolinians who arrived at her hospital, complaining they had not received food or medical treatment for four days. According to John Apperson, Dr. Hunter McGuire, medical director for Jackson's corps, protested the starvation of the sick under Apperson's and Dr. Harvey Black's care. The sick were left to their own devices at Bunker Hill when the Corps moved in October 1862. "[T]hey were running over the country to obtain something to eat." Apperson recorded later, acknowledging that the soldiers were in a poor situation, "but I did not know what else we could do," he confided in his diary.[10]

8 Lee, *Memoirs of William Nelson Pendleton*, 228; Wood & Jackson, *"Kiss Sweet Little Lillah for me,"* 30.

9 David Maxwell, "Some Letters to His Parents by a Floridian in the Confederate Army," in Gilbert Wright, ed., *The Florida Historical Quarterly* (Apr. 1958), 362; Roper, *Repairing the "March of Mars,"* 225–226.

10 Jean Berlin, ed., *A Confederate Nurse: The Diary of Ada W. Bacot, 1860–1863* (Columbia, SC, 1994), 102; Roper, *Repairing the "March of Mars,"* 225–226.

Bailey McClellan, 10th Alabama Infantry, was wounded in the arm during the fight at Sharpsburg in September 1862. McClellan made his way to Shepherdstown, and with "orders and no rations," started walking toward Winchester. The next day, "verbal orders and no rations" sent him toward Staunton, ninety miles away. McClellan found it "pretty tough on wounded soldiers and no rations, and through a country overrun by soldiers of both armies." He and the other walking wounded became separated, and McClellan came across one of the black cooks from his regiment, heading to Richmond. While McClellan had no money, the cook did and "used his money as freely for me as he did for himself." Thanks to the generosity of his traveling companion, McClellan was not forced to beg for eatables as he worked his way to Staunton. Other campaigns brought additional sufferers. Later, the army established depots every twenty miles or so. Confederate soldiers drew rations and then bartered with people along the road. However, at times, conditions were horrible, especially when the army was on retreat. Brigadier General John Imboden wrote of starving men as the Confederate wagon train made its way from Gettysburg to Williamsport. On the same retreat, Mississippi surgeon LeGrand Wilson noted beginning with a haversack full of food, which he distributed to the wounded. At Williamsport, he confessed having not eaten for thirty hours.[11]

Many combat wounded found themselves in dire straits, as the water was quickly contaminated. In a lull in the fighting at First Manassas, a member of the 1st Maryland Infantry recalled rushing down to a small brook "only to find the water tinged with blood." Regardless, many drank as if "it was the clearest." Not everyone possessed such disregard. Charles Blackford, a Virginia cavalryman, attached to the staff, wrote of feeling about in the dark on a marshy ground for some water following the battle of Cedar Mountain. He found a full horse hoof indention and drank from it, only to find the same indention the next morning tainted with blood from a deceased Federal soldier. "The thought that I had slaked my thirst on such water made me very sick," he confided to his wife.[12]

Water was the first thing a wounded man wanted. A Virginia soldier recalled the cry from the wounded for water as soon as the guns fell silent at Malvern Hill. A detail from his regiment provided water for everyone who needed it. At a field hospital after Second Manassas, a South Carolina surgeon observed a wounded

11 Norman Rourke, ed., *I Saw the Elephant* (Shippensburg, PA, 1995), 30–31; Westwood A. Todd "Reminiscences of the Civil War," *SHSP*, 68–69; John Imboden, "The Confederate Retreat from Gettysburg," *Battles & Leaders*, 3:420–429; Legrand Wilson, *The Confederate Soldier* (Memphis, TN, 1973), 127.

12 McKim, *A Soldier's Recollections*, 36; Blackford & Blackford, *Letters from Lee's Army*, 109.

man, shot in the bowels, crying for water. A good water supply was paramount to hospital placement during battle. Surgeon LeGrand Wilson wrote of establishing a field hospital on Willoughby's Run at Gettysburg on July 1, a site with cool, fresh water. He also said he kept his canteen full as he roamed the field, seeking the wounded. Two days later, John Apperson, serving as a clerk for the Second Corps hospital, was sent out to locate a suitable site for a new hospital on the Confederate left, but confessed he found "water very scarce wherever I went."[13]

Once battle commenced, the wounded started trickling into the hospital. Initially, the ambulatory wounded came on foot. Later, stretchers and ambulances brought in the more serious cases. Doctors and their staff, including nurses and cooks, began caring for the wounded, hauling pots out of the wagons, tending the fires, and boiling soups. However, sometimes even hospital stores were interrupted by the fighting. A chaplain in the 12th Mississippi Infantry recollected that during the battle of Chancellorsville, the hospital had no rations, as a Federal cavalry raid had intercepted the hospital's commissary wagons. Two wagons arrived later that evening. "There was great rejoicing, the poor fellows looked longingly out of their hollow sunken eyes as the barrels, bacon and sacks were taken out of the wagons." The wagons only contained bacon and hardtack, which even the healthy found rough. Chaplain Brinsfield recalled that the hardtack was boiled until soft and then fried with bacon grease and a little onion. This "was not a savory dish, but it filled up, and that was what we needed, only the poor fellows who were wounded required nourishing food."[14]

Gettysburg, the largest battle of the war, produced thousands of wounded men who were quartered in division hospitals, and in private homes and public buildings. Major Charles Blacknall, 23rd North Carolina, recalled being placed on the porch of the Hankey farm after his wounding. The family well was pumped dry by thirsty soldiers, and a guard was eventually placed until it was replenished. The Hankey family recalled staying up all day and night to "cook and bake for the Rebels." Some citizens were sympathetic to their uninvited guests. The wounded Henry Kyd Douglas was taken to the Henry Picking farm, recalling that Charlotte Picking brought "a bowl of the best chicken soup that culinary skill ever devised."[15]

13 Westwood A. Todd, "Reminiscences of the Civil War," *SHSP*, 24; Wilson, *The Confederate Soldier*, 117, 119; Welch, *A Confederate Surgeon's Letters*, 26–27; Roper, *Repairing the "March of Mars*," 486

14 Brinsfield, *The Spirit Divided*, 53–54.

15 Gregory Coco, *A Vast Sea of Misery* (Gettysburg, PA, 1988), 131; Douglas, *I Rode with Stonewall*, 252.

Sick and wounded soldiers were often met by civilians in the streets of Richmond, bringing them food and water. *Battles and Leaders*

Locals continued to care for wounded Confederates long after the armies had moved on. The Hankey family baked bread and supplied milk from their farm for five weeks after the end of the battle. Likewise, members of the Cunningham family, with soldiers of McLaws's command quartered on their property, baked all the bread their brick oven would hold every day for several weeks. "Every wounded man who could walk found his way to the house when the odor of baking bread floated out from the oven. . . . When Cassie would bake up one barrel, a hospital attendant would roll out a fresh one," until twenty barrels had been consumed.[16]

Wounded men, or those too sick to remain with the army, were transported across the state to various hospitals. Virginia only held a handful of hospitals before the war. Most medical care was private, with a doctor called to the home of the sick. As tens of thousands of men from across the South flooded into Virginia, hospitals began springing up overnight, with more than 100 Confederate hospitals in Richmond alone during the war. Many were temporary, a vacant store or church used when the wounded overwhelmed existing structures. There were hospital complexes in Petersburg, Danville, Lynchburg, Fredericksburg, Staunton, Charlottesville, and Winchester. Some were official general hospitals, while others,

16 Coco, *A Vast Sea of Misery*, 130, 152.

like the facility at the Exchange Hotel in Gordonsville, were receiving hospitals. At the latter, the sick and wounded were assessed and transferred to additional general hospitals throughout the state. The Confederacy went on to establish general and wayside hospitals to help with the sick and wounded throughout the Carolinas.[17]

When it became apparent that the Confederate government could not keep up with the health care crisis confronting the armies, concerned men and women stepped forward. They established hospitals and aid societies to fill the void. Emily Mason organized a hospital at the Greenbrier Hotel in White Sulphur Springs in late 1861, with a servant assisting with the cooking and nursing. Ada Bacot was sent from the South Carolina Hospital Aid Association to the hospitals being organized in Charlottesville. Within a few weeks of her arrival in December, Bacot served as assistant matron and dietician in one facility. Sally Tompkins operated a very successful hospital in Richmond from July 1861 until June 1865. Tompkins, the only female commissioned officer in the Confederate Army, ran the Robertson Hospital, noted for its cleanliness and quality of care.[18]

Not only did women grow, box, and ship food items to soldiers in the field and hospitals in larger cities, but they also created and staffed wayside hospitals across the South. Wayside hospitals, located at railroad depots, were charged with providing food, a brief rest, and a change of bandages for sick or wounded soldiers traveling home. In June 1862, Dr. Richard Gregory was assigned as a post doctor in Charlotte, North Carolina, and asked the ladies in the surrounding communities to supply old sheets, pillow slips, counterpanes, and lint, along with "any delicacies, such as would gratify and be suitable for the sick and wounded." Later, the Ladies Aid Society in Charlotte took up the daily task of providing food for traveling soldiers. One local newspaper ran lists of women detailed for work on given days. A servant or slave traveled daily to society members' homes to collect food. In October 1862, Louise Medway estimated that the Soldier's Aid Society in Wilmington had fed and changed the dressings of 6,000 to 8,000 soldiers in just one month. A few counties northwest, local women fed sick and wounded soldiers at the depot in Hillsboro. Later they developed a plan to board the train with baskets of provisions, feeding traveling soldiers and performing the same service on a returning train. Over to the east, Catherine Edmondston wrote in February

---

17 Freemon, *Gangrene and Glory*, 126.

18 Mason listed "Jim" as a servant. It is unclear if he was a slave or hired free person of color. Emily Mason, "Memories of a Hospital Matron," *Atlantic Monthly* (1902), 314; Berlin, *A Confederate Nurse*, 6–7; Rebecca Calcutt, *Richmond's Wartime Hospitals* (Gretna, LA, 2005), 172–174. Peter Houck notes that Lucy Wilhelmina Otey of Lynchburg might also have been commissioned by Jefferson Davis. *A Prototype of a Confederate Hospital Center in Lynchburg, Virginia* (Lynchburg, VA, 1986), 75–77.

1864 that she was purchasing thirty-eight dozen eggs from a local lady for the hospital, presumably the one beside the tracks in Weldon. The eggs were $1 a dozen. Twenty-five dollars had been donated, while Edmondston had contributed the remainder.[19]

Over time, Confederate hospital care was reorganized, closing many private hospitals, and placing the government in charge of the others. In September 1862, the Confederate Congress passed an act "to better provide for the sick and wounded of the army in hospitals." The act set guidelines for many different areas, including commutation for rations, which was $1 a day per soldier, paid to the hospital fund; it authorized the secretary of war to contract with railroad and boat companies for the transportation of supplies purchased by hospital agents; and designated the number of matrons and assistant matrons while defining their duties and fixing the pay of cooks at $25 per month. Hospital matrons-in-chief were issued rations, provided with quarters, and paid up to $40 a month. They were responsible for the "domestic economy of the hospital." Food for the sick and wounded was their top priority, ensuring it was properly prepared and served. Of course, direct supervision was delegated to the ward matrons.[20]

Confederate hospitals were typically divided into wards. General Hospital Number Two, in Lynchburg, had three divisions, divided into seven wards, with one chief matron, three assistant matrons, and seven ward matrons in attendance. They oversaw twenty-one cooks. This was only one of three general hospitals, and three specialty hospitals, in Lynchburg in 1864. Richmond had a much larger hospital system, with twenty-eight general hospitals, twenty more state hospitals, and many temporary hospitals as needs arose. Chimborazo could house 3,000 patients in five divisions and 150 wards. Supporting facilities included five soup houses, five icehouses, a bakery capable of producing 10,000 loaves daily, and a brewery that produced 400 kegs of beer at a time. Connected to Chimborazo was a large farm pasturing 300 to 500 goats and 200 milk cows. Also in Richmond

---

19 *Charlotte Daily Bulletin*, Jul. 17, 1862, Nov. 27, 1862, Dec. 3, 1863; Louise Medway to Jefferson Davis, Sep. 13, 1864, Jefferson Davis Papers, DU; Luck Anderson, *North Carolina Women of the Confederacy* (Fayetteville, NC, 1936), 29–30; Beth Crabtree & James Patton, eds., *Journal of a Secesh Lady* (Raleigh, NC, 1999), 518. There was a proposal from citizens in Alabama and Mississippi to create a Confederate Soldiers Aid Society forwarded to Jefferson Davis in October 1862. Davis sent the request to the Quartermaster General for his thoughts, but the proposal went no further. The Confederacy never organized anything like the United States Sanitary Commission. Crist, *The Papers of Jefferson Davis*, 8:445.

20 *OR* Series 4, 2, 199–200. Originally, the commuted value of rations was $.75 a day. This was increased to $1.00 in September 1862, $1.25 in May 1863, and $2.50 in February 1864. Cunningham, *Doctors in Gray*, 80–82. Officers in Confederate general hospitals had to pay $1.00 to $2.00 per diem for rations. Peter Houck, Chapter VI, Vol. 416, *Medical Department* (Lynchburg, VA, 1991), 34.

The Moore Hospital in Richmond was also known as General Hospital #24 and the North Carolina Hospital. *Library of Congress*

was Winder Hospital, able to handle nearly 5,000 patients in six divisions and equipped with a bakery, icehouse, and sixteen-acre garden worked by patients. Jackson Hospital could accommodate 2,500 patients and had two icehouses, a bakery, and a garden, with sixty cows pastured nearby.[21]

Life as a ward matron was fraught with difficulties. When Phoebe Pember arrived at Chimborazo, she was shown a corner of a ward as her office. Pember later wrote that she found a small, rusty stove more suitable for a family of six than the 600 on the diet list. She sent "Jim" to the steward for a pair of chickens, which were cut up and put in a borrowed pot to boil. She felt her "office did not rise above that of chief cook, for I dared not leave my kitchen unattended for a moment." Later, a doctor came by and saw Pember peeling potatoes. She then learned that the cooking of food was left to those hired as cooks, not the ward matrons. Chimborazo alone employed 86 African American cooks from 1863 through 1865. The vast majority were enslaved males. With some variance, most were paid $240 per year in 1863 and $300 in 1864, although a few earned $400

---

21 Houck, *A Prototype of a Confederate Hospital*, 114, 145; Cunningham, *Doctors in Gray*, 51–52; Several of the bakers at Confederate hospitals in Richmond were former Federal prisoners, released from Castle Thunder. Ash, *Rebel Richmond*, 91–92.

The Chimborazo Hospital in Richmond had its own bakery, brewery, icehouses, and farm with dairy cows and goats. *Library of Congress*

per year. Seven were women, and at least two were free people of color. The women earned the same as the men.[22]

Surgeons and their assistants visited the wards daily, prescribing a diet list for the matrons to follow for bedridden soldiers. The matron sat "at her table, the diet list arranged before her. . . . Any necessary instructions of the surgeon were noted and attended to, sometimes with observations of her own. . . . The orders ran somewhat in this fashion: 'Chicken soup for twenty—beef tea for forty—tea and toast for fifty.'" The nurses fed the bedridden first while ambulatory patients went to the dining halls. An Alabama soldier at Howard's Grove Hospital noted in May 1864 that breakfast was at 7:00 a.m., dinner at 1:00 p.m., and supper at 7:00 p.m. Early in the war, breakfast at Chimborazo consisted of "Baker's bread, ¾ pint of coffee, fish & Molasses." Dinner consisted of bacon on Sundays and Wednesdays, then "on all other days, Beef, fresh and corned, with ample allowance of vegetables: Irish and Sweet Potatoes, cabbage, Turnips, peas, stewed Peaches, apples & cold slaw." Supper consisted of coffee and biscuits. Large boilers from local tobacco factories were used to make soups.[23]

22 Bell Wiley, ed., *A Southern Woman's Story* (St. Simons Island, 1988), 19–20; Chimborazo Records, chapter 6, volumes 92, 98, 301, 307, 316, NA.

23 Berlin, *A Confederate Nurse*, 171; Wiley, *Southern Woman's Story*, 23; Hubbs, *Voices from Company D*, 269; Carol Green, *Chimborazo* (Knoxville, TN, 2004), 69.

Hospitals were typically better supplied than the troops in camp or on campaigns. There were non-perishables from the commissary department and fresh items from the onsite gardens and dairy farms. However, there was often more demand than could be met. Hospital agents traveled the countryside, using hospital funds to purchase foodstuffs. At the same time, local farmers and business owners frequented the hospitals with provisions to sell. Brown and Company supplied mostly fish, sturgeon and shad, to General Hospital No. 24 in Richmond in the spring of 1863; Todd Britton and Company supplied Petersburg hospitals with poultry, mutton, and eggs in late 1862 through 1863. Bennett and Cain supplied General Hospital No. 26 with beef during those same months; Cables and Nimmo delivered bread to Castle Thunder, General Hospital 22, and the Texas Hospital. Batkins and Woodward, in Richmond, made deliveries every few days to different divisions in several hospitals, including Howard's Grove and Jackson. They delivered diverse products: dozens of eggs, chickens, radishes, onions, butter, squash, beets, corn, wheat, cucumbers, blackberries, tomatoes, potatoes, lima beans, and ducks. Both Chimborazo and Winder hospitals used a boat to ply the waters as far away as Lynchburg and Lexington, seeking supplies and trading cotton, yarn, shoes, and other items for fresh vegetables, food, and provisions. The vessels were primarily crewed by enslaved men hired by the government. In August 1864, Surgeon General Moore urged hospital directors to stop buying food at the overpriced markets in town and patronize farmers in the countryside.[24]

As with soldiers in the field, there were times of shortages. Worn-out railroads, poorly maintained local roads, and a canal system subject to freezing and Federal raids hampered the transportation of food supplies. Often, shortages were temporary. In Charlottesville, Ada Bacot noted in November 1861 that she was short on beef for her convalescent patients and tried to find chickens at the market. "[T]hey were not to be had," she confessed in her diary, "so I had to get Eggs. . . . I succeeded much better than I had any idea I could in getting up a dinner." Years later, Emily Mason reflected that food was plentiful early on. The Georgia soldier

---

24 Brown & Company, Confederate Papers Related to Citizens or Business Firms, 1861–1865, Roll 98, M346, RG109, NA; Britton, Todd & Company, Confederate Papers Related to Citizens or Business Firms, 1861–1865, Roll 98, M346, RG109, NA; Cables & Nimmo, Confederate Papers Related to Citizens or Business Firms, 1861–1865, Roll 132, M346, RG109, NA. Bennett & Cain, Confederate Papers Related to Citizens or Business Firms, 1861–1865, Roll 59, M346, RG109, NA; Green, *Chimborazo*, 100; James Brewer, *The Confederate Negro: Virginia's Craftsmen and Military Laborers, 1861–1865* (Durham, NC, 1969), 97. The records for Batkins & Woodward end in May 1864. In November, an advertisement appeared in the *Richmond Dispatch*, stating that the previous July, they had closed out their store "through the necessity of the military law," likely referring to new schedule of prices that the government would pay for goods, published on Jan. 27, 1864. Batkins & Woodward, Confederate Papers Related to Citizens or Business Firms, 1861–1865, Roll 48, M346, RG109, NA; *Richmond Dispatch*, Nov. 5, 1864; *OR* Series 4, 3, 54–57.

was able to have his "sweet-'tater pudding" and the Tar Heel his biscuit "dark inside and white outside."

> But as the war went on, only peas, dried peas, seemed plentiful, and we made them up in every variety . . . of which dried peas are capable. In soup they appeared one day; the second day we had cold peas; then they were fried (when we had the grease); baked peas came on the fourth day, and then we began with soup. Toward the last we lived on corn meal and sorghum, a very coarse molasses, with a happy interval when a blockade runner brought up dried vegetables for soup from our sympathetic English friends. A pint of corn meal and a gill of sorgum was the daily ration. . . . If beans and corn bread were not always wholesome, they certainly made a cheerful diet; and full of fun were the "tea parties," which we drank an infusion of strawberry and raspberry leaves. I never heard any one complain save those greedy fellows the convalescents, who could have eaten a whole beef.[25]

But many soldiers did complain. Dick Simpson, 3rd South Carolina Infantry, wrote from a Richmond hospital in November 1861: This is "the nastiest eating you ever heard of. We have here stale baker's bread, cold boiled mutton, and rye water for coffee. I can't eat a mouthful of it." In a Winchester hospital, a Tar Heel cavalryman noted that he "received only tolerably fare." In May 1864, a soldier in the Jackson Hospital complained the fare was "quite poor," and an Alabama soldier at Howard's Grove, writing the same day, found that he did not get enough: "Moreover it is very coarse for sick & wounded men. . . . No lucuries such as eggs, chickens, butter, &c., can not be had."[26]

Soldiers purchased food to supplement their hospital rations from the markets or private homes when possible. After complaining about the "stale Baker's bread," Dick Simpson confessed that he bought everything he could to eat, paying exorbitant prices. An Alabama soldier at Howard's Grove hospital in June 1864 wrote of walking and buying cherries, sponge cake, ginger cake, pie, and milk, not only for himself but also for an ill messmate. At times, these forays did not meet with the approval of hospital staff. Ada Bacot recalled walking into a ward at her hospital and finding a couple of patients trying to cover up two watermelons lying on a cot.[27]

Citizens from the surrounding countryside frequently sent food to hospitals. The YMCA in Richmond was a receiving point, frequently running a column

---

25 Berlin, *A Confederate Nurse*, 159; Mason, "Memories of a Hospital Matron," 476.

26 Everson & Simpson, *Far, Far from Home*, 92; Calvin Leach Diary, Oct. 5, 1863, SHC; Wyckoff, *The Civil War Letters of Alexander McNeill*, 440; Hubbs, *Voices from Company D*, 272.

27 Everson & Simpson, *Far, Far from Home*, 92; Hubbs, *Voices from Company D*, 289, 290; Berlin, *A Confederate Nurse*, 138.

in local newspapers thanking contributors, whose donations varied depending on the time of year. In August 1862, the YMCA received a jug of honey, dried fruit, eggs, tomatoes, onions, potatoes, butter, several coop chickens, blackberry cordial, pickles, coffee, all sorts of spiritous liquors, lemon syrup, and sugar. Donors from further away, such as in North Carolina, whose food might spoil in transit, sent cash.[28]

There were times convalescing soldiers stole food from neighboring houses. "Numerous complaints [have] been made to these Hd Qtrs of continual depredations committed by solders of this command on property of citizens in this city & vicinity of Lynchburg," Brig. Gen. Raleigh Colston wrote to the surgeons under his command in August 1864. Colston limited passes for soldiers to two hours, and men were prohibited from possessing firearms. In Richmond, Phoebe Pember complained that food scarcity led to thefts at Chimborazo. Across town at Winder, riots occurred over food shortages. Patients accused the steward of stealing funds earmarked for food and believed the baker was incompetent. They stormed the bakery, thrashed the baker, threatened to hang the steward, and left the grounds strewn with half-baked bread. Others resorted to theft. Private William Jones, 17th Mississippi Infantry, spent most of the war sick at various Richmond hospitals. While a patient at the Jackson Hospital, he was convicted of larceny and sent to Castle Thunder.[29]

The lack of a consistently nutritious diet prolonged recovery times. Twentieth-century studies prove that the lack of vitamin C led to poor wound healing and a general physical or mental weariness. Night blindness was caused by a lack of vitamin A, as was bronchitis and pneumonia. Low vitamin B caused pellagra and led to dementia, diarrhea, and dermatitis. As Lee prepared his army for new campaigns, inadequate diets, especially during the winter and early spring, could dampen plans and combat effectiveness. Confederate medical practitioners, from field surgeons to ward doctors and matrons, practiced as well as their conditions afforded, but a dearth of beneficial foodstuffs led to many Confederate deaths or permanent disability.[30]

28 *Richmond Dispatch*, Sep. 4, 1862.

29 R. E. Colston, Aug. 8, 1864, General Hospital No. 2, Lynchburg, VA, Supplies and Order Book, 262–263, MOC; Wiley, *A Southern Woman's Story*, 59; *Richmond Dispatch*, Jul. 22, 1864; *Richmond Sentinel*, Dec. 21, 1864.

30 Alfred Bollet, "Scurvy and Chronic Diarrhea in Civil War Troops," *Journal of the History of Medicine and Allied Sciences* (Jan. 1992), 52; Glenda Schroeder-Lein, *The Encyclopedia of Civil War Medicine* (New York, 2008), 194–195.

Chapter 5

"[O]ur hunger is appeased, and I am satisfied"

Feeding Robert E. Lee and
the Confederate High Command

After three grueling days in battle at Gettysburg, one of the strangest sights reported in the aftermath was that of Robert E. Lee seeking his lost laying hen. According to a post-war story, as Lee began retreating his army toward Virginia, he could not find his chicken. This chicken had been with Lee for months. She laid an egg under the general's cot daily, leaving the tent with a "gratified cackle." Lee left the flap of his tent open for the chicken, and Bryan Lynch, Lee's mess steward, gathered the egg for Lee's breakfast. "During battle she seemed too much disturbed to lay, but as soon as the engagement was over she fell at once into her regular routine." The hen accompanied the headquarters staff to Gettysburg but could not be located as they prepared to leave, prompting a search by everyone, including Lee. Eventually, she was found "perched on the wagon, where she had taken her place of her own accord." The hen continued laying eggs for Lee through the winter of 1864.[1]

While Lee grew up in antebellum Virginia with a more varied diet, his years in the army undoubtedly acquainted him with a spartan fare. Once in Confederate service, he could have purchased rations for himself and the two enslaved men he brought. In 1864, the Confederate government changed the law, and officers were issued rations like the men in the ranks rather than buying food. This saved time but created a hardship for those with enslaved or hired free men to support. Lee received the same sustenance that the soldiers were issued. However, this was Robert E. Lee, and the public revered him. He seldom went hungry.

1 A. L. Long, *Memoirs of Robert E. Lee* (New York, 1886), 241–242.

When Lee left Richmond at the end of July 1861, he brought Meredith and Perry, servants from the White House plantation on the Pamunkey River. In western Virginia, their fare was simple. One staff officer noted they often soaked their hardtack in coffee to make it soft enough to eat. On another occasion, Lt. Col. John Washington wrote that he and Lee had "bread and mutton, or beef, rice and tea or coffee, a little brown sugar. We have been out of butter and potatoes for some time and am now getting short of sugar, coffee, and salt." Washington recalled that breakfast was at 6:00 a.m., and dinner/supper was at 6:00 p.m. The winter campaign in western Virginia was a disaster, and Jefferson Davis soon ordered Lee to the Department of South Carolina, Georgia, and Florida. A late December letter to his wife, Mary, noted that breakfast usually came at 8:00 a.m., lunch was whatever could be cobbled together, with dinner around 6:00 p.m.[2]

Both Meredith and Perry accompanied Lee when he was reassigned to the deep South in November 1861, following the general back to Richmond in March 1862. On May 31, Lee learned from Davis that he had been assigned temporary command of the main Confederate army in Virginia. Its leader, Joseph E. Johnston, was wounded during the battle of Seven Pines. Lee never relinquished command of what became the ANV.[3]

Lee seldom wrote about food in his letters home. The young men who served on his staff, such as Walter Taylor, Charles Marshall, and Armistead Long, filled in the gaps. Campaigning in 1862 kept the men busy and in the saddle. In January 1863, Lee filed the paperwork in Richmond to complete the manumission of the Arlington slaves, including Meredith and Perry. Lee wrote home in February 1863 that he had hired George to be his cook, paying him and Perry $8.20 each per month. Writing a month later, he noted that George was a better cook than Meredith, adding that more ham and coffee were available. George did not stay long, as on March 9, Lee's letter stated that Bryan Lynch had arrived to cook. Lynch was an Irish national, probably not subject to the draft, and remained with Lee the rest of the war.[4]

Taylor noted that Lynch, like other camp cooks, was adept at scavenging the countryside to supplement the meager government-issued rations. Taylor believed

---

2 Douglas Freeman notes that Meredith was a cook at White House and Perry worked in the dining room at Arlington. Freeman, *R. E. Lee*, 4 vols. (New York, 1935), 1:541, 608. J. A. Washington to G. A. Myers, Aug. 12, 1861, Myers papers, W&M; J. A. Washington to aunt, Aug. 31, 1861, James A. Washington papers, VHS; REL to Mary, Dec. 22, 1861, REL papers, LOC.

3 Freeman, *R. E. Lee*, 1:608.

4 Dowdey & Manarin, *The Wartime Papers of R. E. Lee*, 402, 412; REL to Mrs. REL, Mar. 6, 1863, REL papers, LOC; Walter Taylor wrote that Bryan Lynch's name was actually Bernard Lynch. *Four Years with General Lee* (New York, 1877), 221.

Robert E. Lee, center, with his son G. W. C. Lee to the left and Richard Taylor to the right. *Library of Congress*

that Lynch pleaded "the gineral's" poor state of health when soliciting "edibles." Since many adored Lee, a steady stream of "edibles" arrived frequently. In November 1863, Taylor wrote that they had received "fresh butter, irish and sweet potatoes, turnips, & venison." Taylor noted in March that headquarters staff had been very fortunate during the past two months. "Box after box has been sent to the General containing all sorts of nice things, and indeed but for these presents we would indeed be in a fair way to starve on the one ration order." In July 1864, a lady near the general's camp sent ice cream. There were two watermelons in August. Taylor realized that his position greatly enhanced the possibilities of better food. He advised his fiancée to keep the donations secret; otherwise, people may not be as generous in the future. "Our table could not boast any great variety, but we had enough to eat," Taylor wrote after the war. "[F]requently after a meal the general would rest both hands on the table and say, 'Well, Colonel Taylor, we are just as well off as if we had feasted on the best in the land; our hunger is appeased, and I am satisfied.'"[5]

That is not to say that Lee and his staff did not, at times, suffer for more substantial subsistence. Taylor noted in February 1864 that sometimes, for a day or two, the mess was without meat "at times from necessity, at times from choice & on principle." The employed camp servants around headquarters complained that they could not continue with short rations. A correspondent, writing immediately after the war, noted how Lee's headquarters ate meat only twice a week. According to the correspondent, Lee's normal fare was a head of cabbage boiled in saltwater and a pone of cornbread. It was probably during this time that Lee's laying hen met its demise. According to Long, Bryan Lynch, needing to produce a meal for a distinguished visitor, killed the hen and cooked it. "At the dinner the general

5 Taylor, *Four Years with General Lee*, 222; R. Lockwood Tower, ed., *Lee's Adjutant: The Wartime Letters of Colonel Walter Herron Taylor, 1862–1865* (Columbia, SC, 1995), 90, 143, 174, 180.

was much surprised to see so fine a fowl; all enjoyed it, not dreaming of the great sacrifice made upon the altar of hospitality." When the hen was missed, Lynch had to acknowledge his deed.[6]

Lee was often generous with the food he received. Bean Campbell, serving at a signal post on Clark Mountain in mid-1862, recalled Lee taking a ham sandwich out of his coat pocket and sharing it with the courier. In March 1863, Walter Taylor wrote of a group of horseback-riding ladies coming near their camp. Lee invited them for "a slice of cake" that had been sent to him. In February 1864, Lee received a box from the aunt and uncle of Col. Briscoe Baldwin and shared it with his staff. Later that year, Gen. James Lane, reporting for duty after being wounded, recalled Lee pulling a box of peaches from under his cot and giving several to Lane, as the "ladies are always sending me nice things and I want to share these with you." Lee even sent some edible gifts to his wife in Richmond. At times, Lee tried to deter citizens from sending food. He wrote to Mary in August 1863 that their camp was near the home of Erasmus Taylor, whose wife had sent vegetables, buttermilk, bread, and ice to his camp. Twice the general had visited their home, attempting to stop the food, but "I cannot get her to desist," he wrote. The following March, he arrived in camp and found a box containing hams, "which I had rather they had eaten," he told Mary. Years after the war, Richard Ewell recalled Lee sharing his lunch—two cold sweet potatoes—right before the evacuation of Petersburg.[7]

At times, Lee was expected to entertain guests at his headquarters, often at great cost, like the hen that followed the army to Gettysburg, only to be served to a visitor. Another story emerged two years after the war, involving a pot of boiled cabbage and a piece of middling, usually pork, about four inches long and two inches wide. No one ate the middling at dinner. The following day, Lee asked for the middling, and the cook confessed it had been borrowed, and uneaten, returned to the owner. In August of 1862, J. E. B. Stuart and his staff arrived at Brandy Station, pitching their tents near Lee's headquarters. Discovering they had not had breakfast, Lee invited them to join him for some "rye coffee, bread, and

---

6 Tower, *Lee's Adjutant*, 112; *Native Virginian*, Dec. 6, 1867; Long, *Memoirs of General Lee*, 242. William Mack Lee, writing in 1918, claimed to be the cook and body servant of Lee, and the one who cooked the hen. Alas, none of Lee's staff, nor Lee's letters home, ever mention a "William Mack Lee." It seems the story was borrowed from Long's account. *History of the Life of Rev. Wm. Mack Lee* (Norfolk, 1918).

7 Katherine Greene, *Stony Mead* (Strasburg, VA, 1929), 21; Tower, *Lee's Adjutant*, 143; Briscoe Baldwin to William & Mary Donaghe, Feb. 27, 1864, Robertson family papers, VHS; Lane, "Personal Reminiscences of General Lee," 311; Jones, *Life and Letters of Robert Edward Lee*, 285, 444; Dowdey & Manarin, *The Wartime Papers of R. E. Lee*, 679.

wild honey." Jefferson Davis and two of his aides visited with Lee while the army was headquartered in the Orange Court House area in November 1863. They had breakfast once and dinner twice while together. A little over a year later, in December 1864, Col. John S. Mosby visited Lee at his headquarters at Edge Hill, near Petersburg. When served a leg of mutton, Lee joked that the meat must have been stolen, as it was a rare treat.[8]

Like the common soldier, Lee was susceptible to poor food and water. During the battle of Gettysburg, he suffered a bout of diarrhea. One of Richard Ewell's staff members arrived with a message, only to find Lee confined to his cot. W. W. Blackford, of J. E. B. Stuart's staff, recalled being at Lee's headquarters during the battle and seeing Lee leave his tent for the rear several times. Blackford consulted other staff members, learning Lee "was suffering a good deal from an attack of diarrhea." On the afternoon of May 23, while the Overland campaign raged, Lee stopped at a house and consumed a glass of buttermilk. By that evening, he had a "violent intestinal complaint." Another historian described it as "bilious dysentery," which confined Lee to his tent for several days. Charles Venable, writing in 1873, lamented the lost opportunity: "[I]n the midst of these operations on the North Anna, Gen. Lee was taken sick and confined to his tent. As he lay prostrated by his sickness, he often repeated: 'We must strike them a blow—we must never let them pass us again—we must strike them a blow.'" It is impossible to say that the buttermilk was the sole contributor, but, coupled with long hours in the saddle and poor food, it surely did not help. Both cases came at times of great responsibility for Lee. They undoubtedly contributed to poor command performances during the battle of Gettysburg in July 1863 and along the banks of the North Anna River in May 1864. "Lee confined to his tent was not Lee on the battlefield," concluded Venable.[9]

Lee, of course, was not the only general requiring food. There were scores of others, from men who commanded corps to those leading brigades, plus their staff and servants. These officers were, like Lee, able to purchase rations until 1864, when rations became issued. The sizes of headquarter staff varied by the general and the time of the war. By regulation, staff was limited, but there were

8 *Native Virginian*, Dec. 6, 1897; Borcke, *Memoirs of the Confederate War*, 1:100; Tower, *Lee's Adjutant*, 90; Adele Mitchell, ed., *Mosby Letters* (n.p., 1986), 125.

9 Jones, *Campbell Brown's Civil War*, 218 n75; W. W. Blackford, *War Years with JEB Stuart* (New York, 1946), 230; Freeman, *R. E. Lee*, 3:356. For a more complete look at Lee's health, see Jack D. Walsh, *Medical Histories of Confederate Generals* (Kent, OH, 1995), 134–36; C. S. Venable, "The Campaign from the Wilderness to Petersburg," *SHSP*, (1886), 535. Charles Blackford also noted that on May 25, 1864, Lee was unwell and a better diet might restore him. Blackford & Blackford, *Letters from Lee's Army*, 126.

volunteer aides-de-camp who served at each general's pleasure. In November 1862, James Longstreet, commanding several divisions in the ANV, reported a staff of thirteen commissioned officers. J. E. B. Stuart's staff numbered up to twenty during this time. These numbers do not include enlisted men, civilians, or those serving as provosts, couriers, telegraph operators, clerks, teamsters, or in a host of other capacities.[10]

One of the most high-profile officers with peculiar dietary restrictions was Thomas J. Jackson. Dubbed "Stonewall" Jackson following his stand during the first battle at Manassas, he once told a staff officer that he had been a dyspeptic for almost twenty years. Henry Kyd Douglas wrote that Jackson

> governed his appetite with severity. He liked a great many things he did not eat, and ate some things he did not like. He was not a hearty eater, although at times he had a good appetite. Whatever might be the variety before him he generally selected one or two things only for his meal and ate of them abundantly. He seemed to know what agreed with him, and often puzzled others by his selections. I knew him to make a very hearty dinner of raspberries, milk and bread. He was, therefore, at times a great disappointment to hospitable housewives, who, after skillfully providing various handiworks of choice food for his enjoyment, looked on regretfully when he selected one or two simple things and declined all the rest.[11]

Like Lee and most Confederate generals, Jackson had a camp servant prepare his meals, hiring Jim Lewis from W. C. Lewis of Lynchburg. Sandie Pendleton, of Jackson's staff, wrote in October 1862 that after ten days of nothing but beef and bread, the staff "rebelled," sending an aid out in an ambulance to forage from the surrounding farms around Bunker Hill. The ambulance returned with turkey, bacon, cabbage, tomatoes, potatoes, apple butter, and bread. None of the food was prepared, "but Jim Lewis did that in very good style."[12]

At times, Jackson could be as unbending with his staff as he was with the men who served under him. At Harrison's Landing, on July 4, 1862, right after the Seven Days Campaign, Jim appeared in the room where the staff slept, announcing that breakfast was ready, and that Stonewall was asking where they were. Douglas was up and dressed quickly but found Jackson in ill humor. Couriers he wanted dispatched early were just waking. "I was about to propose that we breakfast without waiting when the General turned on Jim quickly and ordered him to put everything into

10 J. Boone Bartholomees Jr., *Buff Facings and Gilt Buttons* (Columbia, SC, 1998), 9–10.

11 Douglas, *I Rode with Stonewall*, 122.

12 Bean, *Stonewall's Man*, 81.

Stonewall Jackson's headquarters, based on a war-time sketch. *Library of Congress*

the wagon at once and have it on the road in ten minutes, remarking, 'If my staff will not get up, they must go without their breakfast; let's ride!'" "Why, pray, should the General and I go without breakfast?'" Douglas questioned.[13]

Every general undoubtedly had favorite foods. Lee favored sweet potatoes and buttermilk, while for Jackson, it seemed to be peaches, rather than the legendary lemons. Lemons were scarce, and only one war-time story has emerged documenting Jackson with one. During the Seven Days, in June 1862, Douglas wrote that someone handed Jackson a lemon, "a fruit of which he was specially fond." Jackson bit off a piece and began to slurp out the juice. "From that moment until darkness ended the battle, that lemon scarcely left his lips except to be used as a baton to emphasize an order." It could be that the lemon was a gift from J. E. B. Stuart, salvaged from the Federal depot at White Hall. A post-war account has Jackson sucking on lemons during his Shenandoah Valley campaign. When questioned on how Jackson obtained the fruit, the answer was "from his commissary." But Jackson's commissary did not have lemons, the soldiers replied. "From his other commissary" was the answer. What other commissary? "Old Jack

---

13 Bean, *Stonewall's Man*, 48; Douglas, *I Rode with Stonewall*, 111. Another version of this story appears in Henderson. Lewis, after being instructed to pack the wagon, told Robert Dabney, "My stars, but de general is just mad dis time; most like lightnin' strike him!" G. F. R Henderson, *Stonewall Jackson*, 2 vols. (New York, 1906), 2:72.

William Mahone's gastrological peculiarities were just as odd as Stonewall Jackson's. *AHEC*

drawn all our rations from Banks," the Federal general attempting to corral Jackson in the Valley.[14]

If there was a general as peculiar as Jackson in the culinary department, it was William Mahone. Moxley Sorrel, of Longstreet's staff, described Mahone as a small man, "a mere atom with little flesh." He was "[d]elicate in physique" and "had to nourish himself carefully." While eating breakfast at Mahone's headquarters, Sorrel noted that Mahone had a milk cow and laying hens nearby. In late December 1862, Mahone built a pen outside his tent and purchased several turkeys, which he fattened. On Christmas morning, when selecting a turkey for dinner, Mahone found them gone. "Who stole Mahone's turkeys? was a favorite 'conundrum' in the Division the balance of the war. Our fellows laid it on the Florida Brigade," a 12th Virginia soldier wrote. Mahone managed to keep his milk cow until it was captured, along with his headquarters wagon, during the retreat toward Appomattox. He considered it "a most serious loss, for he was not able, in the delicate condition of his health, to eat anything but tea and crackers and fresh milk," he told an artillery officer.[15]

Being an officer led to a certain degree of mobility. Chances for better food and dinner invitations were frequent. Some of those invitations were with other officers. Then-colonel William Dorsey Pender wrote of having tea with Army of the Potomac commander Joseph E. Johnston and his wife in late August 1861 while stationed near Manassas. James Longstreet, commanding a brigade near Centerville in October 1861, hosted a dinner party that included generals Johnston, P. G. T. Beauregard, Gustavus Smith, and David Jones, along with

14 Douglas, *I Rode with Stonewall*, 103; *CV* 20:58.

15 Sorrel, *Recollections of a Staff Officer*, 276, 277; Westwood A. Todd, "Reminiscences of the Civil War," *SHSP*, 81, SHC; Cockrell, *Gunner with Stonewall*, 118. Freeman wrote that Mahone strapped his cooking utensils to the back of the cow while on campaign. *Lee's Lieutenants: A Study in Command*, 3 vols. (New York, 1942–1944), 3:552.

two politicians. Thomas Goree, also on Longstreet's staff, mentioned two dinner parties on the first of December 1861. He ate "a large ham, a fat turkey, chickens, beef, oysters, salad, pickles, light bread, and a variety of other things," with Brig. Gen. D. R. Jones. A second party, at the camp of Earl Van Dorn, featured speeches by Johnston, Beauregard, Smith, Van Dorn, and others, "all of whom can fight much better than they can speak." These invitations continued through the war. Colonel James Conner wrote that in February 1864, he received an invitation to dine with Richard Ewell. Conner "Pitched into the vegetables in a way that must have astonished Madam Ewell," he confessed. Robert E. Lee dined with J. E. B. Stuart several times in 1864. In March, at Stuart's headquarters, Lee found the cavalier, Mrs. Stuart, William Wickham, and members of Stuart's staff. At the end of the month, Lee and Stuart ate together again, this time accompanied by Rooney Lee, and then again on April 6.[16]

When camps were close to towns and cities, invitations flowed freely. Henry Kyd Douglas recalled in December 1864 visiting the home of a Mrs. Gilliam in Petersburg along with citizens and generals W. H. F. Lee and Robert D. Johnson. Douglas remained all night, enjoying eggnog before leaving the following day. Robert E. Lee shared Christmas dinner at the Bannister home, having turkey and potatoes. Mrs. Bannister saw Lee picking at his turkey and inquired if he preferred dark meat. Lee told his hostess he was saving a portion for an ill staff member back in camp. "He has had nothing to eat but corn bread and sweet potato coffee." She insisted he finish his dinner, and as Lee made his way back to camp, he carried a linen napkin with potatoes and turkey.[17]

Some dinner parties were elaborate affairs. Moxley Sorrel described entertaining three Englishmen in November 1862. Two hospital tents were pitched together, "embellished with trophies of arms and flags" and flowers. Food was sought from the surrounding countryside. Covering the bare boards of the table were a "young pig well fattened, turkey, fowls, fresh beef, and vegetables topped the commissary's pork and hardtack." The camp servants delighted in preparing the meal. "The absence of wine was conspicuous, but no one lacked for good whiskey." Stonewall Jackson hosted a Christmas dinner a month later, attended by Robert E. Lee, J. E. B. Stuart, artillery chief William Pendleton, and a half dozen staff officers. During the evening, Stuart observed that the butter was imprinted with

16 Hassler, *One of Lee's Best Men*, 51; Cuter, *Longstreet's Aide*, 51, 58; Moffett, *Letters of General James Conner*, 110; J. E. Cooke diary, Mar. 9, 1864, Duke; F. G. Walter diary, Apr. 5, 1864, LVA; It is possible the March 30 dinner took place at Lee's Headquarters. Dowdey & Manarin, *Wartime Papers*, 687.

17 Douglas, *I Rode with Stonewall*, 321; A. Wilson Greene, *Civil War Petersburg* (Charlottesville, VA, 2006), 228.

gamecocks and declared the bird Jackson's coat of arms. The following January, Brig. Gen. William Paxton hosted a dinner that included "wild goose, oysters, and scrambled eggs."[18]

While in somewhat stationary camps, officers often hunted birds. "Birdhunting [sic] seems to be quite the rage among a certain class of men, and not satisfied with the thunder of guns during an engagement, seem to be most anxious to prolong the sound of bursting villainous saltpeter," noted Capt. Oscar Hinrichs, serving on Second Corps staff during the second Shenandoah Valley campaign in late summer 1864. Two years prior, E. Porter Alexander wrote of acquiring an old rifle and having his camp servant mash bullets flat and then cut them into squares to use for shot. "[W]ith these I killed quantities of quail, & I nearly lived on them," he wrote after killing 120 in one two-acre field of broom corn. Alexander continued to hunt and make shot in the field into 1864. Now they heated the lead and poured it through a piece of tin with small holes, and into a bucket of water. Later, the Confederate government, according to Alexander, offered to trade 100 pounds of lead for a bag of shot brought through the blockade. Alexander recalled prying open unexploded Federal artillery shells to remove the lead for the trade. Eventually, they traded 700 pounds of lead for seven bags of shot. Alexander even had a pointer named Baxter who flushed birds. Heros von Borcke recalled hunting in January 1863, and Richard Ewell wrote home in February 1864 regarding the "whereabouts of [my] gun" he wanted for hunting.[19]

During campaigns, there was significant food sharing within the high command. Isaac Trimble recalled that on June 24, 1863, as he caught up to Lee near Berryville, Lee sent him to join his staff in eating because Trimble looked "tired and hungry" and "some remains of a fine mutton which fine friends have sent us." In May 1864, as the Overland campaign raged, Jedediah Hotchkiss recalled having breakfast with Lee, Richard Ewell, George Anderson, and other staff officers.[20]

Very few in the army were strict teetotalers. A neighboring general's headquarters could be a haven for those whose generals forbade alcohol. Heros von Borcke enjoyed visiting Longstreet's headquarters when he found the staff around J. E. B. Stuart a little dry. Longstreet's headquarters were well known for hard drinking.

18 Sorrel, *Recollections of a Confederate Staff Officer*, 127; James Smith, "Stonewall Jackson at Chancellorsville," (Richmond, VA, no date), 7; Douglas, *I Rode with Stonewall*, 211.

19 Richard Williams, ed., *Stonewall's Prussian Mapmaker* (Chapel Hill, NC, 2014), 167; Gallagher, *Fighting for the Confederacy*, 156, 340; Borcke, *Memoirs of the Confederate War*, 2:172; Donald Pfanz, ed., *Letters of General Richard S. Ewell* (Knoxville, TN, 2012), 271.

20 Isaac Trimble, "The Battle and Campaign of Gettysburg," *SHSP* (1898), 26:118; McDonald, *Make Me a Map of the Valley*, 207.

J. E. B. Stuart and his Confederate troopers usually had access to superior foodstuff, much of it gleaned from the Federals. *AHEC*

There were many nights when officers gathered for card games and indulgence. One staff officer recalled Brig. Gen. William Pendleton taking a "thimble full" of whiskey at Gettysburg. Even Stonewall Jackson, when visiting a farmer near Tabler's Mill in October 1862, shocked his staff when he invited them to take a drink with the farmer. Jackson mixed the whiskey with a little sugar and water and drank it, complimenting his host on the flavor. At one point, he told a staff member, "I differ with you and most men. I like the taste of all spirituous liquors. I can sip whiskey or brandy with a spoon with the same pleasure the most delicious coffee or cordial would give you . . . and if I had indulged my appetite I would have been a drunkard." The staffer observed Jackson taking a glass of wine every so often.[21]

Feeding generals and their staffs on campaigns and in battles was as challenging as feeding men in the ranks. E. Porter Alexander, serving on Beauregard's staff early in the war, recalled being shelled in July 1861. Two Federal shells came close, but the third crashed into the kitchen where camp servants were preparing dinner. Mud chinking between the logs fell into the soup just as it was being dished up, and "we went without dinner that day." In May 1862, in the first Shenandoah Valley campaign, Robert Dabney recalled Jackson coming in late one night and being offered food but telling Lewis: "I want none; nothing but sleep." During the same campaign, Henry Kyd Douglas recalled Jackson eating hardtack from an overturned wagon, as they had eaten nothing since early that morning. A month later, during the Seven Days campaign, Bryan Grimes first met Stonewall and invited the famed general to dinner, which came from a sutler's wagon captured the day before. General Branch complained in a letter home right after the battle of Ox Hill that all they had to eat was beef. Their wagon train could not keep

---

21 Borcke, *Memoirs of the Confederate War*, 2:162; Elmore, "Revelations of a Confederate Artillery Staff Officer," 78; Douglas, *I Rode with Stonewall*, 185–186.

up with their respective commands. William Pendleton complained of a lack of food for both him and his horse for more than a day during the retreat from Gettysburg, while E. Porter Alexander recalled finding a sheep that had fallen out due to exhaustion on the retreat from Gettysburg. He stowed it away in the headquarters wagon and had "some fine mutton" once they arrived in camp. Combat interrupted the routines established in camp or during a march. During the first day of the battle of the Wilderness in May 1864, Henry McClellan, of Stuart's staff, recalled arriving with a message for Lee at 10:00 p.m., just as the general sat down for dinner. Richard Stiles recalled finding Richard Ewell that same morning, and the general invited him to dismount and share a cup of coffee. Ewell confessed that someone had sent him a "turkey leg." Ewell invited Stiles to join him that evening to share the treat.[22]

J. E. B. Stuart, Wade Hampton, and their staff at times had easier ways to provision themselves. Raids on Federal wagon trains were frequent. After the first battle of Manassas, Stuart's staff made mention of the battle plunder taken. The route of the July 1861 retreat was strewn with "barrels of sugar, crackers, ground coffee . . . [and] cooking utensils." Heros von Borcke was amazed by the food left at the Federal Depot at White House, which was abandoned during their "change of base" in June 1862. While some supplies were destroyed, there were still crates of oranges and lemons, barrels of white and brown sugar, salt fish, hams, bacon, and barrels of eggs. During a November 1862 raid, another staff member recalled plundering sutler stores in Warrenton, seizing cans of condensed milk, fresh tomatoes, cherries, "in fact everything I wanted." A month later, near Occoquan, they captured "boxes of champagne, claret, cheese and numerous other items." However, times were not always bountiful. If the troopers were unable to raid, they and their mounts fasted. This was especially true while on the Peninsula in April and May 1862, and the spring of 1863.[23]

Like Lee, the high command was susceptible to poor food and tainted water. Many generals suffered from diarrhea and dysentery. North Carolina brigade commander Lawrence Branch's bout began in June 1862, and he suffered through August. During the fighting at Cedar Mountain, Branch was hauled in an ambulance due to his weakened state, only emerging to lead his brigade at the last moment. While in camp in January 1863, Brig. Gen. Frank Paxton complained of

22 Gallagher, *Fighting for the Confederacy*, 48, 273; Henderson, *Stonewall Jackson*, 1:300; Douglas, *I Rode with Stonewall*, 54–55; Gallagher, *Letters of Bryan Grimes*, 17; Lane, "History of Lane's brigade," *SHSP*, 10:242; Lee, *Memoirs of William Nelson Pendleton*, 297; Freeman, *R. E. Lee*, 3:283-4; Robert Stiles, *Four Years Under Marse Robert* (New York, 1903), 245.

23 Trout, *With Pen & Saber*, 20–21, 61, 114, 128, 178; Borcke, *Memoirs of the Confederate War*, 1:66–67.

Colonel John S. Mosby's men, along with other Confederate cavalry commands, raided behind the lines, capturing supply trains, and as pictured here, sutlers' wagons. *Harper's Weekly*

being sick in bed with an illness that started about the time of the Cedar Mountain campaign. "It is in some measure owing to a want of vegetables and fruit, and to bad bread," he wrote home. Paxton planned to send to Richmond for crackers, dried peaches, and other items to improve his health. Even though Paxton had a leave of absence, he was little better when he returned to the army. If he ate rice and bread, he fared "pretty well." However, a "hearty meal . . . puts me out of order again."

Richard Ewell was so ill with diarrhea that he missed the battle of Cold Harbor in June 1864. He recovered within a few days, but Lee used the opportunity to replace Ewell with Jubal Early as commander of the Second Corps.[24]

Much like the men in the ranks, generals sometimes requested items from home. James Conner, arriving near Culpeper Court House to command a brigade in the fall of 1864, asked his relatives to send cups, forks, knives, and "German silver forks and table spoons," to accompany the tomato catsup, Worcestershire sauce, brandy, French mustard, grits, and cowpeas he requested in other missives. Richard Corbin, a staff officer in Charles Field's division, Longstreet's corps, wrote to his mother in France, requesting a long list of items to be sent through the blockade, including cheeses and cognac.[25]

Also, like their soldiers, generals and their staff were subject to the whims of war and the commissary department. Unlike men in the ranks, the high command had better avenues to supplement army-issued rations. Enlisted privates earned eleven dollars a month at the beginning of the war. Generals earned $301 per month. A captain on staff might earn $130. Of course, officers had to buy their rations and forage for horses, were not issued uniforms, and paid cooks and camp servants or their owners if they hired help. There were also more opportunities for general officers, or their staff members or servants, to slip off to Richmond or another municipality on business, picking up items from markets to supplement the rations issued by the army. While the food sometimes made generals sick with diarrhea or dysentery, there were chances for better medical care at a private home or officer's hospital, with more wholesome, appealing, and nutritious food. Keeping generals healthy was a top priority, as a poorly fed general, or one sick from poor food and polluted water, was of little use when combat commenced.

---

24 Walsh makes mention of several Confederate ANV generals who suffered bouts of dysentery and diarrhea through the war. These include Turner Ashby, Bryan Goode, Bryan Grimes, Daniel H. Hill, John B. Hood, Benjamin Humphreys, Eppa Hunton, Lewis Little, William D. Pender, William Pendleton, and Cadmus Wilcox. *Medical Histories of Confederate Generals*, 4, 24, 30, 90, 101, 105, 107, 108, 141 167, 168, 235; John Paxton, ed., *The Civil War Letters of General Frank "Bull" Paxton* (Hillsboro, TX, 1978), 72, 76; Pfanz, *Ewell*, 396–397.

25 Moffett, *Letters of General James Conner*, 124, 145, 152, 154; Corbin, *Letters of a Confederate Officer*, 86–87.

Chapter 6

"His whole mind and soul seemed bent on trying
to get and prepare something for his mess to eat"

Camp Servants

D r. Abner McGarity, 44th Georgia, experienced a conundrum in early August
1863. During the battle of Gettysburg, a member of his mess was wounded
and left to be captured. The wounded man owned the mess's young cook. The
wounded man's brother arrived to take the cook home, much to the chagrin of
McGarity and the others. After asking those at home if a cook could be sent to
Virginia, McGarity confessed that it was "difficult to hire one here even at Thirty
Dollars per month." While many Confederate soldiers cooked their own meals,
others employed slaves, free men of color, or brought slaves from home to forage
for food, prepare meals, and handle other camp chores.[1]

The number of camp servants and cooks brought or employed by Confederate
soldiers is unknown. There were undoubtedly thousands. Soldiers from wealthier
families brought trusted slaves, while others hired servants from various
communities or waited to hire local enslaved or free men when arriving in Virginia.
The latter practice quickly produced a shortage. A captain in the 48th Virginia
noted in the summer of 1861 that he needed "a great many things in camp" that he
did not have, including a "servant to look up provisions and cook for me, but no
possible chance to have one here." A 3rd Georgia Infantry member, writing from
near Portsmouth in January 1862, told of hiring eighteen-year-old "Sam" to serve
as a cook. He "makes excellent biscuits and is very convenient." Another Georgia
officer, writing in August 1862, complained of not being able to hire a servant.

1 Burnett, "Letters of a Confederate Surgeon, McGarity," 2:169.

Surgeon Harvey Black also sought a servant, noting that those not already hired had "been taken from this county." One officer even advertised in a Richmond newspaper, seeking a camp servant. A limited supply of camp cooks was a problem that persisted throughout the war.[2]

Often, soldiers pooled their resources to hire cooks. William Morris, then major of the 37th North Carolina, wrote in November 1862 of sharing a mess with the regiment's lieutenant colonel, chaplain, and sergeant major. They hired "a free boy" to cook and wash, paying him $12 a month. In October 1864, four men in the 53rd Georgia hired a Black man for $20 a month to wash, cook, start fires, and bring water. "He is a good cook, his plate of beefsteak this morning would have done credit to most any cook. He can bake as nice biscuits as any cook women."[3]

Letters home instructed wives to teach servants to cook. One North Carolina officer, who had hired a free man to help on his farm during his absence, wrote his wife in June 1863 that as soon as the corn was ready, he intended to have Jesse sent to him. "Let him be about the kitchen when at the house, that he may get a notion of cooking for we may at some time be obligated to force that office upon him." In another letter, the same officer asked for "Johnson," adding that he needed to be taught how to "make first rate biscuits with lard and to cook beef without salt so that it will be palatable. . . . Teach him to make good steak, to bake beef & to make hash, to fry pan cakes and to prepare other such dishes as we are likely to have in camp."[4]

Not all servants were effective, and some were sent home or not rehired. A surgeon in the 13th South Carolina wrote home of a fellow officer and his servant, Tony. Tony was caught stealing syrup to give to a local girl, and his owner intended to send him home. A Rockbridge Artillery member found his hired cook "worthless and dirty," and fired him. John Apperson, a hospital steward on Second Corps staff, several times wrote that their hired servant, James Cooley, was undependable. Finally, in March 1863, Cooley went home. "I am glad he is gone as it saves me the trouble of refusing to hire him . . . and I will save my money," Apperson concluded. An Alabama soldier recalled breaking up a fight between their cook and another. Camps were just as deadly for servants as they were for soldiers. A

2 Chapla, *48th Virginia Infantry*, 9; E. B. Duffee Jr., ed., "War Letters of S. F. Tenney," *The Georgia Historical Quarterly* (Summer 1973), 279; Allen & Bohannon, *"Campaigning with 'Old Stonewall,'"* 132; Glenn McMullen, ed., *The Civil War Letters of Dr. Harvey Black* (Baltimore, 1995), 41. *Richmond Dispatch*, Jul. 30, 1862. Glatthaar speculates that in the first months of the war, new regiments arriving in Virginia had one camp servant for every thirty soldiers, with a few instances of one in ten. *General Lee's Army*, 309.

3 William G. Morris Letters, 77, SHC; Ronald, *The Stilwell Letters*, 286.

4 Foley, *Letters Home*, 52, 73.

A post-war rendition of what a camp servant on campaign might have looked like. *Battles and Leaders*

member of the 5th Alabama described the death of a fellow officer's servant from typhoid in September 1861. Captain R. E. Park, 12th Alabama, described his cook, Banks, falling sick. A surgeon gave Banks medicine, but a few days later, Park transported him by ambulance to a doctor's home. The cooks had to manage with the same scanty rations as the soldiers. In February 1864, Robert E. Lee noted that the rations had been cut and some days there was no meat. "[O]ur servants complain of it more than anyone else," Lee wrote home. Staff officer Walter Taylor wrote the same: "Recently our col. boys declared . . . that they couldn't stay if such short rations were continued."[5]

Camp servant cooks were entrusted with money and a degree of autonomy. Frequently, they were given funds, a pass from owners or employers, and sent into the countryside or to some major city to purchase food to supplement army-issued rations. A 5th Alabama soldier, writing on picket duty near Sangster's Station in October 1861, complained they had spent their month's wages in just a few days while buying provisions. Their servant had paid $2.40 for six pounds of butter plus 75 cents for two dozen eggs. Colonel William Pender, 6th North Carolina, echoed his Alabama compatriots, saying he trusted "Harris entirely with my money in mess business." At times, camp servants resorted to stealing. A sick soldier from the 3rd South Carolina recalled feeling it was wrong for fellow soldiers to kill hogs and enter farmer's fields until his own slave came with an armful of corn. Since the

5 Welsh, *A Confederate Surgeon's Letters to his Wife*, 87; Williams, *Rebel Brothers*, 47; Roper, *Repairing the "March of Mars,"* 379; Hubbs, *Voices from Company D*, 14, 43; Park, "Diary of Capt. R. E. Park," *SHSP* 26:27; Dowdey & Manarin, *The Wartime Papers of R. E. Lee*, 667–668; Tower, *Lee's Adjutant*, 112.

cornfield lacked a fence, allowing horses and hogs to enter at will, a hungry, broke-down soldier could do the same.[6]

Their passes also provided the cooks with a surprising level of mobility. Black Pete, a freeman who cooked for one company's officers in the 4th Virginia, was sent ahead of the command in November 1861 to purchase and prepare food as they moved from near Fairfax toward the Shenandoah Valley. Samuel Walkup, lieutenant colonel, 48th North Carolina, described sending his servant, Tom, to Fredericksburg, on his horse, for sugar, tobacco, and rice. Artillery chief William N. Pendleton recalled sending his servant on horseback to "Brother Hugh's" for a supply of cherries. In April 1863, famed topographer Jedediah Hotchkiss wrote of his servant William bringing a box of provisions from home. A surgeon noted in September 1863 that his new servant Gabriel arrived from South Carolina, buying a watermelon in Richmond as he passed through. Samuel Pickens, 5th Alabama, seemed despondent, with "low spirits & homesick," when he could not procure a furlough while his servant John started home in December 1863. An "inexpressible pleasure is denied me. Oh! What [would] I give to be as free to go there as John is!!!" he lamented. John Preston, serving on Stonewall Jackson's staff, had the same feeling in December 1861. Preston wrote that Jim Lewis, whom Stonewall Jackson hired, was going home on furlough. "White people here have no chance of getting a furlough; it is only our colored friends who can escape for a time the evils of war."[7]

Many found the eatables rounded up and prepared by cooks better than their own culinary attempts. Early in the war, and the summers and falls of 1862 and 1863, there was plenty to buy. An Alabama soldier stationed near Fairfax in August 1861 remembered ample "corn, tomatoes, onions and . . . a mess of cucumbers," all supplied by a slave. In February 1863, Charles Blackford, on Longstreet's staff, wrote that a fellow officer's servant was "a good cook," supplying them with "soup, fritters and cherry roll, all of which seems to be of the highest grade of gastronomic excellence." Colonel James Conner, 22nd North Carolina Troops, wrote in March 1864 that William was a "tip-top cook. Capital biscuits; pretty fair loaf bread; and

6 Hubbs, *Voices from Company D*, 64; Hassler, *One of Lee's Best Men*, 109; Everson & Simpson, *Far, Far from Home*, 147.

7 Bean, *The Liberty Hall Volunteers*, 52, 73; S. H. Walkup diary, Nov. 29, 1862, Walkup Papers, SHC; Lee, *Memoirs of William Nelson Pendleton*, 279; McDonald, *Make Me a Map of the Valley*, 134; Welch, *A Confederate Surgeon's Letters*, 76–77; Hubbs, *Voices from Company D*, 205; Allan, *The Life and Letters of Margaret Junkin Preston*, 122. Colin Woodward argues that "Southern whites could exert greater control over slaves," when the slaves were in the army. Yet hundreds, if not more, camp servants roamed the countryside every day, looking for food. Colin Woodward, *Marching Masters: Slavery, Race, and the Confederate Army, 1861–1865* (Charlottesville, VA, 2014), 80.

splendid on puffs and fritters. He promises wonders when the okra comes out." Cooking was a skill learned in camp. In most families, both White and Black, women were the chief cooks.[8]

The services from the camp cooks were long remembered. Writing in 1912, George Christian, a former sergeant in the Richmond Howitzers, recalled a servant by the name of Aleck Kean. Not long after the war began, Kean became the cook of the "Renfrew" mess. "His whole mind and soul seemed bent on trying to get and prepare something for his mess to eat; and if there was anything to be gotten honestly, Aleck always got the share which was coming to his mess." He had food prepared "in the shortest time possible and in the most delicious way it could have been prepared in camp." In the fall of 1863, Kean's owner died. While he could have returned home, Kean asked to stay with the mess. He surrendered at Appomattox Court House. In 1911, Christian and two other members of the Richmond Howitzers attended Kean's funeral.[9]

Occasionally, these servants used the opportunity to seek freedom within Federal lines. In February 1864, Walter Taylor, on Robert E. Lee's staff, complained that many slaves employed by officers had taken "French leave." Former cooks and camp servants could sometimes provide information to the enemy. The information could be about local geography or more military in nature. In April 1862, a man claiming to be a cook for high-ranking Confederates came through Federal lines. "The colored man described Johnston and Magruder so accurately that he must know them," a Pennsylvania newspaper reported. During the 1864 Shenandoah Valley campaign, Union high command employed a free person of color as a spy, who held permission to enter Confederate lines three times a week to sell vegetables. Some servants were captured in the performance of their duties. Lieutenant Robert Park, 12th Alabama Infantry, wrote in July 1864, while near Washington, D.C., that his "negro cook" Charlie was missing. Park believed he had been enticed to leave or "forcibly detained by some negro worshipper." Park discovered in December that Charlie was being held as a prisoner of war at Fort McHenry, refusing to take the oath. Many servants were captured and imprisoned with their masters. The Federal government's official policy was that these servants were camp followers who became prisoners of war when captured. They were given the choice of taking the Oath of Allegiance and seeking employment with the army

---

8 Hubbs, *Voices from Company D*, 43; Blackford & Blackford, *Letters from Lee's Army*, 166; Moffett, *Letters of General James Conner*,117.

9 *CV*, 20:293. See also "Death of a Colored Ex-Confederate," *The Tennessean*, Mar. 28, 1883; "A Colored Ex-Confederate." *Kansas Jewelite*, Mar. 28, 1883; "Colored Confederate Soldiers." *St. Louis Post-Dispatch*, Dec. 25, 1885; *Jacksonville Republican*, Jul. 27, 1889; "A Colored Confederate Veteran" *Vicksburg Evening Post*, May 21, 1890; "A Colored Confederate." *Greensboro Patriot*, Nov. 25, 1891.

or enlisting in the Federal Army. Those refusing the oath could remain prisoners. It is unclear how many were captured or remained imprisoned at the war's end.[10]

In April 1862, the government stepped into the cooking fray, passing a law allowing each company to hire, or enlist, four cooks. One was a chief cook, making $20 per month, while the assistant cooks earned $15, with allowances for clothing. Slaves could be hired with the permission of their owners, as could free men or White men not liable for conscription. While numerous examples of service records and pension applications exist for these enlisted cooks, an exact number is unknown. In 1864, policy changes in the rationing system prevented officers from purchasing extra rations for their servants, and many officers complained. Richard Ewell, commanding Jackson's old corps, wrote the Adjutant and Inspector General's Office in Richmond that it was "absolutely necessary that officers should keep servants." Regulations kept enlisted men from serving in that capacity, and what little food was available to purchase in the countryside was beyond the pay of officers.[11]

Both slaves and free men of color worked as army cooks, but the Commissary Department also employed them to fill various jobs. They worked as butchers, porters, freight hands, drovers, teamsters, boatmen, bakers, and packers. In Richmond, the meat and packing house employed fifty slaves in 1862 and 1863. Robert E. Lee continuously advocated for using Black laborers in places where White men were employed, freeing these men up for military service. There were calls for volunteers, and later, impressments. Men in the Commissary Department often earned $20 a month, more than front-line soldiers. Unfortunately, most records on the commissary department were lost in the fires that swept through Richmond on April 2–3, 1865. Regardless of this void, African Americans, both slave and free, played enormous and all-too-often underappreciated roles in the Confederate Army.[12]

---

10 Tower, *Lee's Adjutant*, 112; *Philadelphia Public Ledger*, Apr. 22, 1862; Philip Sheridan, *Personal Memoirs of P. H. Sheridan, General, United States Army*. 2 vols. (New York, 1888), 2:3–4; Park, "Diary of Robert E. Park," *SHSP*, 1:379, 2:179; Peter A. Porter to William Huffman, Oct. 6, 1863, quoted in James Paradis, *African Americans and the Gettysburg Campaign* (Lanham, MD, 2013), 62. For another account of Black Confederates being held at Fort McHenry, see *Staunton Spectator*, Oct. 13, 1863.

11 *OR* Series 4, 2, 1079–1080. For examples of service records, see Chief Cook Oscar Carrell, Company K, 32nd Virginia Infantry; Chief Cook Spencer Hineman, Company H, 25th Virginia Battalion; Chief Cook Henry Trent, Company C, 19th Virginia Heavy Artillery; Cook William Read, Company C, 18th Georgia Battalion; and, Cook William Lynch, 5th North Carolina Cavalry, all found in Record Group 109, National Archives. For a listing of those receiving pensions, see Ricardo Rodriguez, *Black Confederates in the US Civil War* (Charleston, SC, 2010); George Kundahl, *The Bravest of the Brave: The Correspondence of Stephen Dodson Ramseur* (Chapel Hill, NC, 2010), 204.

12 Brewer, *The Confederate Negro*, 29–30.

Chapter 7

"[T]hey cannot fight with nothing to eat"

Food, Morale, and Memory

It had been a long winter for William T. Jackson. His regiment, the 8th Alabama, had been in service for twenty months, seeing action during many 1862 campaigns. "You wanted to know something about what I thought of the war's closen," he wrote, answering a missive from home on March 21, 1863. "Although starvation it seems like is stairing us in the face & a great many think that we will have to give it up on that account but they will never give it up as long as they can get as much as three buiscuits to the man A day. Yet I still hope that it will close soon. I have not given over to dispair." While Jackson continued fighting until November 8, 1864, when he died of disease at Howard's Grove Hospital in Richmond, many of his comrades did not. The constant stream of poor, inadequate rations sent many a Johnny Reb home, or to the Federals.[1]

Historians and writers have long debated what caused the demise of the Confederacy. Southern political weakness, superior Union generalship, the moral superiority of the Union cause, and economic difficulties that eroded Confederate morale are some various schools of thought. These theories are each correct to certain degrees. For the men in camp, writing letters on box tops or knees, it was rarely the poor clothing and shoes, commanding generals, or the ongoing states' rights debate between President Jefferson Davis, Governors Joseph Brown, and Zebulon B. Vance that caused them thoughts of despair. It was food.[2]

1 Wood & Jackson, *"Kiss Sweet Little Lillah for me,"* 30–31.

2 For a further explanation of the different philosophies of the cause for South's capitulation, see Beringer, et al., *Why the South Lost the Civil War*, 4–34.

The fortunes of war linked food, morale, and the success of the ANV. Even if rations were monotonous, many men believed in an eventual Confederate victory. However, as winter and Federal advances restricted the flow of supplies, soldiers grumbled, complained, and for some, eventually deserted. Even in the earliest months of the war, their letters show glimpses of discontent. "We are all in a bad fix for something to eat," wrote one Alabama soldier at the end of July 1861. "The camp in general is ranting and some have made complaints," scrawled a South Carolina soldier a few days later. "Our men are willing and anxious to be in the first battle, but they cannot fight with nothing to eat," concluded a Georgia soldier in September. The war was not yet a year old.[3]

The Georgia soldier wrote of the heart of the matter. His thoughts echoed across those four years: How can the soldiers fight if they have nothing to eat? A Confederate soldier on campaign could easily burn through 5,000 calories a day. The regulation ration supplied to each soldier typically provided close to that level of caloric intake. Yet soldiers seldom received those amounts. They often marched with wagons of provisions far in the rear, through lands stripped of foodstuffs by the soldiers in advance. Two ears of corn, such as those issued during the Appomattox campaign, provided about 150 calories. Two pieces of hardtack contained about the same. Writing in mid-May 1862, following the retreat from Yorktown, a member of the 6th North Carolina did not believe the war would last much longer "for if they don't give us more to eat, the war will have to quit." General McLaws echoed the private's remarks: "If our armies can be fed, there is every reason to believe that victory will once more crown our efforts."[4]

Ration reductions usually occurred during the winter, as inactive soldiers required fewer calories, theoretically. However, idle soldiers had time to think and ponder their dismal circumstances. "There is more anxiety felt on the provision subject than all others just at this time," one South Carolina surgeon wrote in March 1863. When it came to "sour bread and bacon," one Virginia soldier professed that he had "become so tired of it I can hardly eat it at all." Even generals complained. For artillery commander William Pendleton in July 1864, the food was costly and insufficient. By the second half of 1864, real cracks were beginning to show. Writing from near Chaffin's Farm in August 1864, a member of Longstreet's staff complained of poor living conditions. "I merely eat to live,

3 Hubbs, *Voices from Company D*, 25–26; Everson & Simpson, *Far, Far from Home*, 38; Burnett, "Letters of Barnett Hardeman Cody and Others," 290.

4 B. Rondal Mull, ed., *David's Letters* (n.p., no date), 25; Oeffinger, *A Soldier's Generals*, 142. For a summary of caloric requirements and intake of Civil War soldiers, see Judkin Browning & Tim Silver, "Nature and Human Race," *Journal of the Civil War Era* (Sep. 2018), 396–397, 412, n22.

and live on as little as possible. You would laugh, or cry, when you see me eating my supper—a pone of corn bread and a tin cup of water. . . . It is hard to maintain one's patriotism on ashcake and water." Food shortages led to stealing and mutiny. More than sixty men in the 31st North Carolina Troops refused to answer roll call one night after being issued one pound of flour and one third of a pound of bacon. Some of the bacon was spoiled. In December, a member of the 54th North Carolina wrote that many men in his regiment threatened to desert if rations were not more forthcoming.[5]

Lee was aware of the problem on campaigns and in camp. Following the march from the Shenandoah Valley to Fredericksburg in November 1862, he complained that straggling resulted from "insufficiency of the ration to appease the hunger of the men." Straggling plagued the army, denying generals thousands of men during battles. Some fell behind because their scanty rations did not provide the energy needed to maintain the pace, or they were foraging in the areas they were passing. These stragglers, such as the 16,000-plus absent during the battle of Sharpsburg, undoubtedly influenced battle outcomes. When winter doldrums set in, men deserted by the hundreds. There were many reasons a soldier might leave, and Joseph Johnston, early in the war, and later Robert E. Lee, realized that insufficient rations were just one of those causes. Johnston often complained of the scarcity of supplies as one factor that impeded capitalizing on the victory of First Manassas. In January 1864, Lee linked small issues of rations to desertions to the enemy. Again, in January 1865, it was partly the "insufficiency of food" that was leading to a frequency of absentees.[6]

The Federals and environmental concerns also played roles. Early in the war, Federal commander-in-chief Winfield Scott proposed the Anaconda Plan, a strategy of blockading seaports, retaking the Mississippi River, and then driving inland. Slowly each port was captured, the most important for the ANV being Wilmington in January 1865. This deprived the Confederacy of imported foodstuffs and other supplies. The Federals were quick to capture central and western Tennessee in early 1862, seizing important pork- and corn-production areas. In September 1863, east Tennessee, with the all-important links to the Deep South, and the East Tennessee & Georgia and East Tennessee & Virginia railroads, fell to the Federals. Now, foodstuffs coming from the Deep South had to take longer routes through North Carolina.

---

5 Burnett, "Letters of a Confederate Surgeon, McGarity," 1:98; Dayton, *The Diary of a Confederate Soldier*, 72; Lee, *Memoirs of William Nelson Pendleton*, 354; Blackford & Blackford, *Letters from Lee's Army*, 272; Hess, *In the Trenches at Petersburg*, 219; Henry, *Pen in Hand*, 133.

6 *OR* 5, 789, 790; 21, 1016; Dowdey & Manarin, *The Wartime Papers of R. E. Lee*, 660, 887.

In 1864, the Federals launched new campaigns that captured and despoiled much of Georgia, South Carolina, and North Carolina. Coupled with the loss of the Shenandoah Valley, little remained for soldiers fighting in the trenches at Petersburg. The environment also affected farmers with droughts, floods, and diseases such as wheat rust and hog cholera. Transportation woes, such as worn-out trains and tracks, along with roads once maintained by the men, contributed to problems of getting foodstuffs to the troops. This all took its toll, and in the last four months of the war, January–April 1865, the ANV lost 25,000 men to desertion.[7]

The post-war writings of Confederate soldiers tended to coincide with their war-time letters and diaries. Gordon Bradwell served in the 31st Georgia Infantry. In the 1910s and 1920s, he wrote a series of articles for *Confederate Veteran* magazine, mentioning foodstuffs, messmates, foraging parties, and prison food. In 1923, Bradwell wrote an entire article, "Cooking in the Army," detailing unpreparedness for camp chores, the organization of messes, issues of cooking utensils, and soldiers making poor cooks. Bradwell stated that during the war he often only ate one meal a day, and later in life continued that practice. His other articles describe a company member robbing a citizen after crossing over into Pennsylvania, an attempted raid to capture Federal foodstuffs during the post-Gettysburg lull, and guarding a family during the 1864 Shenandoah Valley campaign. Bradwell returned to the Petersburg front and slim rations. One day, he saved his rations for the following day so he could have "a double supply," but some person, or a rat, absconded with his small stockpile. His descriptions of rations "reduced that we could hardly exist on them," and of men in good health, despite being "weak from lack of food," echo war-time letters.[8]

Old soldiers wrote articles for newspapers and journals and published their memoirs in book form. Many commented on the food, often remembering the highlights, such as the capture of the Federal stores at Harpers Ferry or the desperate winters of thin rations. In 1914, William A. Smith published a history of his regiment, the 14th North Carolina State Troops. Following the surrender at Appomattox, the soldiers began their walk home. At various forks in the road, there were partings that Smith found "sad." His comrades had "all things in common for four long years," including "common thirst, hunger . . . common cush, flapjacks and mess tables . . . [and] a common Lost Cause." Foodstuffs during the war

7 Horn, *The Petersburg Campaign*, 220.

8 Bradwell's post-war writings were collected and published in Pharris Johnson, ed., *Under the Southern Cross: Soldier Life with Gordon Bradwell and the Army of Northern Virginia* (Macon, GA, 1999), 27–32, 121, 213, 230.

changed the Southern soldier boys. Many were exposed to new foods, such as barbecue, gumbo, rice, and even captured canned foods.[9]

For armies, food is often considered an essential supply item. Rations keep the troops going, willing to endure the trials of combat and the drudgery of everyday camp life. While many factors contributed to the demise of the ANV, foodstuffs rank near the top. The Federal army's ability to capture or destroy farmland limited the growth of new crops. Also, the demise of the railroad system in the South, from Federal raids and the inability to replace failing rails and rolling stock, hampered transportation of goods. The slow capture of Southern ports also strangled the ability to import items. All of these deprived the army in Virginia of food. Poor rations led to sickness and, at times, death. During campaigns, straggling robbed army commanders of essential troops. The lack of rations, especially during the winter when soldiers had abundant time on their hands, led to low morale. Thousands of hungry soldiers simply walked away from the war, heading back home or into Federal lines. The tens of thousands of deserters, caused by a lack of essential supplies, deprived the Confederate armies of the ability to win engagements or to exploit victories.

While far less glamorous than glinting bayonets, glorious cavalry charges, or spectacular cannonades, the humble skillet of the hungry private, whether greasy with bacon or mercilessly bare, was, in many ways, the crucible of the ANV. Here lies the center of their struggle and tragedy, at the campfires of hungry men. In the end, it mattered far less if they were patriotic to a cause or passionate about victory when their bellies were empty. The Confederacy may have fueled the spirit of the ANV, but it could not always feed the men who made up that army, and that may have made all the difference.

9 W. A. Smith, *The Anson Guards* (Charlotte, NC, 1914), 308.

Appendix 1

The Confederate Commissaries of Subsistence

A man serving as a Confederate commissary of subsistence performed a thankless task. These men were responsible for seeing that those commands to which they were assigned received the proscribed rations. When the army was on the move, the commissaries moved as well, attempting to distribute foodstuffs to an army in motion. There were 207 Confederate generals who served in the Army of the Potomac, later re-christened the Army of Northern Virginia. Some generals were there for a short amount of time, like Earl Van Dorn and E. Kirby Smith. Others, like James Longstreet and Richard Ewell, served the entire four years of the war connected with the Virginia armies. Although Longstreet was in Georgia and Tennessee from September 1863 to April 1864, his troops were still identified with the Army of Northern Virginia.

Every one of these commanders had at least one assistant commissary of subsistence or commissary of subsistence under his command. The assistant commissaries of subsistence all bore the rank of captain and served on the brigade level, while the commissaries of subsistence positioned at division and corps level were commissioned as majors. Many of the men who filled the position as staff officers to various generals in the commissary department had pre-war business experience that certainly would have been helpful in their management of foodstuffs. Henry H. Miller, who served as commissary of subsistence to Thomas Clingman, Stephen D. Ramseur, and William R. Cox, was a clerk at an express company prior to the war. Thomas B. Hutchison, serving as commissary of subsistence under Eppa Hunton, was a pre-war merchant in Fauquier County, Virginia. Francis T. Forbes, a pre-war merchant in Spotsylvania County, served on the staff of Richard Ewell. While turnover was frequent the first year of the war, many generals found commissaries who stuck with the job for longer than two years. Jubal Early had William W. Thorton; A. P. Hill used his brother Edward as commissary from May 1, 1862, through the end of the war; William J. Johnston served in the role on the staff of J. E. B. Stuart from July 17, 1862, until Stuart's death, and then he occupied the same role on the staff of Wade Hampton through the end of the war.[1]

There were hundreds of men who served in the role of commissary within the ANV. They all reported to the chief commissary of the army. General P. G. T. Beauregard, commanding forces in Northern Virginia in 1861, had several commissaries on his staff. They included Richard B. Lee, Jr., as commissary of subsistence and William H. Fowle as assistant. Lee was a graduate of the United States Military Academy and a veteran of the Seminole Indian Wars. Fowle was a graduate of Harvard University and a commission merchant prior to the war. Lee and Fowle worked hard on buying foodstuffs in Northern Virginia for the army. Confederate Commissary General Lucius Northrop wanted the food for the army to come from Richmond, while his agents bought foodstuffs in the area, shipping them back to Richmond for distribution. The verbal sparring between Joseph E. Johnston, Jefferson Davis, and Northrop following the battle of Manassas in July 1861 led to the removal of Lee and Fowle.[2]

They were replaced by William B. Blair as Chief Commissary of the Army. Blair was in the same graduating class with General Beauregard at the United States Military Academy. Breveted for gallantry during the Mexican War, Blair served as a commissary in the old army in Texas. After resigning his commission, he was appointed commissary of general subsistence in the provisional Army of Virginia by Governor Letcher, at the rank of major. On May 31, Blair was ordered to turn over his Virginia Bureau of Subsistence to then-Lt. Col. Lucius B. Northrop. On August 23, 1861, Blair was announced as the Chief Commissary of the Army of Northern Virginia.[3]

Blair stepped in and immediately made improvements. All requisitions for foodstuffs had to be processed through his office. The rations that arrived were then divided up equally and issued to the brigade commissaries. Captain Burr P. Noland was a commissary officer serving as a cattle agent in Northern Virginia. Blair and

---

1 Krick, *Staff Officers in Gray*, 130, 159, 168, 172, 221, 287.

2 Goff, *Confederate Supply*, 21.

3 Louisa Blair, *Blairs of Richmond, Virginia* (Richmond: William Byrd Press, 1933), 111; *OR* 51, pt. 2, 121; Dunbar Rowland, ed., *Jefferson Davis, Constitutionalist: His Letters, Papers, and Speeches* (Jackson, MS, 1923), 7:490.

Noland worked well together. At Northrop's suggestion, Noland proposed a meat processing plant at Thoroughfare Gap in October 1861. While having access to fresh meat so close by was a boon, Joseph E. Johnston, commanding all Confederate forces in the area, was not consulted in the matter. The discord between Johnston and Davis continued to grow.[4]

Due to ill health, Blair was relieved of command on December 9. Temporarily filling the role was Capt. George W. T. Kearsley, Johnston's assistant commissary of subsistence. The permanent replacement was Robert G. Cole. Born in Virginia in 1830, Cole grew up near Palatka, Florida. Based on the recommendation of David Yulee, he was appointed to the United States Military Academy, graduating in 1850. Robert Ransom, Jr., Gouverneur K. Warren, and Charles S. Winder were some of his classmates who were promoted to serve as generals during the war. Cole was stationed in New York and Texas before resigning his commission. On March 16, 1861, he was commissioned a captain of infantry in the Confederate army, assigned to recruiting duty in Augusta, Georgia. In June 1861, Cole was assigned to the brigade of Robert S. Garnett. This assignment was followed with a promotion to major in the Provisional Army of the Confederate States, serving as Garnett's commissary of subsistence. Cole assumed his new responsibility as chief commissary of the army on December 24, 1861, with a promotion to the rank of lieutenant colonel.[5]

Over the next three years, Cole's name sporadically pops up in the surviving records or correspondence with officers like Lee. The commissary department was dragged into the debate regarding the loss of commissary supplies when Johnston abandoned Northern Virginia in March 1862. Cole was able to send forty-five boxcars full of meat away from the Thoroughfare Gap processing plant prior to the evacuation. The lack of additional boxcars led to much of the meat being left behind. Noland was able to transport some via wagon to Warrenton, and some was given to local families before the remainder was torched.[6]

Following the Seven Days battle, thousands of Federal wounded fell into the hands of the Confederates. Lee ordered his medical director, Lafayette Guild, to inform Cole on just how many wounded prisoners needed to be fed, as well as where they were located. In December 1862, Cole was instructed to issue extra rations to the men in anticipation of the move from the Shenandoah Valley to Fredericksburg. Northrop wrote Cole in January 1863 informing him of railroad

4 Moore, *Confederate Commissary General*, 111, 120; Joseph E. Johnston, *Narrative of Military Operations* (New York, NY, 1874), 99.

5 Robert G. Cole, CMSR, M331, Roll 0059, RG109; Krick, *Staff Officers in Gray*, 193.

6 *OR Series* 4, 1, 1,039.

Robert E. Lee and his staff. Chief Commissary of the Army Robert G. Cole is number 2, to the left of Lee. *Miller's Photographic History of the Civil War*

delays in shipping beef from Tennessee. He also asked Cole to help generals to send boxcars back to Richmond, instead of keeping the "cars unemployed to meet expected removal of troops." Cole issued his own circular in December 1863. Division commanders, following a battle, were to send an assistant commissary for temporary duty at various field hospitals. Food for the sick and wounded was to come from the division supply trains. In February 1865, when the men had been without rations for three days, Lee sent Cole "to visit Richmond and see if nothing can be done."[7]

On at least two occasions during the war, Lee mentioned Cole in his official reports. At Fredericksburg, Cole, and the other officers of the general staff, "were always in the field, anticipating, as far as possible, the wants of the troops." Lee repeated the praise for Cole and the others following Chancellorsville as well. When Northrop was forced to resign as commissary general, three Confederate congressmen wrote to the secretary of war recommending Cole as Northrop's replacement. The position went to Isaac M. St. John. Cole was one of the officers who followed Lee all the way to Appomattox, where he received his parole.[8]

No post-war correspondence between Lee and these men seems to have survived. However, when Lee took his post-war trip to improve his health and visit the grave of his father on Cumberland Island, he visited Cole. "We spent a night at Col. Cole's, a beautiful place near Palatka and ate oranges from his trees," Lee wrote to Mary back in Lexington, Virginia. Lee also discussed with Cole and others the need to help financially support Samuel Cooper.[9]

Slowly the old commissaries passed into the pages of an incomplete history. Richard B. Lee, Jr., went on to serve with Albert S. Johnston and Beauregard. He passed away in Alexandria, Virginia, in August 1876. William H. Fowle, Sr., did not return to the service and passed away in Alexandria, Virginia, in October 1869. William B. Blair became the chief commissary in the Trans-Mississippi Department, then taught at the Virginia Military Institute after the war, dying in 1883. George W. T. Kearsley served as commissary at Hanover Junction and Gordonsville before being assigned as commissary to James Dearing's brigade in December 1864. After the war, he resumed his dry goods business. He passed in 1901 and is buried in Charlestown, West Virginia. Robert G. Cole lived in Florida for many years but later moved to Savannah, Georgia, where he died in 1887. Cole was remembered in his obituary as being on the staff of Lee during the war, serving "with signal ability."[10]

---

7 *OR* Series 2, 4, 798; *OR* 21, 1,046; *OR* 51, pt. 2, 675; *OR* Series 4, 3, 612; Long, *Memoirs of Robert E. Lee*, 578. There are scattered other references to Cole in the Frank G. Ruffin Papers, Virginia Historical Society.

8 *OR* 21, 556; *OR* 25, pt. 1, 805; Cole, CMSR.

9 Lee, *Recollections and Letters*, 398, 421.

10 Krick, *Staff Officers in Gray*, 75, 100, 132, 192, 199–200; *Huntsville Gazette*, Nov. 19, 1887.

Transporting the Needs of the Army: The Role of the Wagon

Wagons were the primary conveyance of the nineteenth century. Goods were transported from farmers' fields to markets or depots, stock was brought from a warehouse to merchants' stores, and families were loaded up for a ride to church, all in wagons. Many towns and cities had their own wagon works, which were responsible for manufacturing and repairing wagons. These facilities produced Conestoga wagons for transporting people across the country, as well as farm wagons, buggies, and coaches.

While the Confederate government contracted with some existing wagon makers, like the Lynchburg Coach and Wagon Factory in Lynchburg, operated by John H. Bailey, the Confederacy also established its own wagon works at various sites in Virginia. Some of these included facilities in Farmville, Staunton, Richmond, Danville, and Petersburg. The facilities were responsible for manufacturing and repairing wagons and ambulances. Major Robert P. Archer was placed in charge of the shop near Richmond, located in Bacon's Quarter Branch. Archer employed almost 200 Black and 55 White employees, working from 4:30 a.m. to 8:00 p.m. every day. Much of his workforce was highly skilled—wheelwrights, farriers, carpenters, blacksmiths, and harness makers. Some of the Black workforce was enslaved. Henry, a harness maker owned by John M. Gregrory, was hired at $1,200 annually. There were four enslaved blacksmiths hired annually at the same price, while additional skilled, enslaved blacksmiths were hired at $1,000 a year. The Confederate States Ambulance Works, also in Richmond, was supervised by Capt.

R. C. MacMurdo; 32 White and 23 Black men worked on constructing and repairing ambulances. Eleven of the Black workers were freemen.[1]

Confiscated Federal wagons were also used to transport essential Confederate supplies. One soldier noted that as Lee's army moved into Maryland in 1862, one-third of all wagons in the Confederate army were still marked as "U.S." The importance of a steady supply of wagons and craftsmen needed to produce them can be seen in the Confederacy's priority placed upon all those involved in the creation of wagons. Wagon makers were exempt from conscription, and those with special skills were often detailed from their regiments to work at the government wagon shops.[2]

Early in the war, each company had its own baggage wagon, plus four ambulances and an extra wagon for hospital stores, along with ordnance wagons. The regimental wagon trains were under the command of the regimental quartermaster and, when moving within a larger group, under the brigade or division quartermaster. Men from each regiment were detailed as guards both on the march and when in camp. A Georgia private noted in February 1862 that the detail consisted of merely two men from each company. In February 1865, an Alabama soldier noted he was detailed with six other men to guard four wagons loaded with the baggage of officers, cooking utensils, and forage. Some soldiers called their conveyances "spider wagons," as hauling the cooking equipment, including the useful "spider," was one of the primary tasks of the wagons. Frequently, the men had nothing to cook with as the wagons lagged far behind the men on campaign.[3]

In April 1863 came the first order to reduce the size of the wagon train that accompanied each regiment to thirty-four wagons per 1,000 men. The dearth of available wagons, horses, mules, and forage necessitated the reduction. Other reductions came on June 12 and July 16, the latter to twenty-four wagons per 1,000 men. That same year, a weight limit of 1,800 pounds per wagon was stipulated.[4]

Peter Wellington Alexander, a correspondent for several war-time Southern newspapers, provides several important observations regarding wagons

---

1 Brewer, *The Confederate Negro*, 21–22, 27. The Confederate infantry private was only paid $11 per month until June 1864, when the pay was raised to $13 per month.

2 Glatthaar, *General Lee's Army*, 183.

3 *Regulations of the Confederate Army*, 76, 281; Allen and Bohannon, eds, *Campaigning with 'Old Stonewall,'* 74; Hubbs, *Voices from Company D*, 356; Parks, "Diary of Capt. R. E. Park," *SHSP* 26:18.

4 *Regulations of the Confederate Army*, 76, 281; Edward Hagerman, *The American Civil War and the Origins of Modern Warfare* (Bloomington, IN, 1988), 128–129. Just what the standard was prior to April 1863 is unclear. Ibid., n6, 319.

early in the war. Writing in December 1861, he had this to say about the Quartermaster's Department:

> It is the duty of this department to provide transportation, fuel and quarters for the men, and forage for the teams and staff and cavalry horses. The rules adopted in the Army of the Potomac [later Army of Northern Virginia]—and the same is true, I presume, elsewhere—had been to impress all the transportation and forage in the counties adjacent to Manassas. Where the owners were willing to part with their teams or provender, they received pay for them; otherwise, they were seized and the owners turned over to the government for remuneration. There cannot be fewer than 1,500 to 2,000 wagons, and six to 8,000 horses, in the service of the Quarter-Master's department for that division of the army. . . . At first drivers were impressed with the wagons. Now, they are detailed from the ranks, of the army—young men who have no experience in driving and who complained that they did not enlist to drive wagons. They were required to alternate, and thus every day or two there was a new driver, who was ignorant both of the ability and disposition of the horses, and who soon teaches them bad habits.[5]

Many of the drivers (teamsters) for these wagons came from the ranks. In the ranks of the 39th Battalion Virginia Cavalry, there were fourteen men who served as teamsters. The average age was 36. The youngest teamster was fourteen, and the oldest was forty. One of those men, Anthony S. Butts, was conscripted into the Confederate army and was assigned to ANV headquarters staff. For the rest of the war, right up until Robert E. Lee arrived in Richmond on April 15, 1865, Butts was driving Lee's personal ambulance. In some cases, freemen who voluntarily enlisted in the Confederate army were assigned roles as teamsters. William Henry Cozzens and his brother Franklin enlisted in the 37th North Carolina in September 1861. After Franklin was killed fighting at Second Manassas, William drove a wagon until he was captured on April 2, 1865, and confined at Point Lookout. He took the Oath of Allegiance on June 10, 1865. At other times, those not physically well enough to undergo the rigors of combat could be detailed to serve as teamsters. Corporal Horatio Atham, 10th Virginia Cavalry, spent time sick in the hospital with "gonorrhoea" in 1864, about the same time that he was detailed to serve as a teamster. Soldiers were detailed to drive a wide range of wagons: those supplying the commissary department, the ordnance trains, even those needed for "the infirmary camp."[6]

5 William B. Styple, ed., *Writing and Fighting the Confederate War: The Letters of Peter Wellington Alexander* (Kearny, N.J., 2002), 59.

6 Michael C. Hardy, *Lee's Body Guards: The 39th Battalion Virginia Cavalry* (Charleston, SC, 2019), 25, 85. The Cozzens brothers had quite an adventure. The name is also spelled Cousins. See Michael

Hired enslaved and freed Black men impressed into service served as teamsters as well. In 1864, there was an attempt to get many of the men who had been detailed to serve as teamsters sent back into the ranks. Marion Hill Fitzpatrick wrote in November 1864 that "Jeff Davis recommends the calling out of Forty Thousand able bodied negroes [for teamsters]." Some regiments did have Black teamsters. The 30th Virginia Infantry had six. The members of the 1st Maine Cavalry in late 1864 captured ten Confederate wagons loaded with provisions, along with their "drivers (all colored men)." When Martin Gary's brigade was paroled at Appomattox, the report of persons hired by the quartermaster's department attached to the brigade included six Black teamsters, four of whom were free and two enslaved. James Brewer estimated that while exact numbers will never be known, the army in Virginia alone employed thousands.[7]

Being a teamster could be dangerous work. Enemy cavalry was constantly on the lookout for the lightly defended wagon trains. The capture of such trains carrying foodstuffs, ordnance supplies, wounded soldiers or officers, or fodder could hamper military operations, while at the same time, providing supplies, including foodstuffs, to the Confederates. One Tar Heel wrote of capturing Winchester in June 1863. The Confederates "took all of there [sic] wagons and them loaded with commissaries such as shoes, boots, hats, pants, shirts drawers, bacon, shugar, coffe, beans, dride fruit and several other things too tedious to mention." Probably the most famous capture of wagons came in July 1863 when J. E. B. Stuart captured over a hundred Federal wagons while on the Gettysburg campaign. If a teamster was captured, he could expect to receive prison time. Both teamsters John C. Carpenter and William A. Monroe, 47th Virginia Infantry, were captured at Greencastle while driving wagons in the division commissary train, near Gettysburg on July 5, 1863. Both were imprisoned at Point Lookout. Carpenter survived the war, while Monroe died a prisoner.[8]

Not every teamster was honest. The *Richmond Enquirer* reported in August 1862 that a soldier from North Carolina, Abner B. Perry, who was driving the commissary wagon for the North Carolina Hospital in Petersburg, had been arrested for stealing from the wagon. Administrators at the hospital had noticed

---

C. Hardy, *Watauga County, North Carolina, and the Civil War* (Charleston, SC, 2013) 15, 17, 80; Robert J. Driver, *Tenth Virginia Cavalry* (Lynchburg, VA, 1992) 88, 161.

7 *SHSP*, 14:487; McCrea, *Red Dirt and Isinglass*, 528; Tim Talbott, "Behind the Scenes at Pamplin: Food on the Move," https://www.progress-index.com/story/opinion/columns/2018/07/30/behind-scenes-at-pamplin-food/11204269007/; Brewer, *The Confederate Negro*, 29.

8 Henry, *Pen in Hand*, 91–92; Homer D. Musselman, *47th Virginia Infantry* (Lynchburg, VA, 1991), 110, 143.

Confederate wagons transporting wounded following the battle of Gettysburg. *Battles and Leaders*

that rations were coming up short, and a local police officer began observing Perry. As he neared a stable, Perry stopped his wagon and took "a side of bacon and considerable quantity of sugar and soap, concealing them within." Perry, a member of the 32nd North Carolina Troops, was tried on October 18, 1862, and sentenced to a couple of months of hard labor. He rejoined his company in January or February 1863 but deserted in June that year.[9]

There was both occasional jests and some animosity between those soldiers in the ranks and those serving as teamsters and waggoneers. Joshua Lupton, 39th Battalion Virginia Cavalry, was detailed to serve as the wagon master for ANV Headquarters staff. His brother John thought Joshua's assignment was an easy one. All he had to do was "issue forage to General Lee's horses twice a day." Undoubtedly, there was some resentment over this "easy assignment." At Appomattox, when the time came to surrender, those men who had been detailed as teamsters were sent back to their regiments to march in the proceedings. Brigadier General James H. Lane felt that these men should all be placed in a group together. "I did not wish to

9 *Richmond Enquirer*, Aug. 1, 1862.

surrender any but those brave fellows who had followed us under arms," he wrote after the war.[10]

As the armies disbanded and the men returned to their homes, there was a surplus of wagons to be disposed of. In July 1865, the U.S. Quartermaster Depot in Richmond advertised that they were selling wagons and condemned subsistence stores at auction. A major auction took place in Norfolk in December 1865. For sale were army wagons, lumber wagons, ambulances, carts, wagon saddles, various harnesses, and other items connected to military conveyances. That same month in Farmville, the office of the Freeman's Bureau sold at auction the building used as the Confederate wagon shop. At the same time, they disposed of 400 sets of wagon wheels, "400 parts Wagon Wheels, 1 lot of unfinished wagon bodies and other material." Many of these old wagons undoubtedly wound up on some former Confederate's farm, providing years of service.[11]

Although they may not have been glamorous, the wagons that transported the necessary equipage of the Confederate soldier, and especially those that brought him his food and the tools used to prepare it, were essential.

10 Hardy, *Lee's Body Guard*, 25; *Fayetteville Observer*, June 8, 1897.

11 *Richmond Dispatch*, June 19, 1865; *Norfolk Post*, Dec. 16, 1865; *Daily Express*, Dec. 5, 1865.

Bibliography

Primary Sources

Unpublished Manuscript Collections
Duke University, Durham, NC
    Cooke, J. E. Diary
    Davis, Jefferson. Papers
    Mahone, William. Papers
    Porter, John Richardson. Letter Book and Diaries
Georgia Division of Archives and History, Atlanta, GA
    UDC Transcript, Vol. 4
Library of Virginia, Richmond, VA
    Walter, F. G. Diary
Library of Congress, Washington, D.C.
    Lee, Robert E. Papers
Madison-Mayodan Public Library
    Joyce, John William "A Collection of Confederate Letters"
Museum of the Confederacy, Richmond, VA
    Supplies and Order Book, General Hospital No. 2, Lynchburg, VA.
National Archives, Washington, D.C.
    Chimborazo Records, 138 Volumes, Chapter 6, Record Group 109
North Carolina State Archives, Raleigh, NC
    Collins, Noah. Papers
    Cowles, Calvin J. Papers, 1773–1941.
Petersburg National Battlefield, Petersburg, VA
    Morgan, Timothy. Papers
South Carolina State Library, Columbia, SC
    Elmore, Grace. Diary
Southern Historical Collection, University of North Carolina-Chapel Hill, NC
    Basinger, William Starr. Papers
    Davis, Rebecca Pitchford. Letters
    Jones, Edmund Walter. Papers
    Leach, Calvin. Diary and Letters, 1861–1867
    Lineback, Julius. Papers

Morris, William G. Letters

Todd, Westwood A. Reminiscences of the Civil War

Walkup, S.H. Papers, 1858–1876

Webb Family Papers

Whitehorne, J. E. Diary

University of North Carolina, Charlotte, NC

    Gibbon Family Correspondence

University of South Carolina, Columbia, SC

    Amick, James Joshua. Papers

University of Georgia, Athens, GA

    Duggan, Ivy W. Diary

Virginia Historical Society, Richmond, VA

    Robertson Family Papers

    Washington, John A. Papers

Virginia Military Institute, Lexington, VA

    Dedrick, Henry. Civil War Letters

    McCoy, Andrew J. Civil War Letters, 1863–1864

William and Mary College, Williamsburg, VA

    Myers Papers

Published: Books

Alexander, E. P. "Longstreet at Knoxville." In *Battles & Leaders of the Civil War.* Edited by Robert Johnson & Clarence Buel. New York: The Century Company, 1888.

_____ *Military Memoirs of a Confederate; A Critical Narrative.* New York: C. Scribner's Sons, 1907.

Allan, Elizabeth P., ed. *The Life and Letters of Margaret Junkin Preston.* Boston: Houghton, Mifflin, and Company, 1903.

Allen, Randale & Keith S. Bohannon, eds. *Campaigning with "Old Stonewall": Confederate Captain Ujanirtus Allen's Letters to His Wife.* Baton Rouge: Louisiana State University Press, 1998.

Aycock, Robert & Elsie J., eds. *The Civil War Letters of W. D. Carr of Duplin County, North Carolina.* [n.p., n.d.]

Barrett, John G., ed. *Yankee Rebel: The Civil War Journal of Edmund DeWitt Patterson.* Knoxville: The University of Tennessee Press, 2004.

Battle, Laura E., ed. *Forget-me-nots of the Civil War; A Romance, Containing Reminiscences and Original Letters of Two Confederate Soldiers.* St. Louis: Press A. R. Fleming Print Co., 1909.

Beale, R. L. T. *History of the 9th Virginia Cavalry in the Civil War.* Richmond: B. F. Johnson Publishing Company, 1899.

Benson, Susan W., ed. *Berry Benson's Civil War Book: Memoirs of a Confederate Scout and Sharpshooter.* Athens: The University of Georgia Press, 1992.

Berlin, Jean V., ed. *A Confederate Nurse: The Diary of Ada W. Bacot, 1860–1863.* Columbia: The University of South Carolina Press, 1994.

Blackford, Susan Leigh & Charles M. *Letters from Lee's Army.* Lincoln: University of Nebraska Press, 1998.

Blackford, W. W. *War Years with JEB Stuart.* New York: Charles Scribner's Sons, 1946.

Borcke, Heros von. *Memoirs of the Confederate War for Independence.* New York: P. Smith, 1938.

Brinsfield Jr., John W., ed. *The Spirit Divided: Memoirs of Civil War Chaplains.* Macon, GA: Mercer University Press, 2005.

Buckley, Cornelius M., ed. *A Frenchman, A Chaplain, A Rebel: The War Letters of Pere Louis-Hippolyte Gache, S.J.* Chicago: Loyola University Press, 1981.

Caldwell, J. F. J. *The History of a Brigade of South Carolinians First Known as Gregg's and Subsequently as McGowan's Brigade.* Philadelphia: King & Baird Printers, 1866.

Carroll, Sarah P., ed. *Lifeline to Home for John William McClure, CSA, Union County, S.C.* Greenville, SC: A Press, 1990.

Carter, John C., ed. *Welcome the Hour of Conflict: William Cowan McClellan and the 9th Alabama.* Tuscaloosa: The University of Alabama Press, 2007.

Casler, John, ed. *Four Years in the Stonewall Brigade.* Columbia: University of South Carolina Press, 2005.

Chamberlayne, C. G., ed. *Ham Chamberlayne—Virginia.* Richmond: Press of the Bietz Printing Co., 1932.

Chapman, Sarah B., ed., *Bright and Gloomy Days: The Civil War Correspondence of Captain Charles Frederick Bahnson, A Moravian Confederate.* Knoxville: The University of Tennessee Press, 2003.

Chisolm, J. Julian. *A Manual of Military Surgery for the Use of Surgeons in the Confederate Army* Richmond, VA, 1861.

Clark, Walter, ed. *Histories of the Several Regiments and Battalions from North Carolina in the Great War 1861–'65.* 5 Vols. Raleigh: E. M. Uzzell, Printer & Binder, 1901.

Cockrell, Monroe F., ed. *Gunner with Stonewall: Reminiscences of William Thomas Poage.* Wilmington: Broadfoot Publishing Company, 1987.

Corbin, Richard W. *Letters of a Confederate Officer to his Family in Europe During the Last Year of the War of Secession.* New York: William Abbatt, 1913.

Corson Jr., Blake W., ed., *My Dear Jennie.* Richmond, VA, 1982.

Crabtree, Beth, & James Patton, eds. *Journal of a Secesh Lady: The Diary of Catherine Ann Devereux Edmondston, 1860–1866.* Raleigh: North Carolina Office of Archives & History, 1999.

Crist, Lynda, Mary Dix, Kenneth Williams, & Grady McWhiney, eds. *The Papers of Jefferson Davis.* Vol. 8. Baton Rouge: Louisiana State University Press, 1995.

Cuter, Thomas W., ed. *Longstreet's Aide: The Civil War Letters of Major Thomas J. Goree.* Charlottesville: University Press of Virginia, 1995.

Day, W. A. *A True History of Company I, 49th North Carolina Troops.* Newton, NC: Enterprise Job Office, 1893.

Dayton, Ruth W., ed. *The Diary of a Confederate Soldier.* 1961.

Dickert, D. Augustus. *History of Kershaw's Brigade.* Wilmington: Broadfoot Publishing Company, 1990.

Douglas, Henry K. *I Rode with Stonewall.* Chapel Hill: The University of North Carolina Press, 1940.

Dowdey, Clifford & Louis H. Manarin, eds. *The Wartime Papers of R. E. Lee.* New York: Bramwell House, 1961.

Dunaway, Wayland. *Reminiscences of a Rebel.* New York: The Neale Publishing Co., 1913.

Emmons, Louisa, ed. *Tales from a Civil War Plantation: Creekside.* Hollow Tree Press, 2014.

Everson, Guy R. & Edward W. Simpson Jr., ed. *Far, Far from Home: The Wartime Letters of Dick and Tally Simpson, 3rd South Carolina Volunteers.* New York: Oxford University Press, 1994.

Foley, Bradley R., ed. *Letters Home: The Civil War Correspondence of Lieutenant Colonel Alexander C. McAlister, 46th North Carolina Regiment.* CreateSpace, 2013.

Freemantle, Arthur. *Three Months in the Southern States: April, June 1863.* Mobile: S. H. Goetzel, 1864.

Frontis, Ellen F., ed. *Letters Home to Baughn Mountain.* n.p.: E. F. Frontis, 1979.

Gallagher, Gary W., ed. *Extracts of Letters of Major General Bryan Grimes to his Wife.* Wilmington, NC: Broadfoot Publishing Company, 1986.

_____ *Fighting for the Confederacy: The Personal Recollections of General Edward Porter Alexander.* Chapel Hill: The University Press of North Carolina, 1989.

Hamilton, J. G. de Roulhac, ed. *The Correspondence of Jonathan Worth.* 2 Vols. Raleigh: Edwards & Broughton Printing Company, 1909.

Hancock, M. A., ed. *Four Brothers in Gray.* Sparta, NC: Imaging Specialists, 2013.

Haskell, C. L. *John Bachman, the Pastor of St. John's Lutheran Church, Charleston.* Walker, Evans, & Cogswell Co., 1888.

Hassler, William W., ed. *One of Lee's Best Men: The Civil War Letters of General William Dorsey Pender.* Chapel Hill: The University of North Carolina Press, 1990.

Hatley, Joe M. & Linda B. Huffman, eds. *Letters of William F. Wagner: Confederate Soldier.* Wendell, NC: Broadfoot's Bookmark, 1983.

Henry, Riley, ed. *Pen in Hand: David Parker Civil War Letters.* Morgan Hills, CA: Bookstand Publishing, 2014.

Hickerson, Thomas F. *Echoes of Happy Valley.* Chapel Hill, NC: privately printed, 1962.

Houck, Peter W. *Chapter VI, Vol 416, Medical Department, Confederate Army Records Letters Sent and Received, Medical Director's Office Richmond, VA.* Lynchburg: Warwick House, 1991.

Hubbs, G. Ward., ed. *Voices from Company D: Diaries by the Greensboro Guards, Fifth Alabama Infantry Regiment, Army of Northern Virginia.* Athens: The University of Georgia Press, 2003.

Jessup, Harland R., ed. *The Painful News I Have to Write: Letters and Diaries of Four Hite Brothers of Page County in the Service of the Confederacy.* Baltimore: Butternut & Blue, 1998.

Johnson, Pharris, ed. *Under the Southern Cross: Soldier Life with Gordon Bradwell and the Army of Northern Virginia.* Macon: Mercer University Press, 1999.

Johnston, Joseph E. *Narrative of Military Operations.* New York, NY: D. Appleton and Company, 1874.

Jones, Austin. *The Capture of Harpers Ferry.* n.p., 1922.

Jones, Constance, ed. *The Spirits of Bad Men Made Perfect: The Life and Diary of Confederate Artillerist William Ellis Jones.* Carbondale: Southern Illinois University Press, 2020.

Jones, J. William. *Life and Letters of Robert Edward Lee: Soldier and Man.* New York: The Neal Publishing Company, 1906.

_____ *Personal Reminiscences of General Robert E. Lee.* New York: D. Appleton & Co., 1875.

Jones, J. Keith, ed. *The Boys of Diamond Hill: The Lives and Civil War Letters of the Boyd Family of Abbeville County, South Carolina.* Jefferson: McFarland & Company, 2011.

Jones, Terry L., ed. *Campbell Brown's Civil War: With Ewell and the Army of Northern Virginia.* Baton Rouge: Louisiana State University Press, 2001.

Koonce, Donald B., ed. *Doctor to the Front: The Recollections of Confederate Surgeon Thomas Fanning Wood, 1861-1865.* Knoxville: The University of Tennessee Press, 2000.

Kennedy, Joseph. *Agriculture of the United States in 1860.* Washington: Government Printing Office, 1864.

Kundahl, George G., ed. *The Bravest of the Brave: The Correspondence of Stephen Dodson Ramseur.* Chapel Hill: The University of North Carolina Press, 2010.

Lee Jr., Robert E., *The Recollections and Letters of Robert E. Lee.* New York: Doubleday, Page, & Company, 1904.

Lee, Susan, ed. *Memoirs of William Nelson Pendleton, D. D.* Harrisonburg, VA: Sprinkle Publications, 1991.

Leon, L. *Diary of A Tar Heel Confederate Soldier.* Charlotte, NC: Stone Publishing Company, 1913.

Lohr, Lawrence, ed. *The Mauney Brothers' Civil War: Andrew, Peter, and Jacob.* Kings Mountain, NC: Kings Mountain Historical Museum, 2013.

Long, A. L. *Memoirs of Robert E. Lee.* New York: J. M. Stoddart & Company, 1886.

Lee, William Mack. *History of the Life of Rev. Wm. Mack Lee.* Norfolk: The Smith Printing Company, 1918.

Longstreet, James. *From Manassas to Appomattox: Memoirs of the Civil War in America.* Philadelphia: J. B. Lippincott Company, 1896.

Maurice, Frederick, ed. *An Aide-de-Camp of Lee.* Boston: Little, Brown, & Company, 1927.

McCarthy, Carlton *Detailed Minutiae of Soldier Life in the Army of Northern Virginia, 1861–1865.* Lincoln: University of Nebraska Press, 1993.

McCrea, Henry, ed. *Red Dirt and Isinglass: A Wartime Biography of a Confederate Soldier.* n. p., 1992.

McDonald, Archie P., ed. *Make Me a Map of the Valley: The Civil War Journal of Stonewall Jackson's Topographer.* Dallas: Southern Methodist University Press, 1973.

McKim, Randolph H. *A Soldier's Recollections: Leaves from the Diary of a Young Confederate.* New York: Longmans, Green & Co., 1910.

McMullen, Glenn L., ed. *The Civil War Letters of Dr. Harvey Black.* Baltimore, MD: Butternut & Blue, 1995.

Miers, Earl, ed. *A Rebel War Clerk's Diary.* New York: Sagamore Press, Inc., 1958.

Mitchell, Adele, ed. *The Letters of John S. Mosby.* n.p.: Stuart-Mosby Historical Society, 1986.

Mobley, Joe A., ed. *The Papers of Zebulon Baird Vance.* Raleigh: Office of Archives & History, 2013.

Moffett, Mary C., ed. *Letters of General James Conner.* Columbia, SC: R. L. Bryan Co., 1950.

Moore, Edward. *The Story of a Cannoneer under Stonewall Jackson.* Lynchburg: J. P. Bell, 1910.

Moseley, Ronald, ed. *The Stilwell Letters.* Macon, GA: Mercer University Press, 2002.

Mull, B. Rondal, ed. *David's Letters.* n.p., n.d.

Munson, E. M., ed. *Confederate Incognito: The Civil War Reports of "Long Grabs," a.k.a. Murdoch John McSween, 26th and 35th North Carolina Infantry.* Jefferson, NC: McFarland & Co., 2013.

Oeffinger, John C., ed. *A Soldier's General: The Civil War Letters of Major General Lafayette McLaws.* Chapel Hill: The University of North Carolina Press, 2002.

Paxton, John G., ed. *The Civil War Letters of General Frank "Bull" Paxton.* Hillsboro, TX: Hill Jr. College Press, 1978.

Peace, Laura P., ed. *To Tranquillity, 1861–1865: Civil War Letters of Six North Carolina Brothers.* Charleston, SC: Createspace, 2018.

Pfanz, Donald C., ed. *The Letters of General Richard S. Ewell: Stonewall's Successor.* Knoxville: The University of Tennessee Press, 2012.

Pettijohn, Dyer B. *Gettysburg and Libby Prison.* n.p., 1970.

Pittard, Pen. *Alexander County's Confederates.* n.p., n.d.

Polley, J. B. *A Soldier's Letters to Charming Nellie.* New York: The Neale Publishing Company, 1908.

Randolph, George W. *Regulations for the Army of the Confederate States, 1862.* Richmond: West & Johnson, 1862.

Roper, John H., ed. *Repairing the "March of Mars": The Civil War Diaries of John Samuel Apperson, Hospital Steward in the Stonewall Brigade.* Macon, GA: Mercer University Press, 2001.

Rourke, Norman E., ed. *"I Saw the Elephant:" The Civil War Experiences of Bailey George McClellan, Co D, 10th Alabama Infantry Regiment.* Shippensburg: Burd Street Press, 1995.

Rowland, Dunbar, ed. *Jefferson Davis, Constitutionalist: His Letters, Papers, and Speeches.* 10 vols. Jackson, MS: Mississippi Department of Archives and History, 1923

Runge, William H. ed. *Four Years in the Confederate Artillery: The Diary of Private Henry Robinson Berkeley.* Chapel Hill: University of North Carolina Press, 1961.

Sheridan, Philip. *Personal Memoirs of P. H. Sheridan, General, United States Army.* 2 vols. New York: Charles L. Webster & Company, 1888.

Smith, W.A. *The Anson Guards: History of Company C, 14th Regiment N. C. V. Army of Northern Virginia.* Charlotte: Stone Publishing, 1914.

Sorrel, G. Moxley. *Recollections of a Confederate State Officer.* New York: The Neal Publishing Company, 1905.

Speer, Allen P., ed. *"Voices from Cemetery Hill": The Civil War Diary, Reports, and Letters of Colonel William Henry Asbury Speer* (1861–1864). Johnson City, TN: The Overmountain Press, 1997.

Stiles, Robert. *Four Years Under Marse Robert.* New York: The Neale Publishing Company, 1903.

Stone, Ellen H., ed. *Letters Home to Baughn Mountain, 1862–1865.* n.p., 1979.

Styple, William B., ed. *Writing and Fighting the Confederate War: The Letters of Peter Wellington Alexander.* Kearney, N.J.: Belle Grove Publishing Company, 2002.

Swank, Walbrook. *Raw Pork and Hardtack: A Civil War Memoir from Manassas to Appomattox.* Shippensburg: White Mane Publishing, 1996.

Taylor, Michael W., ed. *"The Cry is War, War, War": The Civil War Correspondence of Lts. Burwell Thomas Cotton and George Job Nuntley, 34th Regiment North Carolina Troops.* Dayton, OH: Morningside, 1994.

Taylor, Walter. *Four Years with General Lee.* New York: D. Appleton & Company, 1877.

The Stranger's Guide and Official Directory for the City of Richmond. Richmond: Geo. P. Evans & Co., 1863.

Toalson, Glenn, ed. *No Soap, No Pay, Diarrhea, Dysentery & Desertion: A Composite Diary of the Last 16 Months of the Confederacy from 1864 to 1865.* iUniverse, 2006.

Tombes, Robert M., ed. *"Tell the Children I'll be Home When the Peaches Get Ripe": Letters Home from Lt. Robert Gaines Haile, Jr., Essex Sharpshooters, 55th Va., 1862.* Richmond: Tizwin, 1999.

Tower, R. Lockwood, ed., *Lee's Adjutant: The Wartime Letters of Colonel Walter Herron Taylor, 1862–1865.* Columbia: University of South Carolina Press, 1995.

Trout, Robert J. *With Pen & Saber: The Letters and Diaries of J. E. B. Stuart's Staff Officers.* Mechanicsburg, PA: Stackpole Books, 1995.

Turner, Charles W., ed. *My Dear Emma: War Letters of Col. James K. Edmondson, 1861–1865.* McClure Press, 1978.

Warren, Edward. *A Doctor's Experiences in Three Continents.* Baltimore: Cushings & Bailey, Publishers, 1885.

Welch, Spencer G. *A Confederate Surgeon's Letters to His Wife.* New York: The Neal Publishing Group, 1911.

West, John C. *A Texan in Search of a Fight: Being the Diary and Letters of a Private Soldier in Hood's Texas Brigade.* Waco, TX: J. S. Hills & Co., 1901.

Wiggins III, Clyde G., ed. *"My Dear Friend: The Civil War Letters of Alva Benjamin Spencer, 3rd Georgia Regiment, Company C.* Macon, GA: Mercer University Press, 2007.

Wiley, Bell, ed. *A South Woman's Story: Life in Confederate Richmond.* St. Simons Island: Mockingbird Books, 1988.

Williams, Edward B., ed., *Rebel Brothers: The Civil War Letters of the Truehearts.* College Station: Texas A&M University Press, 1995.

Williams, Richard B., ed. *Stonewall's Prussian Mapmaker: The Journals of Captain Oscar Hinrichs.* Chapel Hill: The University of North Carolina Press, 2014.

Wilson, LeGrand. *The Confederate Soldier.* Memphis: Memphis State University Press, 1973.

Wood, Wayne & Mary Virginia Jackson, ed. *"Kiss Sweet Little Lillah for me": Civil War Letters of William Thomas Jackson.* Birmingham, AL: Ebsco Media, 2000.

Wright, Stuart T. ed. *The Confederate Letters of Benjamin H. Freeman.* Hicksville, NY: Exposition Press, 1974.

Wyckoff, Mac, ed. *The Civil War Letters of Alexander McNeill.* Columbia: The University of South Carolina Press, 2016.

Government Documents

Confederate Papers Related to Citizens of Business Firms, Record Group 109, National Archives.

Compiled Military Service Records, Record Group 109, National Archives.

General Orders, Army of Northern Virginia, Record Group 109, National Archives.

The Medical & Surgical History of the War of the Rebellion. (1861–1865) Washington, D.C.: Government Printing Office, 1870.

War of the Rebellion: A Compilation of the Official Records of the Union & Confederate Armies, 128 vols. Washington, D.C., 1880–1901.

War of the Rebellion: A Compilation of the Official Records of the Union & Confederate Navies. 30 vols. Washington, D.C.: Government Printing Office, 1892.

Periodical Articles

Brown, Bedford "Personal Experience in Observing the Results of Good and Bad Sanitation in the Confederate Army." *Southern Practitioner* 15, no. 11 (Nov. 1893): 443–453.

Coffman, Alexander S. "Civil War Diary of Alexander Stewart Coffman," edited by Ralph S. Coffman. *Augusta Historical Bulletin.* 28, no. 2 (Fall 1992): 17–28.

Coxe, John. "The Battle of Gettysburg." *Confederate Veteran* 21, no. 9 (Sep. 1913): 433–436.

Davis, Harvey. "Harvey Davis's Unpublished Civil War 'Diary' and the Story of Company D of the First North Carolina Cavalry," edited by Francis B. Dedmond. *Appalachian Journal* (Summer 1986): 368–407.

Fleming, Francis P. "Francis P. Fleming in the War for Southern Independence: Letters to the Front," edited by Edward C. Williamson. *The Florida Historical Quarterly* 38, no. 2 (Oct. 1949): 145–155.

Garnet, James M. "Diary of James M. Garnet, Ordnance Officer of Rodes' Division, 2nd Corps, Army of Northern Virginia." *Southern Historical Society Papers* 27 (1899): 1–16.

Hinson, William G. "The Diary of William G. Hinson during the War of Secession: April 6, 1864, Part 1," edited by Joseph I. Waring. *The South Carolina Historical Magazine* 75, no. 1. (Jan. 1974): 14–23.

Hosford, John. "A Florida Soldier in the Army of Northern Virginia: The Hosford Letters," edited by Knox Mellon. *Florida Historical Quarterly* XLVI, no. 3 (Jan. 1968): 243–271.

Lane, James H. "Personal Reminiscences of General Lee." *The Wake Forest Student* 26, no. 5 (Jan. 1907): 310–311.

_____ "Glimpses of Army Life in 1864." *Southern Historical Society Papers* 18 (1890): 406–422.

Lang, David. "Civil War Letters of Colonel David Lang," edited by Bertram H. Groene. *The Florida Historical Quarterly* 54, no. 3 (Jan. 1976) 340–366.

Lilley, John D. "Diary of Lieutenant Colonel John Doak Lilley: 52nd Regiment Virginia Volunteers 1861–1865, Part 1," edited by Robert Driver. *Augusta Historical Bulletin* 27, no. 2 (Fall 1991): 8–18.

Mason, Emily V. "Memories of a Hospital Matron." *Atlantic Monthly* 90 (1902): 305–318, 475–485.

Maxwell, David E. "Some Letters to His Parents by a Floridian in the Confederate Army," edited by Gilbert Wright. *The Florida Historical Quarterly* 36, no. 4 (Apr. 1958): 353–372.

McGarity, Abner E. "Letters of a Confederate Surgeon: Dr. Abner Embry McGarity, 1862–1865, Part 2," edited by Edmund C. Burnett. *The Georgia Historical Quarterly* 29, no. 3 (Sep. 1945): 159–190.

_____ "Letters of a Confederate Surgeon: Dr. Abner Embry McGarity, 1862–1865, Part 1." *The Georgia Historical Quarterly* 29, no. 2 (Jun. 1945): 76–114.

_____ "Letters of Barnett Hardeman Cody and Others, 1861–1864, Part 2." *The Georgia Historical Quarterly* 23, no. 4 (Dec. 1939) 362–380.

Miller, Robert H. "Letters of Lieutenant Robert H. Miller to His Family, 1861–1862," edited by Forrest P. Conner and Robert H. Miller. *The Virginia Magazine of History & Biography* 70, no. 1 (Jan. 1962) 62–91.

Page, Coupland R. "Revelations of a Confederate Artillery Staff Officer: Coupland R. Page's Reminiscences of the Battle of Gettysburg," edited by Thomas L. Elmore. *Gettysburg Magazine,* no. 54 (Jan. 2016): 69–80.

Park, Robert E. "Diary of Robert E. Park, Macon, Georgia, late Captain Twelfth Alabama Regiment, Confederate States Army." *Southern Historical Society Papers* 1, no. 5 (May 1876): 370–386.

_____ "Diary of Robert E. Park, Macon, Georgia, late Captain Twelfth Alabama Regiment, Confederate States Army." *Southern Historical Society Papers* 1, no. 5 (Jun. 1876): 430–437.

_____ "Diary of Robert E. Park, Macon, Georgia, late Captain Twelfth Alabama Regiment, Confederate States Army." *Southern Historical Society Papers* 2, no. 1 (Jul. 1876): 25–31.

_____ "Diary of Robert E. Park, Macon, Georgia, late Captain Twelfth Alabama Regiment, Confederate States Army." *Southern Historical Society Papers* 2, no. 2 (Aug. 1876): 78–85.

_____ "War Diary of Captain R. E. Park, 12th Alabama Reg't, Jan. 28, 1863–Jan. 27, 1864." *Southern Historical Society Papers* 26 (1898): 1–31.

Parks, J. W. "I am Writing on My Canteen: A Georgia Soldier's Letters Home," edited by Gregory Parks & Steve Baker. *Company Front.* No volume, issue 2 (Jun. 2001): 9–21.

Plane, William F. "Letters of William Fisher Plane, C. S. A. to His Wife," edited by S. Joseph Lewis. *The Georgia Historical Quarterly* 48, no. 2 (Jun. 1964): 215–228.

Setzer, William A. "Your Neighbor Boys That Fell in Defense of their Country: The William A. Setzer Letters," edited by Locke W. Smith, Jr., & Greg Mast. *Company Front* 29, no. 1 (2015): 4–94.

Smith, James P. "Stonewall Jackson and Chancellorsville" Richmond, VA: R. E. Lee Camp No. 1, Confederate Veterans, no date.

Taylor, William H. "Experiences of a Confederate Surgeon." *Transactions of the College of Physicians of Philadelphia.* Series 3, 28 (1906): 91–121.

Tenney, S. F. "War Letters of S. F. Tenney, A Soldier of the Third Georgia Regiment," edited by E.B. Duffee, Jr., *The Georgia Historical Quarterly* 57, no. 2 (Summer 1973): 277–296.

Thompson, James T. "A Georgia Boy with 'Stonewall' Jackson: The Letter of James Thomas Thompson," edited by Aurelia Austin. *The Virginia Magazine of History & Biography* 70, no. 3 (July 1962): 314–331.

Torrence, Leonidas. "The Road to Gettysburg: The Diary and Letters of Leonidas Torrence of the Gaston Guards," edited by Haskell Monroe. *The North Carolina Historical Review* 36, no. 4. (Oct. 1959): 476–517.

Townsend, Harry C. "Townsend's Diary January–May 1865." *Southern Historical Society Papers* 34 (1906): 99–127.

Trimble, Isaac. "The Battle and Campaign of Gettysburg." *Southern Historical Society Papers* 26 (1898): 116–128.

Venable, C. S. "The Campaign from the Wilderness to Petersburg." *Southern Historical Society Papers* 14 (1886): 522–542.

Welsh, John P. & James Welsh. "A House Divided: The Civil War Letters of a Virginia Family," edited by W. G. Bean. *The Virginia Magazine of History & Biography* 59, no. 4 (Oct. 1951): 397–422.

White, W. S. "Stray Leaves from a Soldier's Journal." *Southern Historical Society Papers* 11, 552–559.

Newspapers

Asheville News

Atlanta Appeal

Brooklyn Evening Star

Buffalo Courier

Charleston Courier

Charleston Mercury

Charlotte Daily Bulletin

Daily Express

Democratic Watchtower

Edgefield Advertiser

Evening Courier and Republic

Greensboro Patriot

Huntsville Gazette

Jacksonville Republican

Kansas Jewelite

Native Virginian

New York Times

Norfolk Post

Philadelphia Public Ledger

St. Louis Post-Dispatch

Staunton Spectator

Richmond Dispatch

Richmond Enquirer

Richmond Whig

Southern Confederacy

Tipton Gazette

Vicksburg Evening Post

Western Democrat

Secondary Sources

Books

Altmayer, Bud. *A Family History of Watauga County.* Boone: Minor's Printing Co., 1994.

Anderson, Luck. *North Carolina Women of the Confederacy.* Fayetteville: United Daughters of the Confederacy, 1936.

Ash, Stephen V. *Rebel Richmond: Life and Death in the Confederate Capital.* Chapel Hill: The University of North Carolina Press, 2019.

Ballard, Sandra L. & Leila E. Weinstein. *Neighbor to Neighbor: A Memoir of Family, Community, and Civil War in Appalachian North Carolina.* Boone: Center for Appalachian Studies, 2007.

Bartholomees Jr., J. Boone. *Buff Facings and Gilt Buttons.* Columbia: The University of South Carolina Press, 1998.

Bean, W. G. *Stonewall's Man: Sandie Pendleton.* Chapel Hill: University of North Carolina Press, 1959.

_____ *The Liberty Hall Volunteers: Stonewall's College Boys.* Charlottesville: The University of Virginia Press, 1964.

Beringer, Richard E., Herman Hattaway, Archer Jones, & William N. Still Jr. *Why the South Lost the Civil War.* Athens: The University of Georgia Press, 1986.

Black III, Robert C. *The Railroads of the Confederacy.* Chapel Hill: University of North Carolina Press, 1998.

Blair, Louisa. *Blairs of Richmond, Virginia.* Richmond: William Byrd Press, 1933.

Blair, William. *Virginia's Private War: Feeding Body and Soul in the Confederacy, 1861–1865.* New York: Oxford University Press, 1998.

Blanton, Wyndham. *Medicine in Virginia in the Nineteenth Century.* Richmond: Garrett & Massie, 1933.

Brewer, James H. *The Confederate Negro: Virginia's Craftsmen and Military Laborers, 1861–1865.* Durham: Duke University Press, 1969.

Brown, Kent Masterson. *Retreat from Gettysburg.* Chapel Hill: University of North Carolina Press, 2005.

Browning, Judkin & Timothy Silver. *An Environmental History of the Civil War.* Chapel Hill: University of North Carolina Press, 2020.

Calcutt, Rebecca B. *Richmond's Wartime Hospitals.* Gretna: Pelican Publishing Company, 2005.

Cashin, Joan E. *War Stuff: The Struggle for Human and Environmental Resources in the American Civil War.* Cambridge: Cambridge University Press, 2018.

Chapla, John D. *48th Virginia Infantry.* Lynchburg: H. E. Howard, 1989.

Coco, Gregory A. *A Vast Sea of Misery: A History and Guide to the Union and Confederate Field Hospitals at Gettysburg.* Gettysburg: Thomas Publications, 1988.

Cornier, Steven. *The Siege of Suffolk: The Forgotten Campaign April 11–May 4, 1863.* Lynchburg: H. E. Howard, 1989.

Cunningham, H. H. *Doctors in Gray: The Confederate Medical Service.* Baton Rouge: Louisiana State University, 1958.

Driver, Robert J. *Tenth Virginia Cavalry.* Lynchburg, VA: H.E. Howard, 1992.

Driver Jr., Robert, & Kevin Ruffner. *1st Battalion Virginia Infantry, 39th Battalion Virginia Cavalry, and 24th Battalion Virginia Partisan Rangers.* Lynchburg: H. E. Howard, [1996].

Faust, James P. *The Fighting Fifteenth Alabama Infantry: A Civil War History and Roster.* Jefferson: McFarland & Company, 2015.

Freeman, Douglas. S. *R. E. Lee.* 4 Vols. New York: Charles Scribner's Sons, 1935.

_____ *Lee's Lieutenants: A Study in Command.* 3 Vols. New York: Charles Scribner's Sons, 1942.

Freemon, Frank R. *Gangrene and Glory: Medical Care During the American Civil War.* Cranbury, NJ: Associated University Presses, 1998.

Furgurson, Ernest B. *Ashes of Glory: Richmond at War.* New York: Alfred A. Knopf, 1996.

Glatthaar, Joseph T. *General Lee's Army: From Victory to Collapse.* New York: Free Press, 2008.

Glasgow, William. *Northern Virginia's Own: A History of the 17th Virginia Infantry Regiment.* Alexandria, VA: Gobill Press, 1989.

Goff, Richard. *Confederate Supply.* Durham: Duke University Press, 1969.

Green, Carol C. *Chimborazo: The Confederacy's Largest Hospital.* Knoxville: The University of Tennessee Press, 2004.

Greene, Katherine G. *Stony Mead: A Sketch.* Strasburg, Virginia: Shenandoah Publishing House, Inc., 1929.

Greene, A. Wilson. *Civil War Petersburg: Confederate City in the Crucible of War.* Charlottesville: The University of Virginia Press, 2006.

Hagerman, Edward. *The American Civil War and the Origins of Modern Warfare.* Bloomington, IN: Indiana University Press, 1988.

Hall, Harry. *A Johnny Reb Band from Salem.* Raleigh: Office of Archives & History, 2006.

Hardy, Michael C. *General Lee's Immortals: The Battles and Campaigns of the Branch-Lane Brigade in the Army of Northern Virginia, 1861–1865.* El Dorado Hills, CA: Savas Beatie, 2018.

_____ *Lee's Body Guards: The 39th Battalion Virginia Cavalry.* Charleston, SC,: The History Press, 2019.

_____ *Watauga County, North Carolina, and the Civil War.* Charleston, SC: The History Press, 2013.

Harsh, Joseph. *Taken at the Flood: Robert E. Lee and Confederate Strategy in the Maryland Campaign of 1862.* Kent: The Kent State University Press, 1999.

Hartwig, D. Scott. *To Antietam Creek: The Maryland Campaign of September 1862.* Baltimore: The John Hopkins University Press, 2012.

Henderson, G. F. R. *Stonewall Jackson and the American Civil War.* 2 vols. New York: Longmans, Green, & Co., 1906.

Hess, Earl J. *In the Trenches at Petersburg: Field Fortifications & Confederate Defeat.* Chapel Hill: The University of North Carolina Press, 2009.

Hilliard, Sam. *Hog Meat and Hoecake: Food Supply in the Old South, 1840–1860.* Athens: The University of Georgia Press, 1972.

Hoke, Jacob. *The Great Invasion of 1863, or General Lee in Pennsylvania.* Dayton, OH: W. J. Shuey Pub., 1887.

Horn, John. *The Petersburg Campaign.* Pennsylvania: Combined Books, 1993.

Houck, Peter W. *A Prototype of a Confederate Hospital Center in Lynchburg, Virginia.* Lynchburg: Warwick House Publishing, 1986.

Humphreys, Margaret. *Marrow of Tragedy: The Health Crisis of the American Civil War.* Baltimore: The John Hopkins University Press, 2013.

Hurt, R. Douglas. *Agriculture and the Confederacy: Policy, Productivity, and the Power in the Civil War South.* Chapel Hill: The University of North Carolina Press, 2015.

Iobst, Richard W. & Louis H. Manarin. *The Bloody Sixth: The Sixth North Carolina Regiment, Confederate States of America.* Raleigh: North Carolina Confederate Centennial Commission, 1965.

Krick, Robert E. L. *Staff Officers in Gray.* Chapel Hill: The University of North Carolina Press, 2003.

Krick, Robert K. *Civil War Weather in Virginia.* Tuscaloosa: The University of Alabama Press, 2007.

Kautz, August V. *Customs of Service for Non-Commissioned Officers and Soldiers.* Philadelphia: J. B. Lippincott & Co., 1864.

Marvel, William. *Lee's Last Retreat: The Flight to Appomattox.* Chapel Hill: The University of North Carolina Press, 2002.

Massey, Mary Elizabeth. *Ersatz in the Confederacy: Shortages and Substitutes on the Southern Home Front.* Columbia: University of South Carolina Press, 1993.

Moore, Jerrold. *Confederate Commissary General: Lucius Bellinger Northrop and the Subsistence Bureau of the Southern Army.* Shippensburg: White Mane Publishing Company, 1996.

Musselman, Homer D. *47th Virginia Infantry.* Lynchburg, VA: H. E. Howard, 1991.

O'Sullivan, Richard. *55th Virginia Infantry.* Lynchburg: H. E. Howard, 1989.

Owsley, Frank L. *King Cotton Diplomacy: Foreign Relations of the Confederate States of America.* Tuscaloosa: University of Alabama Press, 2008.

Paradis, James M. *African Americans and the Gettysburg Campaign.* Lanham, MD: Scarecrow Press, 2013.

Reid, J. W. *History of the Fourth Regiment of S.C. Volunteers.* Dayton: Morningside Bookshop, 1975.

Rodriguez, Ricardo J. *Black Confederates in the US Civil War: A Compiled List of African-Americans Who Served the Confederacy.* Createspace, 2010.

Roman, Alfred. *The Military Operations of General Beauregard.* 2 Vols. New York: Harper, 1884.

Scheel, Eugene. *The Civil War in Fauquier County, Virginia.* Warrington, VA: The Fauquier National Bank, 1985.

Schroeder-Lein, Glenna. *The Encyclopedia of Civil War Medicine.* New York: M. E. Sharpe, 2008.

Sears, Stephen. *To the Gates of Richmond: The Peninsula Campaign.* New York: Ticknor & Fields, 1983.

Smith, Andrew F. *Starving the South: How the North Won the Civil War.* New York: St. Martin's Press, 2011.

Spaulding, Brett W. *Last Chance for Victory: Jubal Early's 1864 Maryland Invasion.* Thomas Publications, 2010.

Starr, Stephen. *The Union Cavalry in the Civil War.* 3 vols. Baton Rouge: Louisiana State University Press, 1979.

Taylor, Sally, & Sallie Conner. *South Carolina Women in the Confederacy.* Columbia, SC: State Co., 1903.

Thomas, Emory. *Robert E. Lee: A Biography.* New York: W. W. Norton, 1995.

Vandiver, Frank. *Confederate Blockade Running Through Bermuda, 1861–1865: Letters and Cargo Manifests.* Austin: The University of Texas Press, 1947.

Walsh, Jack D. *Medical Histories of Confederate Generals.* Kent, OH: The Kent State University Press, 1995.

Weitz, Mark A. *More Damning than Slaughter: Desertion in the Confederate Army.* Lincoln: University of Nebraska Press, 2005.

Wiley, Bell. *The Life of Johnny Reb: The Common Soldier of the Confederacy.* Baton Rouge: Louisiana State University Press, 1943, 1978.

Wise, Stephen R. *Lifeline of the Confederacy: Blockade Running During the Civil War.* Columbia: University of South Carolina Press, 1988.

Woodward, Colin E. *Marching Masters: Slavery, Race, and the Confederate Army, 1861–1865.* Charlottesville: University of Virginia Press, 2014.

Periodical Articles

Bollet, Alfred Jay. "Scurvy and Chronic Diarrhea in Civil War Troops: Were They Both Nutritional Deficiency Syndromes?" *Journal of the History of Medicine and Allied Sciences* 47, no. 1 (Jan. 1992): 46–67.

Browning, Judkin & Timothy Silver. "Nature and Human Nature: Environmental Influences on the Union's Failed Peninsula Campaign, 1862." *Journal of the Civil War Era* 8, no. 3 (Sep. 2018): 388–415.

Bryan, T. Conn. "The Churches in Georgia During the Civil War." *The Georgia Historical Quarterly* 33, no. 4 (Dec. 1949): 283–302.

Daniel, John. "General A. Early." *Southern Historical Society Papers* 22: 281–335.

Escott, Paul. "Joseph E. Brown, Jefferson Davis, and the Problem of Poverty in the Confederacy." *The Georgia Historical Quarterly* 61, no. 1 (Spring 1977): 59–71.

Kennon, L. W. V. "The Valley Campaign of 1864." *Confederate Veteran* 26, no. 12 (Dec. 1918): 517–523.

Johnson, Dudley S. "The Southern Express Company: A Georgia Corporation." *The Georgia Historical Quarterly* 56, No. 2 (Summer 1972): 224–42.

Johnson, Ludwell H. "Contraband Trade During the Last Year of the Civil War." *The Mississippi Valley Historical Review* 49, no. 4 (March 1963): 635–652.

McGee, David H. "Home and Friends": Kinship, Community, Elite Women in Caldwell County, North Carolina, During the Civil War." The *North Carolina Historical Review* 74, no. 4 (Oct. 1997): 363–388.

Wilson, Harold S. "Virginia's Industry and the Conduct of War." *Virginia at War* 1862. William C. Davis & James I. Robertson, Jr., eds. Lexington: The University Press of Kentucky, 2007.

Index

Greensboro, NC, railroad, 33, 39; rations in, 40; ladies passing out water, 62

Gregg, Brig. Gen. Maxy, 69

Grimes, Maj. Gen. Bryan, has blacksmith make oven, 79; men without rations, 81, 84, 86; eating with Jackson out of sutler's wagon, 115

Guiney's Station, VA, 48

Hagerstown, MD, 69, 70

Hampton, Lt. Gen. Wade, beefsteak raid, 35; capture of depot at Manassas Junction, 44; rations while Legion is traveling, 62; permits foraging, 70; raiding enemy 116; commissary on staff, 134

Hanover Junction, VA, bridges not destroyed, 22; rations at, 23, 32; depot commander, 137

Harper's Ferry, WV, 15, 69; Federals removing rations from, 81

Harrisonburg, VA, 51

Hill, Lt. Gen. Ambrose P., division commissary, 66; left at Harper's Ferry, 70; Sharpsburg, 70; becomes corps commander, 73; brother on staff, 134

Hood, Lt. Gen. John B., looking for rations at Sharpsburg, 70

Hospitals, coffee for, 10; confiscated liquor sent to, 21; wounded from Chancellorsville sent to Richmond, 22; boxes sent to, 51; Ladies Aid Societies supporting, 55, 97; division hospitals at Gettysburg, 75; cleanliness, 90; brigade hospitals, 91; hospitals early in war, 92; field hospitals, 94; and Gettysburg, 95; in Richmond, 96, 97, 98-102; in Gordonsville, 97; in Charlottesville, 97; wayside hospitals in Charlotte, 97; reorganization, 98; in Lynchburg, 98; in Petersburg, 101; in Winchester, 101; wagons for, 139; stealing from, 141-142

Imboden, Brig. Gen. John, 94

Jackson, Lt. Gen. Thomas J. 16, 61, Romney Campaign, 63; eating captured food, 65; capturing depot at Manassas, 67; ordering Branch into a cornfield, 69; capturing Harper's Ferry, 69-70; Antietam battle,

70; death of, 73; compared to Early, 81; dietary restrictions, 110; cook, 110, 122; and lemons, 111; hosting dinner party, 113; taking a drink with farmer, 115

James River, VA, 33, 80, 84, 91

Jenkins, Brig. Gen. Micah, 69

Johnson, Maj. Gen. Bushrod, 40

Johnston, Gen. Joseph E., post Manassas, 7; ordering railroad extended, 11; stockpiling supplies, 12; meets with Davis, 12; replaced by Lee, 106; dining with Pender, 112; dining with Longstreet, 112; aware of food problems, 129; discord with Davis and Northrop, 135

Johnston, Brig. Gen. Robert J., 113

Jones, Maj. Gen. David R., 113

Jones, Maj. Gen. William, 18

Ladies Aid Societies, in South Carolina, 51; 55-58; hospital work, 97

Lane, Brig. Gen. James H., building road to get to supply depot, 19; soldiers distributing rations, 28; wants camp servants to be counted as soldiers, 31; desertion due to food, 39; boxes at Christmas time, 52; getting rations to the men at Spotsylvania, 79; getting peaches from Lee, 108; feelings against teamsters, 142-3

Lang, Col. David, 24

Lee, Lt. Col. Richard B., Jr., 6, 134, 137

Lee, Gen. Robert E., 1, staff complains of food during western Rich Mountain campaign, 11; takes command of the Army of Northern Virginia, 14-15; restores rations after Maryland Campaign, 16; complains to War Department about food reduction, 18; offers to send men to Virginia to fix railroad, 18; agrees to loan some wagons to Northrop, 25; writes Seddon regarding short rations, 28; writes Seddon on purchasing rations from the enemy, 29; gets letter from Lane regarding change in officers' ration, 31; writes Seddon regarding rations and 1864 campaign season, 31; wants whiskey ration in 1864, 32; appeals to local farmers in 1865; writing to Seddon, complains about the

About the Author

After three decades and more than two dozen books, Michael C. Hardy is still finding unexplored corners of history. His books, articles, and popular blog posts cover the history of people, places, and events across the southern United States. A graduate of the University of Alabama, Michael is fascinated with the life of the Confederate soldier from the boots up. When he is not researching and writing, he spends his time at historic sites volunteering as a historic interpreter.